PRAISE FOR FROM HARLEM WITH LOVE

"Joseph Holland writes a personally riveting, articulate, and extraordinary, almost excruciatingly honest, confession of his on-going, passionate, unmitigated love-affair with Harlem. Mr. Holland's sincere passion for Harlem is evidenced in his descriptions of her and her history in fascinating detail."

—**Paul de Vries**, Ph.D., President,
New York Divinity School

"A gem. Joe Holland gives a compelling account of his career, leavened by humor, motivated by a deep social compassion, and undergirded by an unflagging Christian commitment. An inspiration." —**Frank Rhodes**, President Emeritus,
Cornell University

"Joseph Holland reveals the complex dynamism of Harlem—the cultural heartbeat of Black America. His insightful details of the community's historical transitions make *From Harlem with Love* essential reading for all those who would Americanize Harlem. Holland's vision of Harlem is priceless, endowing this African-American Mecca with a cultural authenticity that raises the bar for old-timers and newcomers alike.

—**Wyatt Tee Walker**, Former Chief of Staff,
Rev. Dr. Martin Luther King, Jr.; author; cultural historian

"Joseph Holland's experience in Harlem, the Black Metropolis, better focused his already keen sense of W.E.B. Du Bois' Talented Tenth. Like Du Bois, Holland was educated in America's best institutions of higher learning and dropped anchor in Harlem thereafter with an undeniable love of blackness and a thorough understanding of white America. To read his memoir is to take a journey with Holland and learn the ways of black folks—their history, their politics, and their cultural life, and, indeed, emerge a fuller and richer individual."   —**Woodie King, Jr.**, Founder, Producing Director, New Federal Theater

"Joe Holland's book is an epic of a faith-based entrepreneur in Harlem. Holland weaves Harlem's faith, history, culture, politics, troubles, and personalities into his love story with Harlem. The book is honest, engaging, challenging, and wonderful."
                    —**Tony Carnes**, Publisher and Editor,
                    A Journey through NYC Religions

FROM HARLEM
with love

An Ivy Leaguer's Inner-City Odyssey

A MEMOIR

Joseph H. Holland

LANTERN BOOKS • NEW YORK • A DIVISION OF BOOKLIGHT INC.

Lantern Books
128 Second Place
Brooklyn, NY 11231
www.lanternbooks.com

Permission to use "If we must die" by Claude McKay is made possible
through the courtesy of the Literary Representative for the Works of Claude
McKay, Schomburg Center for Research in Black Culture, The New York
Public Library, Astor, Lenox and Tilden Foundations.

Printed in the United States of America

Library of Congress Cataloging-in-Publication Data
Holland, Joseph H.
From Harlem with love : an Ivy Leaguer's inner city odyssey :
a memoir / Joseph H. Holland.
p. cm.
ISBN 978-1-59056-322-9 (alk. paper)—ISBN 978-1-59056-323-6 (ebook)
1. Holland, Joseph H. 2. Harlem (New York, N.Y.)—History—20th century.
3. Harlem (New York, N.Y.)—Economic conditions—20th century. 4. Urban
renewal—New York (State)—New York. 5. Community development—
New York (State)—New York. 6. African American businesspeople—New
York (State)—New York—Biography. 7. Real estate developers—New York
(State)—New York—Biography. 8. African American lawyers—New York
(State)—New York—Biography. 9. Harlem (New York, N.Y.)—Biography.
I. Title.
F128.68.H3H65 2012
974.7'043092—dc23
[B]

2011036029

MIX
Paper from
responsible sources
FSC   FSC® C011935
www.fsc.org

We are pressed hard on every side, but not crushed;
perplexed, but not in despair;
persecuted, but not abandoned;
plummeted, but not destroyed.

—II Corinthians 4:8, 9

2011

Publisher certification awarded by Green Press Initiative.
www.greenpressinitiative.org

Lantern Books has elected to print this title on Rolland Enviro, a 100%
post-consumer recycled paper, processed chlorine-free. As a result,
we have saved the following resources:

27 trees, 1,256 lbs of solid waste, 11,349 gallons of water,
19,000,000 BTUs of energy, 2,472 lbs of net greenhouse gases

As part of Lantern Books' commitment to the environment we have joined the
Green Press Initiative, a nonprofit organization supporting publishers in using
fiber that is not sourced from ancient or endangered forests. We hope that you, the
reader, will support Lantern and the GPI in our endeavor to preserve the ancient
forests and the natural systems on which all life depends. One way is to buy books
that cost a little more but make a positive commitment to the environment not only
in their words, but in the paper that they are printed on.
For more information, visit www.greenpressinitiative.org.

In memory of my mother
Laura Mitchell Holland
Whose love for her son
Ripened into Love for his community

CONTENTS

x   *Contents*

Have Faith, Mrs. Stokes, Harlem Will Rise Again!

THE LATE SPRING sunshine dances through the breeze, illuminating the immaculate lawn of Langdell Hall, perfecting the physical conditions for the Harvard Law School graduation ceremony. The social conditions are far less ideal, but I'm hoping my anxieties melt away with the noonday sun.

As I inch forward in the line to receive my diploma from the dean, I look out over the sparkling green and the panoply of proud parents—and my ambivalent ones. Trying to put it all in perspective, I flash back to a time when I was ambivalent about one of their missions, a dozen years before, thousands of miles across the Atlantic: the day we arrived in Sweden to begin Dad's tenure as U. S. ambassador.

Anguished over having to give up the familiar, like football, for foreign things like soccer, I'd cried throughout the flight to Scandinavia. As our plane had landed at Stockholm's Arlanda Airport, my tears had quickly dried. I'd looked out of the window at hundreds of riot-ready police officers and military troops that surrounded protesters, who were waving placards and brightly colored banners and signs:

HOLLAND = USA IMPERIALISM
THE GENOCIDE CONTINUES
DID YOU ALSO FLY A B-52?

Dad was assuming a controversial post that had been left vacant for over a year in a diplomatic snub. The Nixon White House had cold-shouldered the Swedes because they'd switched their diplomatic ties in Vietnam from Saigon to Hanoi, and had pledged millions of dollars in humanitarian aid to North Vietnam as well as defiantly granting asylum to U.S. draft dodgers. But I'd had no idea we'd be entering hostile territory.

We had descended from our jet onto the tarmac, Dad leading the way, followed by Mother and my sister Lucy. I had intentionally trailed behind, providing the rear guard in our precarious circumstance, my only frame of reference for such perilous international settings being *From Russia with Love*, a James Bond movie I had finally persuaded my parents to let me see.

I was struck by the dozens of photographers, the phalanx of TV cameras, and the gauntlet of dignitaries, soldiers, protesters, reporters, and cops that lined the couple of hundred yards between the aircraft and the terminal, which now loomed before me as a safe harbor.

Suddenly a large, blond demonstrator had broken through the security line and had sprinted toward us. I'd grabbed Lucy's and Mother's arms and had leaned in toward Dad, knowing his still bulky frame (the legacy of his days as a football player) was the best available shield. Before a host of soldiers and cops had tackled the rebel, he'd screamed in English, "You are not wanted here!" Then, "Nigger, go home!"

Nigger, go home? Had I traveled from one continent to another only to land on the battlefield gladly left behind in the American South—in "tolerant" Sweden, no less?

FIGURE 1: My family inside the airport terminal after we had walked the gauntlet

• • •

The graduates mingle with diplomas in hand, relishing the moment of accomplishment—except for me. I dread the inevitable question. A smiling parent approaches; it's too late to disappear. Here it comes.

"So, young man, which firm will you be joining in the fall?" I hesitate and rub my forehead. Dad clears his throat. Mom looks away. How quickly I turn from hero to fool.

"Well . . . I don't have a job yet," I offer weakly. There is an awkward silence.

The inquisitive father chuckles. "Decided to take a year to travel? I did the same thing after law school. Best year of my life, cycling around Europe." I glance at Dad, sense his temperature rising.

Adding fuel to the fire, this father pats Dad on the shoulder. "You're a braver man than me. My boy got a clerkship. I insisted he take it. Times are tougher now. I told him Paris will still be there down the line. Then it will be on his own nickel, not mine."

The dad laughs; mine tries to feign a smile. I know I'd better beat him to the punch, but before I can offer my obligatory explanation, the other father is whisked away by his graduating daughter to greet a friend. But before I can finish my sigh of relief, another parent presses the inquiry, forcing my hand.

"I'm moving to Harlem to give back to my community," I announce.

"Oh," the inquirer remarks, trying to figure out what to say. "Well . . . that's different."

"Why Harlem?" queries another parent.

My hopes for a mercifully brief exchange are dashed. Should I delay or declare my hand? Okay, I'll let the truth come out so I can nip the conversation in the bud.

"Harlem is still the cultural capital of black America," I affirm. "If you can make a difference there, the benefits will spread to other needy communities."

Somebody's mom—sincerely: "That sounds like a very noble thing to do."

Somebody's dad—sarcastically: "Good luck."

A classmate beckons, offering me an escape, and I walk away to meet her fiancé.

As I shake hands, my mind races to the day I made the decision—or rather the decision was made for me. I was crossing the manicured grounds of a suburban country club on a humid afternoon. I had slipped away from my peers and the partners at the Wall Street law firm, who were enjoying the exquisite décor, extensive wine lists, splendid floral displays, elegant buffets, and consummate service of the firm's annual summer associate outing. I was having difficulty seeing myself climbing the corporate ladder to a high-flying career as the firm's first black partner (it had already been hinted at). Walking along the fairway, I glanced at my watch and quickened my pace, concerned that my mentor Joe Strauss might send out a search party if I stayed away from the Clubhouse much longer. Making a shortcut across a green, I had Harlem on my mind, although Harlem was as distant for me as Stockholm.

I'd grown up in southern Virginia on the campus of Hampton Institute, a historically black college founded to educate ex-slaves in the wake of the Civil War. As the son of a college president, I'd been sheltered in the bosom of the black elite. I'd been insulated from the violent realities of the civil rights movement: I'd participated in no bus boycotts, diner sit-ins, or freedom rides. I'd never been bitten by dogs, knocked down by fire hoses, battered by police clubs, or terrorized by swinging nooses and burning crosses. Yet a seed of social consciousness had been planted, which I cultivated through my Cornell University history-and-English double major. I'd been captivated by the literature and politics of the Harlem Renaissance—the decades from roughly 1905 to 1935, when Harlem was in vogue.

I maneuvered around a huge sand trap and summoned my Renaissance muse in the verse of my favorite poet Langston Hughes and favorite poem "Harlem" to distract myself from the banality awaiting me just beyond the eighteenth hole.

But I never got beyond the first line: "What happens to a dream deferred?" I was thinking about the meaning of Hughes' question, when . . .

"Fore!"

I looked up and around. An errant golf ball was coming straight at me. I ducked in the nick of time. The ball just missed striking me in the head.

That certainly got my attention! I stopped to ponder the serious possibility that God was trying to speak to me about direction for my life, and I kept ducking. In that moment, the thought of Harlem took on colors and shapes and places and people. I saw myself amid the bustle of an embittered urban landscape: 125th Street; black people, all the hues of the diaspora, in dashikis and Afros, hustling by me, passing under the Apollo marquee, ignoring its beckoning. The poetry of Hughes and the music of Ellington and Strayhorn's "Take the A Train" rang in my ears.

For a silver-spoon member of the black elite like me, the choice could not have been starker: a smooth transition to New York's downtown white upper class versus a defiant detour to its uptown black underclass.

In my imagination, I tried to flee the vision and the sense of calling that encircled me. However, I stumbled over a beggar on the sidewalk. One of his hands held a plastic bucket, the other clutched at me. I pulled away, resolving to fend off notions of community service and urban renewal, of social justice and divine destiny.

The clubhouse loomed ahead as a refuge from my reverie, and my stroll turned into a jog. I began to sweat, slowed down, and pulled out my handkerchief to mop my brow.

"Joe!" The voice startled me. It was one of the partners, on his way back from the links. "Glad I ran into you. Got a matter I want your help with. Pro bono case, uptown in Harlem."

My mouth dropped open. I closed it quickly to cloak my astonishment. The partner had never uttered more than hello to me until this moment—and his first real communication was punctuated with Harlem?! The partner rambled on, but I was preoccupied with this bizarre confluence of Harlem moments at a suburban country club, coming at me like a cultural train to ride as an escape from the all-consuming Wall Street world for which I seemed destined.

"Time to go." Lucy's whisper breaks my musing. She nods in the direction of Mom and Dad, noting their agitation. My expectation of a silent, tense walk to the car is unfortunately fulfilled. Lucy and Mother ride with Grandma, Aunt Doris, and Uncle Joe, strategically setting me up for the climactic one-on-one with Dad that I'd hoped to avoid. I brace myself, sensing his impending last stand against my Harlem move. Though Dad is no stranger to idealism, past exchanges have revealed he's not seduced by my quixotic notions of community service, divinely inspired or otherwise.

I haven't even closed the car door when Dad starts in. "Unlike me when I finished school, you can go anywhere and do anything and you come up with this silly mission in Harlem?!"

It's a familiar point that tends to find its way into every major discussion about my career. His generation of African Americans didn't have the opportunities that mine possessed. He's just more emphatic about it today. Though offended by Dad's constant characterization of my Harlem direction as "silly," I respond with a moral argument I've not used before. "There's nothing silly about serving the urban poor. It's the right thing to do. If we don't take care of our own communities, who will? If we leave it in the hands of whites, we end up with paternalism. If we leave it to the government, we have dependency."

My college research had helped me understand the dynamics of Harlem's devastating decline. The influx of African Americans into Harlem during the Renaissance had become an exodus of middle-class blacks during the years of economic and social dislocation that had followed. This reverse had yielded a greater concentration of poverty in Harlem and other cities across the nation, and had left in its wake a new frontier in the quest for American social justice—the plight of the inner-city underclass. While the passage of civil rights legislation in the sixties had advanced the fortunes of the middle class, the spread of the welfare system had worsened the plight of those left behind. My studies had left me both aware of and intimidated by the magnitude of the problem.

My father's frustration grows. "Where did you get such a crazy Harlem idea?" We pull into a gas station and Dad begins to refuel the car.

As I focus on how best to respond, I recall the mysterious turning point in the genesis of my "silly" mission. I had been up late one night in Langdell Library, brooding over my future instead of writing a constitutional law brief. My current assignment at the Harvard Legal Aid Bureau had caused me to research housing-discrimination cases, which was eerily similar to the file I'd been given by the partner at the Wall Street law firm—namely, investigating unfair housing practices that had been uncovered by a Harlem nonprofit. Even though the research for the pro bono case had been library-based, I'd used the project as an excuse to make innumerable trips to Harlem, where I'd walked the streets and breathed the uptown air. I'd looked for confirming signs and found none. This had left me wondering whether I'd lost my mind. I still resisted any impulse—divine or otherwise—that insisted that the path from Harvard to Harlem was one I was destined to travel.

Despite my best efforts to escape, however, I'd been besieged by signs directing me to Harlem. They'd started in the classroom. My Real Property Law professor's lectures had been about land-use entanglements in Harlem. An Evidence lecture had featured a defendant from Harlem. Business Planning had used a case study on Harlem. And my Race and the Law seminar had highlighted a discrimination suit with a Harlem complainant. My very first Legal Aid Bureau client, a middle-aged alcoholic facing eviction, had regaled me with stories from his hometown—Harlem. In a lively discussion in our weekly Black Christian Fellowship group about taking personal responsibility for the problems of our communities, a fellow student had lectured us on "The Return of the Native Sons to the Ghettos of America—If We Don't, Who Will?" And there had been those from the fellowship who'd embraced the vision: James O'Neal, Leslie Walker, Dennis Henderson, and Jacqueline Patton. We'd prayed, fasted, and strategized about relocating to Harlem.

The signs had kept on manifesting themselves. A sermon by my pastor, Reverend Michael Haynes of Roxbury's Twelfth Baptist Church, had enthralled me. His theme rose from the divine commission of Isaiah, in the Old Testament: *Whom shall I send? Who will go for us?* Reverend Haynes had implored us to respond to the providential call just as Isaiah had. *Here I am. Send me.*

The most riveting encounter had come through John Perkins, a Christian community developer from Mississippi, who'd come to Boston to talk about his grassroots, holistic work to uplift the poor of the Deep South. Perkins had emphasized community institution–building to empower people economically, just as nonviolent civil rights–protest marches had empowered them politically. He'd explained his unlikely relocation from California to Mississippi as obedience to divine calling. He'd described the sacrifice of leaving his career, uprooting his family, and traveling thousands of miles, not because of a better job or lifestyle but because God had told him to do it.

Harvard still seemed like light-years away from Harlem, so I'd cornered Perkins afterwards for some frank discussion.

"Why did you do it?" I'd asked him.

"Obeying God's call is the most important thing you can do in your life. I did and got no regrets," was his response.

"But how do you know it's God's call?"

"Sometimes you don't know until you go. Harlem isn't as far away as you think. Remember, with God, all things are possible."

I had consequently bought Perkins' book *Let Justice Roll Down*, detailing how he'd endured unemployment, physical violence, imprisonment, and the discrimination of the 1960s South to create educational programs, a health-care clinic, and businesses that generated jobs. Perkins was part of a generation of black church leaders who debated whether to fight racial segregation and injustice primarily through politics or with the Gospel, whether by changing the law or altering hearts and minds. Perkins rejected this false dichotomy, believing both were imperative. He argued that redemption must encompass not just individuals but entire communities. This vision resonated with my own perspective.

Nonetheless, my pragmatism had prevailed. I had rationalized all the signs and support for my vision as peculiar happenstance. I'd continued to cling to my plan of taking the best Wall Street job offer and pursuing an international law career with an office in Stockholm.

Back in Langdell Library, I glanced at the clock, distressed that my mental woolgathering had squandered so much studying time. Rubbing my eyes, I put down my casebook and noticed that the student who'd been sitting across from me had gone, and had left a newspaper on the table. I yawned, and slid the paper toward me.

The paper had been opened to the comics page. I was about to turn it when a *Doonesbury* strip caught my eye. It depicted two ladies—Mrs. D., a white senior citizen, and Mrs. Stokes, her

black maid—talking about Harlem! I rubbed my eyes again to make sure I was still awake.

"Tell me, Mrs. Stokes, where are you from originally?" the white boss asked.

"I'm from Harlem, Mrs. D.," Mrs. Stokes replied.

"Harlem? Really? Why, it's been years since I've been to Harlem!"

"Say what?"

I picked the paper up and held it to the light, making sure not to miss a word of this captivating conversation.

Mrs. D. continued: "Dick and I used to go up to the Cotton Club in the 30's to hear Billie Holiday. What a marvelous, exciting place it was then! Everyone called it Harlem's Golden Age."

Mrs. Stokes turned away: "I don't know nothin' about no Golden Age, ma'am. Seems like Harlem always been just a place to give up hope."

This declaration deflated me, and her boss: "Yes, I know. The riots of '35 brought that home to us. It was very sobering."

In the concluding frame, Mrs. D. tried to encourage me—and Mrs. Stokes.

"Have faith, Mrs. Stokes," she affirmed. "Harlem will rise again."

"Yes, ma'am," Mrs. Stokes counters. "So will Jesus, but I ain't waitin' up nights."

I read this strip over and over, mystified over its meaning for my own life. As I identified with the skeptical Mrs. Stokes, her elderly employer took on a divine voice: *Are you going to have faith or listen to Mrs. Stokes?*

I smiled. God did have a sense of humor, resorting to cartoon characters to foster my resolve about Harlem. But my chuckle had quickly turned to fear. Moving from Harvard to Harlem was no laughing matter.

As Dad returns to the car, I decide against disclosing my *Doonesbury* inspiration. I would risk not only his disdain but a likely referral for a mental-health examination. I hate this negative turn in our relationship. Having followed in his footsteps, I became a Cornell All-American football player. I could do no wrong, until now. What a filial fall! My Harlem decision threatens to drop me from favored offspring into the ranks of the disinherited.

Dad goes for the jugular, using arguments from the professional ("I didn't raise you with the best of everything, send you to the top schools, and open doors for you, for you to be a struggling community lawyer"), to the political ("We're Republicans. Those Democrats in Harlem will never help you"), and the practical ("Take care of yourself first, then maybe you'll be able to take care of the less fortunate").

Dad's pragmatism was always his most challenging argument: make money first; give back later. His conventional wisdom, however, begged the key question: Must community service take a back seat to more lucrative career opportunities? I could have counterargued from Gandhi (unearned suffering is redemptive), King (risk-taking for social justice is liberating), Christ (humble self-sacrifice is leadership). But I resisted. The key now was not to win an argument but to discover common ground.

I float a compromise. "You agree that Harlem needs help, right?" He looks askance, wary of my approach. "So look at my time in Harlem as the Peace Corps or military service—my giving something of value to the country."

"That's a big stretch."

"C'mon, Dad, work with me on this."

"So why don't you join the army?"

"You really want me to enlist?"

"You'd probably be safer. At least in boot camp you'd learn how to use a gun. You'd need it more in the ghetto than in the military."

I don't like his analogy, but his tone is encouraging. I press on. "If you're really worried, I'll take martial arts."

"Just don't lose your football legs. At least you can run away from trouble."

"I still hold the Ivy League record: carries in a game." I flash a smile, hoping for a return. My reach for levity falls short.

"How much time are we talking here?" His question is the first sign of an imminent breakthrough. I'll probably need at least half a dozen years, but I go light to make a deal.

"Give me five years. If my progress hasn't convinced you by then, I'm out."

"Three," he counters.

"Four," I offer, sensing that it might be unrealistic, but feeling that I may be ready to move on by then, anyway. "Like two tours of duty. Four years."

"Y'know, there's a fine line between vision and fantasy." Our eyes lock. I extend my hand. He grudgingly takes it for what has to be the most satisfying handshake of my life. Silence rules the half-hour ride to my uncle's house in Newton where my graduation dinner awaits. I spy my father's wry smile. I've made a lousy bet, and Dad knows it.

SECTION ONE

PURGATORY

1980s

ONE

The Battle for Harlem's Soul

W ALKING UP CONVENT Avenue—a streetscape less marred than the rest of Harlem—I wonder if James O'Neal is home. Soon after graduation, he and I transformed ourselves from Harvard roommates to Harlem roomers, renting the basement floor-through at 419 Convent Avenue for six hundred dollars a month. James was the first recipient of the Harvard Fellowship in Public Interest Law, awarded for his Legal Outreach proposal to use the law as a vehicle to motivate at-risk teens toward academic success. The Fellowship funding gave him a reliable source of income. I, meanwhile, searched for work uptown.

Having resolved to follow the Perkins paradigm and work in the community, I'd sent out my resume to every Harlem lawyer I could find and knocked on every uptown law office still standing. These endeavors had yielded only a handful of interviews. I'd concluded that these firms were wary of an upper-middle-class guy from Harvard with big ideas but no practical experience. This suspicion had been confirmed by my meeting with legendary Harlem attorney Cora Walker. "You've got a lot of Ivy

FIGURE 3: 419 Convent Avenue, 1982

League on this resume," she'd said, laughing, "but Ivy doesn't grow on Lenox Avenue."

I'd feigned a smile. I felt like an overeducated fool. I expected my three Ivy League degrees to launch a successful career. Instead, they'd become heavy medals of dishonor causing me to sink into the uptown quicksand.

· Frustrated by my search for jobs uptown and having to empty my pockets of bills and coins on the kitchen table to come up with three hundred bucks, which was my share of the month's rent, I accepted Dad's offer to write the speeches he gave to the Red Cross and other charitable groups. This financial lifeline, however, came with a price.

I'd figured that working for Dad would be a challenge—too cozy, paternalistic—and each time I'd come to his Park Avenue suite I'd had to endure another attempt of his to direct my initiative elsewhere. His favorite stratagem was recounting his life story as a case study in how to build a career before being of service to the community. I could have recited it in my sleep. But I always listened dutifully.

Dad had been born the son of a gardener in a small upstate New York town. He'd been the first in his family to attend college and had worked his way through Cornell University shoveling coal in a frat-house furnace to earn room and board. He'd refused financial help even after he'd become a football star. When he graduated as a two-time All-American in 1939, no professional team would offer him a contract because of a color bar in professional sports that didn't fall until Jackie Robinson joined the Brooklyn Dodgers in 1947. Although my father was a top student, none of the corporate recruiters on campus would talk to him, and so he taught and coached football at black colleges—the only schools where he could find employment—until he attained his doctorate in sociology from the University of Pennsylvania. He rose to become a college president, a U.S. ambassador, and the first black person on the board of the New York Stock Exchange. He was now chairman of the American Red Cross.

Each week, Dad found a way to remind me of the values of hard work, achievement, common sense, and leadership that he'd instilled in me—qualities that he expected me to emulate.

As I was leaving Dad's office one afternoon, Cyrus Vance just happened to show up, trumpeting his venerable law firm and passing me his business card. I glared at Dad on my way out, signaling to him that using a former secretary of state as bait was an unfair tactic. Our eyes met, and Dad let a thinly veiled smile cross his lips. He knew he'd touched the nerve of my unfulfilled ambition. I tossed the business card in the trash as I exited the building. It was too great a temptation.

. . .

My greatest hope for a job uptown was Hope Stevens, known as "Harlem's Lawyer" for his half-century crusade against Harlem's decline. Like thousands of others, Hope had emigrated from the Caribbean during the height of the Renaissance. After City College and Brooklyn Law School, he'd been a pioneer attorney and entrepreneur. He'd become chairman of the National Conference of Black Lawyers, a founder of Carver Savings Bank and the United Mutual Life Insurance Company, and president of the Uptown Chamber of Commerce.

The day of my interview with Hope, I'd been so excited that I'd decided to walk the twenty blocks from my Sugar Hill abode to his 125th Street office. Block after block of abandoned, dilapidated brownstones and tenements had distracted me. I'd slowed my pace to observe a couple of homeless men sleeping on the stoops. The incongruity had perplexed me: people in need of housing were lying outside of housing in need of people.

The ragtag retail landscape had also disturbed me: the numerous check-cashing spots, cheap Chinese takeouts, poorly stocked bodegas, shoddy kids' clothing stores, overpriced products, old-school record shops, retail outlets with Arab and Asian workers but no black employees in sight, and the ubiquitous fried-chicken spots. I had expected Kentucky Fried, but Kansas, Southern, Harlem, Mama's, Johnnie's, Community, Lenox? How many greasy fried-chicken joints did a neighborhood really need?

I finally reach 125th Street and find a throng of black people of all shades and dress—dashikis, Afros, headdresses, medallions. I'm confronted by a potpourri of street vendors—selling cheap perfume, five-dollar loop earrings, knock-off designer purses, x-brand watches, ethnic trinkets, incense and oils, and loud neckties. A guy wearing a WE BUY DIAMONDS placard pushes his flyer in my face. The only newsstand has no *New York Times*, but stacks of *Amsterdam News*. The Harlem USA T-shirt vendor brandishes his Malcolm X tchotchkes, his Martin Luther King stock buried. I pause at one of the black book purveyors, struck by a title called *Winning the Black Way*, but decide I'm too broke to make the five-dollar purchase.

I pass by the Apollo. Its signature marquee recalls my fairway vision a couple of years before, and I sense something divine about the moment. I'm now enthralled, drawn to the drumbeats that emanate from 125th Street and Seventh Avenue: African Square, the very heart of Harlem. I cross the street into the Adam Clayton Powell Jr. Building Plaza, where a dozen drummers beat out the rhythms of our heritage.

I check my watch; I'm still too early for the Hope appointment. I linger with the crowd as it grooves to the Afrocentric music, and reflect on how hard it is to imagine that Harlem was not always the center of black culture.

Dutch colonizers settled Harlem in the mid-seventeenth century under the leadership of Peter Stuyvesant, displacing the remaining members of the Weckquaesgeek, part of the Iroquois Nation, the first inhabitants of Manhattan Island. Slaves from the Dutch West India Company turned the Native American trail running through the lush bottomland meadows into the first road to Nieuw Haarlem. It is poetic justice that Africans first paved the way to the place that would eventually become the epicenter of African-American culture. The village was anglicized to Harlem when the British captured the New Netherlands colony in 1674.

Eighteenth-century Harlem was an agricultural town for the "patroons," New York's wealthy, who owned estates overlooking the Hudson River. The tranquility of their holdings was broken by the Revolutionary War skirmishes that raged across the pastoral landscape. The Battle of Harlem Heights in 1776 was General George Washington and the American Continental Army's first victory over the British. Alexander Hamilton, one of Washington's commanders against the Redcoats, bought some of this prized property at the turn of the nineteenth century and built his country home, Hamilton Grange, now the two-story, yellow woodframe national memorial located down the street from my new Harlem abode. It's also poetic justice that Hamilton was Harlem's first famous resident, given the popular although probably apocryphal story that his Caribbean roots entailed some kind of African lineage.

The saga of Hamilton's legacy reflects the vicissitudes of Harlem's history. The Revolutionary War hero who became the first secretary of the treasury built his Federal-style country house in the farmland of Manhattan Island in 1802. His move uptown

FIGURE 4: Hamilton Grange, 1802

epitomized a trend among wealthy New Yorkers to flee the hustle and bustle at the southern tip for the pastures to the north. Hamilton traveled to his Wall Street–area office by horseback or stagecoach around the salt marshes and on through McGowan's Pass, which later became part of Central Park. He didn't live long enough—his life was cut short in 1804 by his infamous duel with Aaron Burr—to experience the downtown commute via the ninety-minute steamboat ride along the East River.

The Hamiltonian landholding didn't survive Harlem's first decline. After the Civil War, crop yields fell as industrialization rose. Like many other Harlem estates, Hamilton's was auctioned off and eventually taken by New York City in the 1870s. Hamilton Grange was eventually shoehorned into its current location on Convent Avenue between a six-story apartment building and St. Luke's Episcopal Church. In this way, even the Grange, the most visible legacy of Harlem's only founding father, was relegated to blink-you-miss-it status.

Mass transit expansion spawned Harlem's recovery in the late 1800s. The elevated railroads reached Harlem in 1880, by which time the planning of the Lexington Avenue subway was already underway. Developers seized the market opportunities and created new commercial buildings like the Corn Exchange Bank at 125th Street and Park Avenue, which opened in 1883. The massive, red-stone structure with bay-window frames and ornamental terra-cotta rosettes housed luxury apartments upstairs and the bank at street level. Builders also developed elegant townhouses, quickly transforming Harlem into New York's first suburb.

Harlem at the turn of the twentieth century possessed only a smattering of African Americans, who were confined to "Negro tenements" around West 130th Street. Instead, Eastern European Jews dominated the emerging uptown merchant class, with Harlem being home to the third largest Jewish settlement in the world. Italians populated the East Side around Pleasant Avenue and flocked uptown for the first two decades of the century. By the 1930s, the Italian community in the area that eventually became known as Spanish Harlem was the largest in the United States. Irish and Finnish immigrants also made their way from Ellis Island to fill the new mid-rise dwellings.

Walking swiftly now back across Seventh Avenue, I look up at the sign for Stevens, Hinds & White. I leap up the steps to the second floor, imagining myself part of a singular legacy. For it is in Harlem in the early twentieth century that the National Association for the Advancement of Colored People (NAACP) established its headquarters. This is where W. E. B. Du Bois published *The Crisis*, A. Phillip Randolph launched his barrier-busting Brotherhood of Sleeping Car Porters, and where artists allowed black culture to bloom, activists rallied the masses, and entrepreneurs uplifted the community.

I enter the small, cluttered office of the honorable Hope Stevens. He's on the phone and waves me toward a chair. My eyes are drawn to a framed quotation on his desk: *You will never discover new dreams if you don't have the courage to lose sight of the shore.*

I chuckle to myself. Hope is mentoring me without saying a word. In coming to Harlem I've unmoored myself from my suburban and Ivy League shores. But have I lost sight of them? I know that having Hope as my first employer will help me navigate this deep water.

Watching Hope as he concludes his phone call, I become clearer about just how far out I may need to sail. His ruffled appearance reflects my own attire, but the elegance of his lilting West Indian accent challenges my pedestrian style.

Hope strokes his straight, thick, white hair with the same firmness of hand with which he shook mine. He describes his experiences and beams about his tenure with the National Negro

Congress, when his advocacy yielded a commitment from private bus companies to hire black drivers in Harlem. He flashes his broken smile. "You're quite a young man. Harlem needs young men like you."

My hopes balloon. Job or no job, I resolve to have him as my mentor.

"Be certain of one thing," he says passionately. "We're in the battle for Harlem's soul. This community was once great and Harlem will rise again."

I think of the cartoon conversation between Mrs. Stokes and Mrs. D. and am uplifted that my soon-to-be boss concurs with Mrs. D. Hope's observation quashes in my mind—at least for the moment—the lingering presence of Mrs. Stokes' pessimism.

"Don't worry. We'll find a place for you here," Hope affirms.

These words are music to my ears, as is Hope's promise to call the following day after discussing me with his partners. I skip to "Take the A Train," humming the melody, happy at last to be at home in Harlem.

The thrill passes quickly. The next day I call to thank Hope and am stunned to learn that he's dead, felled by a heart attack early that morning. So soon after my pivotal meeting with him, just after his promise of employment, my mentor, my employer, my great hope—gone? Overnight?! Was this a cruel twist of fate? Just plain ol' bad luck? Or some divinely sanctioned trial that I must somehow find the faith to endure?

Rounding 148th Street and Convent Avenue, I glance at my watch and rush into the apartment, realizing how little time James and I have to prepare for this evening's fellowship meeting. We've brought with us from Harvard our weekly regimen of Bible study, discussion, sharing of personal challenges, prayer support, and a joint meal. The conversation has shifted, from the intellectual gymnastics of the Ivory Tower to intimate exchanges on how to make a difference in Harlem and survive. Word of mouth about how supportive the environment is has spread, filling our living room from the beginning with friends and neighbors. They serve as the only hope so far that my move here might eventually work out.

James greets me with a letter. I can tell by his tone that it's the one from the New York State Bar I've been waiting for, for weeks. I grab it and hurry to my room, shutting the door behind me. I rip open the letter, looking for the good news.

What?! I don't believe this! I reread the letter, toss it away, lock my door, kick something, and knock files off my radiator-shelf. I fling my sneaker against the wall, so hard I cause a dent. I really don't care right now. I collapse on my bed, hiding under my pillow. I've failed to pass the bar exam.

I blame Harlem: for preoccupying me with routines of survival; for the distraction of living in a home that's become as busy as Grand Central Station; for the anxiety of eking out the money so it lasts to the end of the month; for having to study in the library next to noisy vagrants, then moving to the park in search of quiet but ending up sharing the bench with the noxious homeless, and finding another spot only to witness a drug dealer or pimp at work.

I can hear Mrs. Stokes laughing.

James knocks, calls out. I'm supposed to lead the fellowship meeting. I ignore his entreaties. I will cloister myself in here just like I did the day I lost Hope.

What of my plan to launch my solo law practice? I could pass on the law career, dust off notes from the classes I audited at Harvard Divinity School, and go to seminary. Or maybe now that I was an unemployed failure in Harlem I could flee this godforsaken place.

I pace, pause at my bookshelf, grab *Strength to Love*, a collection of classic sermons from Martin Luther King Jr., and remind myself of an early experience that germinated this misadventure in Harlem. I recall the time I'd met King with his mentor, Morehouse College president Benjamin Mays, and other alumni, who were visiting the Mansion House at Hampton Institute where Dad was president. I was scampering about in our living room in my pajamas, hiding between Dad's legs, before Dad had picked me up for a proper introduction and King's hands had taken mine.

Several years later, when I'd seen on television that King had been assassinated, I'd stared at the TV screen, then at my hand that had once held his. I was disbelieving, then confused, and then indignant. At that young age, I couldn't understand why I was so upset. I had just wanted to do something about the mix of emptiness and anger, but had no idea what. After my fairway vision, I had insisted on connecting this childhood epiphany to that singular summer moment, strengthening my resolve to take the fateful step to Harlem, with no money, no job, no community base, and no family support. What had I been thinking?

Disgusted, I sink into my blanket, bundled up against the frigid temperature. It seems colder in my bedroom than outside. Periodic chill was my reward for moving into an unfinished house that smelled of oil and had a fickle boiler.

Why had I thrown away Cyrus Vance's business card?

I pick up my game ball—a reliable source of consolation— and reach for the heroic gridiron days. I'd wanted to become an elite football player when I was growing up. My three years in Sweden hadn't help fulfill that vision. I'd played goalie for my Swedish soccer team (the coach had liked my quick hands, but not my two left feet) and I'd starred for my Swedish basketball team, which hadn't been hard. Finally, Dad had heeded my pleas and, with Mom on my side, had cut short his ambassadorial

FIGURE 5: With my father

tenure. This decision had allowed time for my abbreviated yet All-American, high school football career under the legendary coach Tony DeMatteo, which had culminated in a "Joe Holland Day" in the City of Yonkers. I had garnered an athletic scholarship to the University of Michigan, but that lasted only a year. The intensity of Big Ten football politics had forced me to beat a hasty retreat to the better academic/athletic balance of the Ivy League.

My best game had been during my final season, leading Cornell to victory over Harvard in the driving rain with fifty-five carries, 244 yards, and four touchdowns—statistics painted on the game ball in my hands. Dad was so proud of me back then. My gridiron accomplishments had placed me second to Heisman Trophy winner Billy Sims of Oklahoma in yards and points per game, leading to All-American distinction. I'd shared the backfield with Joe Montana in the Japan Bowl, and had garnered one Heisman vote of my own, cast by fellow Cornellian and prolific sports journalist, Dick Schaap. With fond memories of big gains through the career of my Ivy League predecessor Calvin Hill, the Dallas Cowboys had courted me with an offer of free agency. On Dad's advice, however, I'd opted for Harvard Law instead. I'd listened to him then. Why hadn't I listened to him about Harlem? And now how would I ever survive his "silly mission" tirade? Or Mother's gloomy glare?

A rescue team from the HARK Fellowship pounds on my door. I'd come up with the name Harlem's Ark of Freedom (nicknamed HARK) from my Old Testament studies, updating Noah's ark into a modern-day vehicle in which we outsiders could ride along with Harlem natives as we journeyed together toward freedom and justice. But how could the ark stay afloat when its captain was sinking fast?

I hear singing. Fellowship has begun. I open *A Quiet Revolution* by John Perkins, and turn to a favorite passage in my favorite book:

> Go to the people.
> Live among them.
> Learn from them.
> Serve them.
> Plan with them.
> Start with what they know.
> Build on what they have.

I pull out the index card I'm using as a bookmark. The long-forgotten quotation on the card—a maternal gift for a rocky time—transfixes me:

> If days do not mock dreams
> Then life would be a fairy tale.

Mother had sent it to me when I was a depressed college sophomore, the season I couldn't play football because of the NCAA transfer rules. It was the most trying time of my life—until now.

I open my Bible to Mark 11:23, my beloved scripture: *I tell you the truth, if anyone says to this mountain, "Go, throw yourself into the sea," and does not doubt in his heart but believes that what he says will happen, it will be done for him.*

It had been shared with me as a college freshman, during a retreat held by the Athletes in Action. It had inspired me to forsake my perfunctory religious upbringing and embrace the Christian faith as a daily commitment. Embarking on this spiritual journey had reawakened my childhood sense of destiny and had spawned a yearning to make a difference with my life. I need my present mountain of fear and doubt to move. I fall to my knees to pray.

A few minutes later, I stagger to my feet, unlock the door, make a pit stop at the bathroom to throw water on my face, and trudge through the kitchen to the meeting. The room is packed with the usual twenty-somethings, and so full that I hope to slip in unnoticed. Instead, I'm inundated with handshakes and hugs. I shroud my suffering with a half smile, hoping to be uplifted by my spiritual brothers and sisters. I clap along with them, but only mouth the words of the chorus:

> What a mighty God we serve.
> Angels bow before him,

Heaven and earth adore him,
How can you ignore him?
What a mighty God we serve.

How do I sing the Lord's song in a strange land?

TWO

Pressed to the Wall, Dying, But Fighting Back!

To PASS THE BAR exam seems such a Pyrrhic victory, given what practicing Harlem law has yielded: a poorly lit cubbyhole of an office buried at the back of a Hotel Theresa office suite and lots of painful decisions, such as turning away another desperately needed client because helping a lowlife landlord evict his tenants is just too much for my paycheck-starved stomach to bear.

I mark up a real estate contract, glad to be drafting in my office instead of representing clients in landlord-tenant court—my least favorite place to be. I check my watch, worried that I'll run out of time. This is my cue to clean things up for Mother's first office visit tomorrow. Dad, of course, won't be coming, but will likely send another card reminding me that the clock is ticking on our Harlem bet. I feared that his absence tomorrow would have less to do with any lingering opposition to my Harlem initiative than with his intensifying struggle with lung cancer.

Recently, Mother has been tweaking me about my lack of social life. She also has been accusing me of being in love with

FIGURE 6: Receiving my mother's post-game notes

Harlem, married to my silly mission. She's been advising me about my lack of paying clients, social life, exercise, time, balanced diet, wardrobe, money, etc. Her critique hasn't been this intense since my football days when she would find me after the final whistle and confront me with her game notes (see Figure 6). Dad and I would share a smile and laugh afterwards about her Monday-morning quarterbacking. Her counsel yields no humor these days.

I'm trying to get her to convince Dad to back my Harlem real estate venture. I've mentioned that we could buy some vacant brownstones for $50,000 apiece. But as the intellectual of the family, with a master's degree in psychology from Harvard, Mother is ambitious for me is to be a professor at an Ivy League university, not an uptown businessman. She herself had been encouraged to follow the professional path of her father, who was a lawyer, and her brother, a judge. But she'd handled her career the old-fashioned, conservative way, sacrificing it in support of family, seeding and nurturing the success of her husband and children. She'd typed every page of her husband's doctoral dissertation for timely submission, and had become the consummate first lady to my Dad's college presidencies at Delaware State and the Hampton Institute and to his diplomatic stint abroad. She'd helped him break into the upper echelons of public service and business.

Since no Harlem job had been forthcoming, I'd moved my office to this erstwhile hotel in order to establish a more professional setting than my brownstone basement apartment for my solo law practice. I sigh, observing the cracked windowpane and leak-stained ceiling and recalling the loose floor tiles I'd tripped over this morning and my walk up six flights, after having waited long enough for the elevator.

There is no greater representation of Harlem's fall from grace than the Hotel Theresa, having morphed from storied bedroom suites to subpar office space, but retaining her name in deference to her glory days. I'd thought that establishing my first law office in Harlem's most famous building would be some sort of plus. However, this was not the Theresa of old.

When it opened in 1913, with three hundred guest rooms and an all-white staff, the Theresa had become the golden girl of Harlem's Golden Age, the grande dame of the Renaissance. Developed by clothing manufacturer Gustavus Sidenberg and designed by the Blum Brothers, it was built for the white elite who were moving uptown. As the tallest building in Harlem for forty years, this "Waldorf of Harlem" featured a striking white brick façade and diamond-shaped terra-cotta. It sported a grand ballroom that hosted New York's high society throughout the Renaissance. For whites only, of course.

When this racist guest and staff policy ceased in 1940, the Theresa welcomed the highest echelon of black society. Over the next few decades, Duke Ellington, Louis Armstrong, Lena Horne, Sugar Ray Robinson, Dorothy Dandridge, Josephine Baker, Ray Charles, Dinah Washington, Muhammad Ali, Little Richard, and Jimi Hendrix walked through the hotel's lobby and made the Theresa the vibrant center of African-American life, solidifying Harlem's place as the capital of black America.

When boxer Joe Louis won his widely anticipated United States vs. Nazi Germany rematch with Max Schmeling in 1938, Harlem flooded her streets to celebrate. Thousands swelled around the Theresa, hoping to catch a glimpse of their national hero returning to the hotel from his first-round knockout at Yankee Stadium.

Perhaps the Theresa's most telling time came in 1960, when she played host to political legends. Fidel Castro, who'd recently ascended to power in Cuba, came to New York City for the opening session of the United Nations. After he'd been evicted from the Shelburne Hotel for allegedly cooking chickens in his room, he'd brought his delegation uptown to the Theresa, where he'd held impromptu press conferences in the grand ballroom and received Soviet leader Nikita Khrushchev, Indian prime minister Jawaharlal Nehru, and Malcolm X. Later in the year John F. Kennedy had brought his presidential campaign to the Theresa for an event with Eleanor Roosevelt. The Theresa closed as a hotel in 1967, beaten down by the increasing commercial deterioration that followed the Harlem riots of 1964 and ironically also due to the end of segregation, which had opened hotel doors for blacks elsewhere in the city.

My stomach growls and distracts me from my legal drafting. I've worked right through lunch again, a frequent occurrence given that my vegetarian diet is incessantly challenged by Harlem's greasy-spoon ubiquity. I became a vegetarian at Harvard, when I was struggling for direction over my Harlem vision. Weekly fasting became my spiritual discipline, as I sought divine guidance. In the process, my meat-and-potatoes habits gave way to yogurt-and-granola preferences. These have put me at odds with Harlem's chicken-and-fries culture.

My solo law practice had an auspicious beginning with my first clients, Yolanda King and Attallah Shabazz. The retainer check for $500 from the daughters of Martin Luther King Jr. and Malcolm X to form Nucleus, their nonprofit theater company, seemed to vindicate my entrepreneurial initiative: I couldn't find a Harlem job, so I created my own. But my pitches to do legal work for Freedom National Bank, Carver Savings Bank, United Mutual Insurance, Harlem Commonwealth Council, and other community institutions bore no fruit. So I was left representing slumlords, which left me with the tortured choice—go broke or go to hell.

Walter Wilson rushes in, excited about a new prospect for the real estate brokerage business we're trying to build. I'd met Walter in the Powell State Office Building at the monthly meeting of MORE, the Motivational Organization Researching Economics. I wasn't sure what the acronym meant, or even why I was there, except for my naïve notion that attending community meetings was a good way to connect to Harlem. The failure of this strategy after countless sessions over innumerable weeks had made me an ambivalent attendee that night.

I'd observed one of the activists who had fingered me as a "traitor to my people for representing white realtors," so I'd settled in a dark corner at the back of the room, and looked at MORE's mission statement that I'd scribbled in my notebook: "to formulate economic developments to create wealth for community residents." The subsequent shouting matches confirmed my suspicion that the others in the room were as clueless as I was about how to pursue this worthy objective. This was no surprise. From the pain of slavery's Middle Passage to emancipation's broken promise of "forty acres and a mule," to the current pathologies of the urban underclass, the paucity of economic power—and what to do about it—continued to plague black America.

Tired of the tirades against "Ivy League interlopers," I was readying myself to leave when I was captivated by a tall, razor-thin, dark-skinned, bearded man, who preached about the need for "modern-day Philip Paytons." The sound of Payton's name made me sit up and take notice.

Blacks moved into Harlem following the opening of the Lexington Avenue subway in 1904. Its much-anticipated completion had made upper Manhattan a boomtown during the mass-transit construction. Speculative residential developments had sprung up like wildflowers, quickly outstripping the demand of prospective white residents, for which they were built.

The housing glut had crashed property values, which in turn opened a door of opportunity for Philip A. Payton Jr., called the "Father of Colored Harlem"—an entrepreneur whose short-lived ventures set in motion the seismic changes that led to the Harlem Renaissance.

Trained as a barber in New England, Payton became the leading black realtor in New York City, managing black tenements for white landlords. With initial capital of half a million dollars (he sold 50,000 shares for $10 each), Payton formed his own company in 1904, the Afro-American Realty Company. He bought a swath of property on West 135th Street and moved African Americans by the hundreds into it and other tenements that had been left vacant because landlords couldn't find enough white renters to fill their new buildings.

Payton recruited his tenants from New York neighborhoods where blacks were suffering worsening conditions: primarily San Juan Hill (now the site of Lincoln Center) and the Tenderloin— both scenes of anti-black riots—and Hell's Kitchen and the nearby West 30s, where "negro tenements" had been razed for the construction of the original Pennsylvania Station.

Payton burst open a demographic dam. The trickle of locals became a flood of Jim Crow–fleeing, Promised Land–seeking blacks, primarily from Virginia, the Carolinas, and Georgia. The migration turned international, with the masses—Hope Stevens among them—streaming into Harlem from the Caribbean.

Despite the support of Booker T. Washington and his other investors, Payton mismanaged his capital needs and went bankrupt within four years. Though he failed to exploit his premier position, Payton paved the way for John Nail, Henry Parker,

Lillian "Pig Foot Mary" Dean, and other African-American entrepreneurs to own and invest in Harlem real estate.

The trail Payton blazed radically shifted the racial demography of Harlem. The more blacks moved in, the more whites fled north to Riverdale and New Rochelle, east to Long Island, or across the Hudson River to New Jersey. Harlem through the 1920s witnessed what was called the Roarin' Reversal: 120,000 whites left; 90,000 blacks arrived. The former kept leaving until they'd all gone; the latter kept coming until there was no more room. The number of blacks grew from 10 percent of Harlem's population in 1910 to 70 percent in 1930.

As I listened to the bearded, razor-thin speaker that evening at the MORE meeting, I appreciated not only his grasp of history but his passion, vernacular, sensibility, and indignation. Therefore, I made the painful decision to stay until the end of the protracted session, after which I introduced myself to him. His name was Walter Wilson, and his skepticism about my Harvard-to-Harlem spiel was obvious. He interrupted me mid-sentence. "What you know 'bout Harlem?"

Spontaneity has never been my strong suit. "I know Harlem needs help," I said. "I've come to help create housing, jobs, and uplift for the Harlem community." Though my sentiments had been heartfelt, I knew they'd missed the mark. I was being shown once again that conviction and wisdom are two very different things.

Walter glared at me. "Forget 'bout all that," he barked. "First you gotta deal with the pain. You know ain't nothing but pain in these streets, lots and lots of pain, for lots and lots of years!"

His voice had become a loud whisper. I could sense the man's compassion had been shackled by his anguished heart. I decided to try again. "Will you help me help Harlem?"

"What? You think I got time to be running around behind some pie-in-the-sky preppy? Your kind done come and gone before. Nothing changed."

His emotion had paralyzed me. He shrugged in disgust and turned to walk away. At that moment, all I could think of was Mrs. D. and Mrs. Stokes. So I floated my vision line: "Have faith, my brother. Harlem will rise again."

He laughed a loud infectious guffaw. Had I said something funny? Should I laugh, too? I risked it. I saw surprise, perhaps a glimmer of hope, in his eyes.

"Okay," he said. "Show me what you got."

"What I got?"

"Want my help? You better show me something!"

Short of options, I'd invited Walter to the 419 Convent Fellowship. I wasn't sure he'd come, even less so what would happen if he did. Nonetheless, one Thursday evening he showed up and, to my shock, didn't say a word. He just studied everything and everybody. The next week he returned and confronted James with, "What you know 'bout Harlem?" Then he did the same with Leslie, Jackie, Cliff, Mimsie, and Mary Ann. . . . Everybody had to pass the Walter test. Though nobody had sailed through with flying colors, the entire fellowship seemed to pass more quickly—and with less aggravation—than I had.

Our backgrounds couldn't have been more different. Born and raised in Harlem in the 1940s and 1950s, Walter had been part of what I call Generation Blight. They had suffered the consequences of slavery's enduring legacy. They'd been perceived as society's failures, but were in fact products of a society that could have—and should have—done more to level the playing field of socioeconomic advancement. Unfortunately, when the government had intervened in their lives it had done so with policies that fostered cycles of dependency, low expectations, and family disintegration, and had turned tough but functional communities into ghettos of crime and isolation.

FIGURE 7: The leadership of HARK Fellowship: *Standing from right*: Dennis Henderson, me, Jacqueline Patton, Sylvia Kinard, James O'Neal, Cliff Royal, and Jacqueline's son David. *Seated from right*: Leslie Walker, Warren Staton, Mary Ann Royal, Walter Wilson.

Walter had grown up in the projects and been raised in a household by a single mother. Peers had pressured him to drop out of school. He'd turned from petty larceny as a teen to doing and dealing drugs; he'd become active in street riots and had fathered children out of wedlock. Seventeen arrests had led to five different stints in jail.

What made Walter great was that he'd survived the body blows of the Blight —the economic and social catastrophe that had plagued Harlem since the 1940s—with the drive to make something out of his life. I was drawn to him by his knowledge that he, as a native son of Harlem, could find a new way for himself and his community. Likewise, I think he was drawn to me by my knowledge as a child of privilege who sought to understand a place he was unprepared to serve. Through this mutuality we became each other's mentors, discovering a similarity greater than our differences—a commitment to work toward Harlem's rebirth.

There was a deeper lesson I had to learn as well. I had chosen Hope Stevens, but God had given me Walter Wilson. The wonderful irony was that this ex-convict, street peddler, and incense-maker had turned out to be the best Harlem shepherd imaginable. He was someone who could keep me out of trouble, and tell me where to go and where not to go and, more importantly, who to trust and who not to trust. I closely followed his advice on places he used to frequent in his former life but now avoided. One of those blocks was 129th Street between Lenox and Fifth avenues.

Although at the time I met Walter he was a thirty-something ex-con with no mainstream work experience, he possessed lots of Harlem contacts and a set of solid people skills. With these, we fashioned an entrepreneurial opportunity. I set up a real estate brokerage under my law license with Walter as my salesperson. At least, that was the plan. Walter not only had to pass the licensing exam, but had to obtain a certificate of good conduct from the parole department. This was no easy task with his multiple convictions.

The phone rings. I'll never finish this contract with all these interruptions. One of these days I'll be able to afford a secretary to screen my calls.

I call out to Walter, only to discover that he's already left to show one of my listings. I decide to pick up. It's Alex Prempeh, the community activist who facilitated my move to this two-room suite when I desperately needed a bona fide office instead of a desk at home. He knows I owe him, and he's always cashing in. He's calling with today's crisis.

"Kofi's on the roof of the Dwyer throwing bricks down," he announces.

"No way."

"Demolition crew called the cops," he reports.

I hesitate. I'll never meet my paying client's deadline if I go running off on another errand of mercy.

"We need you, Joe," Alex importunes.

Let us not become weary in doing good, for at the proper time we will reap a harvest if we do not give up.

I try to dismiss the relevance of this morning's scripture reading, but since I direly need to reap a harvest, I realize I'd better go help the enigmatic Kofi Brown.

"On my way." I'm already heading to the door, ever ambivalent. *When will I finish the contract, clean the office?* one part of me thinks. *Isn't this why I came to Harlem?* asks the other.

I run outside and sprint the two blocks to West 123rd Street and St. Nicholas Avenue, hoping my out-of-shape football legs will support my ambitious pace. I arrive at the Dwyer Warehouse—another troubled Harlem landmark, though not as famous as the Theresa. The Dwyer is a nine-story structure of undulating yellow, red, and orange brick, which opened in 1892 as the O'Reilly Brothers Warehouse, named after the family that developed it. Like other entrepreneurs, the O'Reilly brothers followed the late nineteenth-century real estate boom northward, expanding their warehouse business from midtown. Some were more visionary. The builders of the Polo Grounds—the future home of the New York Giants and later a massive public-housing project—saw Harlem as the hot spot for Manhattan's affluent, and introduced polo uptown. Another entrepreneur, Oscar Hammerstein, brought the Harlem Opera House to 125th Street (the emerging commercial core of the community).

I look up and see the broad silhouette of Kofi Brown on the roof of the Dwyer, a brick in each hand, raised high over his head. I'd met Kofi at a MORE meeting, where he'd told me he needed a lawyer for a real estate matter but couldn't afford one. Since I couldn't afford any more pro bono work, the conversation had been brief. But rumors surrounding his financially strapped nonprofit, Our Families Protection Association, were rampant. After pressure from Alex Prempeh, I'd succumbed and offered Kofi advice. I'd also limited my time, having learned the hard way that big-hearted actions don't pay the bills.

Still breathing hard and more resolved than ever to get to the gym (*Next week*, I told myself), I scan the crowd of bystanders, hard hats, and cops who are standing next to an ominous-looking bulldozer that confronts the Dwyer.

"Put the bricks down," bellows a police officer through a bullhorn, "and come down now!"

Kofi isn't easily intimidated. "Send your wrecking crew home," he yells out. "Or in the name of Marcus Garvey, bricks will rain down from heaven!"

Kofi is a follower of Garvey's philosophy of self-help, race pride, and black nationalism, still so prevalent around here decades after its heyday. The arrival of a young Jamaican named Marcus Garvey in Harlem early in the Renaissance exemplified the change that the O'Reilly brothers and other white entrepreneurs hadn't foreseen.

Garvey electrified Harlem. Through his signature street-corner, soapbox oratory and pompous parades down Harlem's broad boulevards, Garvey exhorted the black poor and working class to join "a mighty race," marching with his African army toward a "glorious destiny in a beautiful Motherland." Garvey spoke of the black man's "place in the sun," and called for the resettlement of Africa, which in effect meant colonizing Liberia. He drew 25,000 uniformed delegates to Madison Square Garden in 1920 for the First International Convention of the Negro Peoples of the World.

Blacks from across the nation were drawn to Garvey in the aftermath of the "Red Summer" of 1919, when racial violence erupted in two dozen cities, including Chicago and Washington,

D.C., but not in Harlem. African Americans embraced "the Negro capitol of the world" as a safe haven in a country where the Ku Klux Klan had been reenergized, lynchings were widespread, and job prospects were diminishing. Garvey was their champion.

Although he was popular among the masses, Garvey was derided as "a Negro with a hat" by W. E. B. Du Bois. Like other black intellectuals, Du Bois feared that Garvey's support among grassroots Harlemites threatened what Du Bois termed the "Talented Tenth"—the potential leaders of the black community. More threatening for Garvey, however, was the opposition of J. Edgar Hoover, who pressed a federal prosecution against him on flimsy evidence. Garvey was convicted of mail fraud in 1923 and spent five years in prison.

As I stand looking up at Kofi I wonder whether I'm not in some way responding to Garvey's call, except instead of Africa I've been summoned back to Harlem. I've always been more of an integrationist than a nationalist; that we're all the same in God's eyes and need to work together to build institutions for the greater good. I've also noticed that, while all the black nationalists are running around Harlem these days at protest marches, the Koreans, Arabs, and whites are the ones who own the businesses and buildings.

Kofi is the exception to this rule. He's fighting for the Dwyer to keep his entrepreneurial dream alive. The O'Reillys had lost the building many decades ago, their business plan wrecked by the demographic and market dynamics of the Renaissance. One of their successors had named the building the Dwyer Warehouse, which had eventually ended up, like most post-Renaissance properties, in the hands of New York City for back taxes. Our Families Protection Association had purchased it at a city auction for $47,000. Kofi's vision—borrowed from Garvey—had been to transform the Dwyer into a training school to empower community residents to own businesses and properties.

I look up at Kofi, regaled in Garvey's spirit, and see him as a defiant and armed African warrior against the demolition crew a dozen stories below. His militancy testifies to Garvey's enduring legacy, whose business failures, imprisonment, and deportation were immaterial if not forgotten details to Kofi.

"This is your last warning!" announces the police officer. "Come down. . . ."

Kofi interrupts him, shouting down pieces of signature verse from Claude McKay as his battle cry:

> If we must die, O let us nobly die,
> So that our precious blood may not be shed
> In vain; then even the monsters we defy
> Shall be constrained to honor us though dead!

Kofi's so high up, some of the words are difficult to make out. But I know them all. I recite the rest of it quietly with him.

> O, kinsmen! we must meet the common foe!
> Though far outnumbered let us show us brave,
> And for their thousand blows deal one deathblow!
> What though before us lies the open grave?
> Like men we'll face the murderous, cowardly pack,
> Pressed to the wall, dying, but fighting back!

That the Renaissance muse would find a mouthpiece in a grizzled, grassroots activist like Kofi Brown astounds not only me, but also everyone within the sound of his voice. For an eerie moment, you can hear a pin drop on St. Nicholas Avenue.

The cops huddle. I approach them and we exchange words. I'm handed the megaphone, which I point skyward.

"Kofi Brown," I yell. "This is your attorney, Joe Holland." I wait for him to look down.

Decades of deferred maintenance on the Dwyer had made today's standoff inevitable. A chemical fire had caused floors to collapse, alarming not only the residents at the contiguous 270 St. Nicholas Avenue but exposing other locals, including police officers at the nearby 28th Precinct, to toxic fumes. The buildings department had issued an unsafe building order and had dispatched the demolition crew. The battle lines had been drawn and the Garveyite had ascended to make his last stand.

"Kofi Brown." I use my most stentorian voice. "I will bring a motion in Supreme Court tomorrow to stay the demolition. The authorities will cease any action today pending that hearing—if you come down now!"

He finally lowers his gaze. Others buttress my pleas, and Kofi eventually descends from his fortress. The cops and the crowd are relieved. I am not. I know what lies ahead. I will go back to the office to put my priorities on hold and instead pull an all-nighter to prepare motion papers and oral argument for my crazy-as-a-fox, nonpaying client, which might buy him and his building plans some precious time.

I hate to say I told you so, but—

Enough already, Mrs. Stokes.

THREE

The Old Repair Man

ON CHRIST the solid rock I stand / All other ground is sinking sand.

As the congregants sing, I process with the clergy to the pulpit of Christ Community Church. On this hot, late summer Sunday afternoon in Harlem, I'm wearing an African robe—Dad's gift from Ghana as a keepsake—over my suit. I feel beads of perspiration on my forehead. Why didn't I bring a handkerchief?

I listen to the invocation, Old and New Testament scriptures, a musical selection, and several greetings. Periodically but discreetly, I dab my brow with the edge of this finely textured piece of clothing. Dad wouldn't have been pleased that I'm turning his favorite ethnic garment into a sweat rag.

He hadn't been pleased with a lot of my decisions, and on the occasion of my ordination he might have been particularly unforgiving. Mother pulled me aside before the service and reminded me in a whisper of my father's admonition during one of my "religious" moments: "Your father and I raised you to be an international statesman, not a Pentecostal preacher," her last two words dripping with disdain.

My father had died the year before, having lost his battle with lung cancer. He'd been pleased when the HARK Fellowship had come to Bronxville to sing and pray for him. He'd even laughed at my joke: "You wouldn't come to Harlem, so Harlem came to you." And he would have been pleased with his memorial service at the Abyssinian Baptist Church, officiated by his old friend Reverend Sam Proctor. Many of his prominent colleagues on the corporate boards had come uptown to speak in his memory, and I had recited my own poem, "A Son's Psalm":

> Then early every morning, rain or shine
> The denizen of discipline
> That he was
> He would walk, sometimes he would call me,
>   and we would walk
> Along the shores of the Hampton Roads
> Through the corridors of his creations
> Dormitories and science buildings
> Gymnasiums and communications centers
> Education complexes with fountain-centered plazas
> Uplifted lives
> An amalgam of advancement
> Shaped by his genius of weaving
> People
> And his love for them
> Places
> And his labor in them
> Powers
> And his load of them
> Into a tapestry of progress.

I flash back to my earliest Harlem moment with Dad—the summer during law school that I'd spent on Wall Street. Mother had driven Dad and me every morning to the tony Bronxville station, and we'd ridden the train together to Grand Central. Back then, except for a conductor or two, we'd been the only riders of color. Although the express train to Harlem was only fifteen minutes, no one ever got off the train at 125th Street. It was as if Harlem didn't exist. The question that nagged me had become more intense after my vision on that country-club fairway.

"Why doesn't the train ever stop at Harlem?" I'd asked Dad.

His response was memorable: "You need fertile soil for crops to grow."

I hadn't understood what Dad had meant until now. I'd learned firsthand how hard it was to cultivate a harvest of progress in an urban wasteland. For people to succeed, they needed character, education, and opportunities. Dad's "fertile soil" represented what is called "civil society," those institutions—family and church, schools and youth clubs, corporations and small businesses, theaters and libraries—that support individual progress. Perhaps my ordination day would be the moment when I finally started to make some headway cultivating such soil.

I reflect on the bitter irony: the only way I could get Dad to Harlem was for posthumous remembrances. I'm still haunted by how lousy (for me) the bet was that I made with him. He didn't live long enough to collect on it, but I could sense how certain he felt he'd triumph by the wry smile that would cross his lips every time we talked about Harlem. He understood far better than I in all my idealism and naïveté that overcoming the Blight was not a Peace Corps–like stint, but a generational mission.

Now I'm beginning to see what he meant—except my escape route out of Harlem is no longer just a phone call away. This "silly mission" has to work out.

• • •

I signal Lenny, one of the homeless men living in the shelter in the church basement, to bring me a towel. He does so, and I bring it toward my sweat-moistened face, only to discover it's dirty! Where did Lenny disappear to so fast? I sigh and use the edge of my robe again.

Sitting next to my sister, Lucy, near the front of the packed church, Mother discreetly shakes her head at me. She disapproves of my "handkerchief." I'm hoping her first visit to my church goes as well as her first to my home. It had taken her eighteen months to make it to 419 Convent. That evening our weekly Bible study/open house morphed into my surprise birthday party with Mother as the mystery guest. I was proud of her.

FIGURE 8: The surprise birthday party

She kept her smile on for the HARK Fellowship the whole time. I see that same faux smile now.

Although she's always hard on me, she nonetheless seems to be softening toward Harlem. I'd almost convinced her to buy a building on St. Nicholas Avenue from one of my clients, and I was twisting her arm to invest in my own Harlem business. At least Mother had given up hope of persuading me to do something "less risky" with my life. But she was still upset with me for having the HARK Fellowship over to her house for a pool party while she was away in Boston visiting her mother.

I listen to the loud but sonorous visiting choir finish another selection, stifle a yawn, and open my eyes wide. I'm trying to combat the effects of the previous night's shelter duty. I let my eyes gaze anew at the humble décor of this large, brownstone parlor floor that has been converted to a sixty-seat church: its inexpensively paneled walls, tattered red curtains, faded black-and-red-patterned rug, and folding chairs to supplement the battered pews.

What a contrast from Harlem's grand houses of worship that I'd looked at when I was gathering intelligence about Harlem! I'd visited St. Luke's, All Saints, Mother Zion, St. Martin's. Among these magnificent edifices, which had been built for the affluent white population of early twentieth-century Harlem, there was even a synagogue—Temple Ansche Chesed, which had opened in 1909. During the Renaissance and for decades afterward, religion became Harlem's big growth industry. Black houses of worship like Abyssinian, Canaan, Convent, St. James's, and Mt. Nebo took over the grand church buildings that the white faithful had abandoned, as well as storefronts, theaters, and converted brownstones like this one. Harlem eventually had become home to over four hundred churches, seemingly one on every block.

I see one of my mentors, Bishop Ezra Williams of Bethel

Gospel Assembly. The church is another Renaissance child, born in resistance to Jim Crow. The founder of Bethel, Lillian Krieger, a white woman, had come to Harlem in 1917 because her downtown church refused to seat the African Americans she'd invited. Bishop Williams' growing congregation had recently purchased from the city an abandoned junior high school building that the Blight had shuttered. In addition to Bethel's sanctuary, it housed a range of community-outreach programs, including the Beth-HARK Crisis Center.

Cofounded by Bethel and HARK, Beth-HARK's mission was to address one of Harlem's most pressing social problems—the plight of substance abusers and ex-offenders. Our strategy was to meet their needs holistically. We would start off with counseling so our clients could understand the underlying issues of their alcoholism, drug addiction, or incarceration. Then we'd develop a plan of action to overcome the crisis and support them as they implemented it. Walter and I were on the board of directors with Bishop Williams and others from Bethel.

"Hallelujah! . . . Praise the Lord! . . . O Glory to God!!" Evangelist Naomi Wright's praise-filled, offertory prayer breaks my reverie. Her passion notwithstanding, I see a handful of folks, even one of my pulpit mates, who've fallen asleep. All are aroused by the insistent usher with the offering plate.

As I scan the now standing-room-only crowd, I return the smiles of Walter and other members of the HARK Fellowship. Walter has a lot to smile about these days. He'd received his certificate of good conduct from the parole department, and was now making his living as a licensed real estate salesperson. He'd started college and he and I had been volunteering at the St. Nicholas Houses, where he was raised and still lives.

The St. Nick is one of eight large public housing developments, containing thousands of units apiece, that was built in Harlem as part of Franklin Roosevelt's New Deal. Among the vast uptown projects was the Riverton, which had been born of MetLife's frankly segregationist attempt to create a separate-but-unequal uptown counterpart to Chelsea's sprawling, pristine Peter Cooper Village–Stuyvesant Town complexes.

Harlem's movement to create more living space for its residents had led to federally subsidized housing developments, which were of a piece with a government-focused, top–down approach to fighting poverty and pathology. By making welfare a permanent entitlement, the government gutted personal initiative and helped displace men, especially young men, as family breadwinners. By providing the poor with direct aid in every arena, the government had driven out grassroots poverty-fighting organizations that offered not just material aid to the disadvantaged but spiritual resources and character development. And by building its own housing for the indigent, the government had crowded out developers with the knowledge, expertise, and local understanding to construct elegant homes, rather than uninviting towers devoid of beauty, individuality, and character.

Invariably, these monstrosities destabilized communities instead of strengthening them. They bred new subcultures of social pathology rather than the dignity of residency. They fostered gangs instead of families, in Harlem and across the nation. The St. Nick is almost paradise compared to Cabrini–Green in Chicago and other travesties that would eventually be vacated and demolished.

Walter and I would walk door-to-door through each building to survey the problems facing tenants: peeling paint, leaky pipes, loose wires, broken elevators, falling bricks, rusty playgrounds, pests, and graffiti. I would write up a report and serve as pro bono counsel to tenant association leaders as they lobbied New York City Housing Authority officials for a larger repair budget.

Through this grassroots outreach, Walter helped me move beyond the Fellowship routine. Studying the Bible and breaking bread together every week had sustained us, but they didn't address the issues that raged outside the walls of 419 Convent. So the HARK Fellowship hit a different corner every Saturday, dispensing food and clothing, performing music and skits, and replacing leather-armchair theories with preaching and serving. My vision of a new movement based on capitalizing, and teaching within, community-based institutions through which the human and financial resources can flow toward individual advancement sounded a whole lot better in a Harvard classroom than on a Harlem street corner.

I look around the church. Is that Kofi Brown standing in the corner? Kofi and I had won the battle but had lost the war over the Dwyer. My motion to stay the demolition had succeeded, but the work needed to shore up the building had been so substantial that a private developer had exploited the exigency by providing the funds but wresting control of the Dwyer from Kofi's group. Thankfully, I'd been able to help preserve a restrictive covenant in the deal, so that whatever the eventual development, it had to include a nonprofit use.

Rev. Linnette Williamson, my pastor, introduces yet another guest soloist. Like all the music ministers today, she prefaces her song with preaching. I'd met Reverend Williamson in my Theresa law office, when she came to discuss the rehabilitation of a building that her church owned. We'd bonded over a shared commitment to manifest a core biblical value—God's love for the poor. Reverend Williamson had been feeding the homeless through her free lunch program, and I'd been reaching out to them during our HARK street missions. One such encounter had taken me in a new direction.

I'd met Henry on Lenox Avenue and had offered him the food, clothing, singing, and preaching we'd brought along. Henry seemed to respond well and returned week after week, even coming to a couple of our fellowship meetings. Then he stopped. He told me he was staying at the City Armory shelter on West 142nd Street. Eventually, I'd decided to go and look for him.

What I saw at the Armory devastated me. Five hundred men were sleeping in cots that crowded the drill-hall floor. I looked for Henry amid the stench and gloom of row after row of desolation. Faces of despair stared back at me. As the staff dragged men out of bed, I moved in for a closer look but a fight broke out over a broken crack-pipe stem. When someone pulled out a gun, I gave up trying to find Henry and hustled out of there. I never saw Henry again.

Distraught at what I'd encountered, I talked with Reverend Williamson. There had to be a better way, I told her. These men were being given a collective roof over their heads and other material sustenance, but little else. No one, it seemed, was acknowledging their humanity. No one was dealing with their uniqueness as people, their wholeness as individuals. No one was even trying to confront the poverty of spirit that gave rise to their pathologies and their material destitution. As far as I was concerned, the approach whereby the government was a direct provider of social services had failed Henry. He had "three hots and a cot" but nothing more.

But HARK, too, had been failing the Henrys of Harlem. They came to our outreaches for the food and clothing but returned to the streets still hungry, needy, and hurting—week after week, month after month. They gladly received our material provisions but our offerings weren't enough to turn them away from chronic crisis to permanent progress. To really make a difference, the intervention had to be holistic, going deeper than the needs of the body to lift the spirit while at the same time imparting practical guidance.

It became clear to me that without the value of personal

responsibility, Henry risked falling into dependency and despair, his dreams forever deferred. Turning Henry's life around would be impossible as long as he remained in the transitory, precarious world of Harlem's streets and city shelters. I would have to connect with Henry and others like him on a deeper level and under different conditions. I would have to create a physical and moral environment in which life-building tools—the material and spiritual resources necessary for personal rehabilitation— would be accessible.

I thus conceived of Harkhomes: housing not as an end in itself but as a means to restore the whole person. The shelter would offer not only housing and food but life skills that could pave the way toward independence and self-sufficiency. With Reverend Williamson's blessing, therefore, I started a fifteen-bed shelter to help homeless men in her church basement on 128th Street just east of Lenox Avenue. It was a far from ideal location. There weren't too many Harlem blocks in worse condition than 128th, which was light-years away from our HARK Fellowship up on Sugar Hill. From the Fellowship I recruited the male volunteers I needed to supervise the residents each night. I moved the weekly meetings to the sanctuary to facilitate volunteer support for the shelter.

Harkhomes became the new Fellowship, with Bible study every morning instead of once a week, breakfast and dinner every day instead of only on Thursday nights, and with the energy of loving support directed to Harlem's neediest instead of to one another. The old Fellowship evolved into a handful of residents occupying two houses—men's and women's. The women remained at 419 Convent; others joined original Harvard-to-Harlem members Leslie and Jackie and filled the entire house. I moved with Walter and others to West 137th Street off Edgecombe, a ten-minute walk down Sugar Hill from the ladies' abode. James, who had relocated to New York from Cambridge with me, got married and moved away. But another Ivy Leaguer, Mimsie Robinson, moved in. A Brown graduate, he'd given up medical school to return to Harlem. Unlike me, he was an authentic returnee, having grown up in Harlem's Polo Grounds housing project.

To my surprise, Reverend Williamson took me under her wing and drafted me as her assistant pastor. She began to groom me as her successor and insisted on my ordination. I hadn't been looking to add pastoral duties to practicing Harlem law and running Harkhomes, which was an already burdensome mix of responsibilities. My prayers for wisdom and grace intensified as I tried to figure out how to manage my increasing load.

His officiating duties running just as long as everything else, Rev. George Perry amazes me with a quote other than from the Bible—"God Is the Old Repair Man" by Fenton Johnson:

> God is the Old Repair Man.
> When we are junk in Nature's storehouse he takes
>   us apart.
> What is good he lays aside; he might use it someday.
> What has decayed he buries in six feet of sod to
>   nurture the weeds.
> Those we leave behind moisten the sod with their
>   tears;
> But their eyes are blind as to where he has placed
>   the good.
> Some day the Old Repair Man
> Will take the good from its secret place
> And with his gentle, strong hands will mold
> A more enduring work—a work that will defy
>   Nature—
> And we will laugh at the old days, the troubled days,
> When we were but a crude piece of craftsmanship,

FIGURE 9: Lucy takes the microphone

When we were but an experiment in Nature's
 laboratory. . . .
It is good we have the Old Repair Man.

"And we have in our midst today," Reverend Perry concludes,
"a young repair man, Joseph Holland, whom the Old Repair
Man has called to help repair our Harlem community." At his

direction I stand, smiling, more pleased that a relatively obscure poet like Fenton Johnson caused the Renaissance muse to show up at my ordination service than with the standing ovation.

Reverend Perry invites Mother and Lucy to join me on the pulpit. Why did he do that? He tries to hand Mother the microphone but she declines, still smiling. Lucy steps up and graciously handles the moment (see Figure 9). I begin to prepare myself for the inevitable, spirited post-service family conversation.

The tempting aroma of fried chicken and collard greens wafts up from the basement kitchen and exacerbates my impatience. The good news is that the length of the service has introduced an early evening cool to the church. I conclude—given the relative brevity of the ordination message—that Rev. Timothy Mitchell must be hungry, too.

"And sometimes God shows up in our lives," Reverend Mitchell exhorts, "as a blessing in disguise. The reality of His blessing does not become real to us until after the fact."

"Amen!" echo several congregants, including me. Reverend Mitchell hands me the microphone, and I relate a mystery of providential provision from my own experience.

The summer after my second year at Harvard Law School, while I was still wrestling with my Harlem decision, I worked at a Washington, D.C., law firm. I lived with a close family friend—she'd been Dad's assistant when he was president of the Hampton Institute—whom I knew as absentminded Aunt Marie. I'd been saving money for a top-of-the-line stereo system to take back with me to Cambridge. When I finally had enough money, I'd withdrawn the twelve hundred dollars, only to find out at the store that my model was out of stock and my salesman had left early for the weekend. It was a Friday afternoon and the bank had closed. I hid the money in my room at Aunt Marie's house, intending either to buy the stereo or redeposit the money the following Monday.

What I didn't know—because she forgot to tell me—was that Aunt Marie was having some rooms painted the next day. When I returned home Saturday evening, I'd found the furniture rearranged and covered, my room painted, and the painters come and gone. My money was missing!

I searched for it in vain. I felt like an idiot. I was angrier at myself than at the painters, for being so stupid as to leave that much cash unsecured. I told Aunt Marie, who called me irresponsible, chided me for accusing her painters, and summarily dismissed my concerns. I searched again, never found the money, and chalked it up as a very tough life lesson.

Eighteen months later, at the nadir of my first year in Harlem—broke, behind on rent, and with no job in sight—Aunt Marie called.

"I found your money," she reported.

I was speechless.

Aunt Marie explained how she'd discovered the twelve hundred dollars in an envelope tucked inside a favorite blouse she'd removed and put to the side before the painters started. She'd been reorganizing her wardrobe, seen the misplaced blouse, picked it up, and my cash had fallen out. She promised to send me a check by overnight mail.

My blessing in disguise! Absentminded Aunt Marie became to me like one of Elijah's ravens. What had seemed like bad luck at the time had actually been God's handiwork. Providence had prevented me from spending the money on a stereo I really didn't need to preserve it for a more important future purpose that I didn't know I had—manna from heaven to survive in Harlem. Four months rent that I didn't have was now on the way.

Reverend Mitchell takes back the microphone. Impassioned, he climaxes his message with the example of my biblical namesake: Joseph dreamed a dream, and his brothers hated him all the more.

"From this vision," the preacher proclaims, "Joseph ended up in the valley of hardship and persecution, betrayed by his brothers, sold into slavery, falsely accused of rape, unjustly thrown into prison. But it was all a blessing in disguise, for in the Lord's time, Joseph rose to prosperity and leadership."

I am the first to rise to my feet, caught up in the powerful hope of this message.

"And we have a Joseph here today destined for prosperity and leadership," the preacher exhorts.

This is much better news than I expected, especially the part about "destined for prosperity." Maybe I would be able to pay rent on time the following month.

All are on their feet, clapping, singing, and dancing, as the organ and drums surge with an upbeat hymn—*In the name of Jesus / We have the victory.*

I sense a penetrating gaze and turn to see Reverend Williamson glaring at me prophetically. Since my seminal Christian experience as a freshman on the athletes' retreat, my walk with God has been one great adventure. Today's service is just the latest wonder. My plan for a globe-trotting law practice is a distant memory. I've had to lose sight of that shore.

"Thank you, Lord, for calling this young man to Harlem," asserts Reverend Perry.

I'm relieved to know that after all I've been through the "silly mission" wasn't just my crazy idea.

Reverend Williamson guides me to the center of the pulpit. The ministers surround me, lay hands on me, and bless me with the prayer of ordination. "I pray, O God," effuses Reverend Williamson, "that you will give Joe the faith to labor so that Harlem, like Jesus, will rise again."

Again that phrase is uttered. I'm excited to hear the victorious Mrs. D. over Mrs. Stokes.

The sweat is pouring from me now, soaking my robe. I've never felt such glorious perspiration before in my life.

"In the name of Jesus Christ, we consecrate this man of God to proclaim the gospel," exclaims Reverend Mitchell.

As the hands press against my flesh and the music and prayers crescendo, I experience the presence of God as never before, flush in the passion of the moment. Yet one question squeezes through the perspiration and inspiration.

What now, Lord?

FOUR

The Gang of Four

WALKING FAST ALONG Lenox Avenue, I bump into someone in front of Sylvia's Restaurant, Harlem's dining landmark. Its blinking neon illuminates a crowded sidewalk. I'm late. I'm supposed to meet Mother in a couple minutes at the Harlem Travel Bureau, our new business. I'd finally persuaded her to go in with me, so we'd bought a travel agency with a fifty-year brand and a great location on Fifth Avenue. We'd been able to acquire the business and the building that housed it with her investment and a loan from real estate developer Jim Fusco. I'd met Jim, also a former Cornell football player, through Dad's classmate Jan Noyes, who'd attended the memorial service at Abyssinian Baptist. Dad's influence had survived his death in ways he would never have sanctioned.

The site of the travel agency includes a parking lot, which fronts Marcus Garvey Park. With a chance finally to pursue my real estate aspirations, my plan is to build housing on the parking lot. I don't have the time, resources, or expertise for such a venture—but visions die hard.

The real agenda of all the entrepreneurship is to create

employment for the men of Harkhomes, some of whom have attained the stability required for the workplace. Yet it's incredibly difficult to place them in jobs. Mother has agreed to help them with an apprenticeship program at Harlem Travel. Our objective now is to expand the agency and garner training funds to support the initiative. She and I are meeting with an American Express representative—facilitated through another one of Dad's contacts—to explore establishing the first uptown AMEX representative office at Harlem Travel.

I slow my gait to check out the commotion at Sylvia's. I maneuver through the throng and ask what's going on. There aren't enough cops for a police action. I peer into Sylvia's: the pedestrian décor bestows a down-home charm for the usual mix of tourists and locals. I've been approached about taking over a competitor of Sylvia's—La Famille Restaurant, another soul-food spot. But I'm challenged enough sustaining my law practice and strengthening Harlem Travel while running Harkhomes. Thoughts of a Wall Street escape and its certain financial stability, however impracticable at this point, still linger.

"They're about to come out." A middle-aged man's remark breaks my despondency.

"Who's inside?" I ask.

"The Gang of Four!" he says excitedly.

I hesitate then nod, feigning affirmation so as not to come off as an outsider. I still have concerns about being seen as a carpet-bagger.

The man looks dismissively at me. "You're not from around here, are you?"

"Moved to Harlem a while back," I respond matter-of-factly, trying to appear more rooted than I feel. That I still get this question even after my four-year exit plan has expired makes me wonder whether I'll always be perceived as coming from another planet.

I conclude he's referring to some group that's part of this hip-hop trend here to announce a new rap. I'm about to leave when he announces, "Look here. They coming out now!"

He presses forward for a better view. His enthusiasm is infectious and my curiosity gets the better of me.

"Been in there for a while," he whispers back to me. "Must be plotting to take over the city."

His proud pronouncement is the pivotal piece of the puzzle. Dad had prophesied to me about the predominance of the Harlem Democrats, but he hadn't told me quite how powerful they were. I'd learned on my own that the so-called Harlem Clubhouse wasn't some smoke-filled cubbyhole in a wood-paneled basement filled with pandering politicians. Nor was the Gang of Four a singing group. Rather, it referred to the most important members of a political dynasty, the personification of a generational movement begun in the Renaissance by the Harlem Fox, aka J. Raymond Jones.

Like Hope Stevens and Marcus Garvey, Jones had immigrated to Harlem from the Caribbean early in the Renaissance. Unlike Garvey, Jones played establishment rather than radical politics, and lasted longer than his pompous peer. He'd created and grown the Carver Democratic Club into the breeding ground for black political high achievers for generations to come.

Jones rose to power during the reign of Tammany Hall, the Democratic Party's patronage mill that controlled New York City's politics from the nineteenth well into the twentieth century. As the "ward boss," Jones gathered votes, dispensed patronage, and distributed aid. In the dog-eat-dog world of Depression politics, he earned his nickname by his savvy at political hardball. With the support of Harlem real estate baron Lloyd Dickens, the Fox had the resources to match his knowhow, surviving long enough to challenge Tammany powerhouse Carmine DeSapio. He eventually became a city councilman, county leader, and Tammany's first black leader in 1964.

Jones was without peer as a kingmaker. The careers he cultivated constitute an African-American political hall of fame: the first black New York City district leader Charles Fillmore; Congressman Adam Powell; Manhattan borough president and federal judge Constance Baker Motley; federal cabinet member Robert Weaver; judges Alexander, Dudley, Watson, Stevens, and Evans—and the Gang of Four.

The first of the gang to emerge from Sylvia's is Percy Sutton, known simply as the Chairman. Sutton is a tall, broad-shouldered, goateed Texan. A Tuskegee airman and son of a former slave, Sutton came to Harlem as a young lawyer—as did the other three—and developed a broad clientele, which included the controversial Malcolm X. Sutton's career rose more quickly than his power-seeking peers. He won the retiring Motley's seat to the Manhattan borough presidency in 1966 with a stunning 80 percent of the vote, and held the office for eleven years.

Sutton's next move, however, brought a premature end to his political career. He threw his hat into the crowded ring for the Democratic nomination for New York City mayor in 1977 against Congressman Ed Koch, New York Secretary of State Mario Cuomo, Mayor Abe Beame, former congresswoman Bella Abzug, and Congressman Herman Badillo. Sutton finished a disappointing fifth to the victorious Koch and gave up electoral politics for a trailblazing career as a media entrepreneur. He founded Inner City Broadcasting, which owns New York City's leading black radio stations—hit-maker WBLS and talk-central WLIB—as well as AM and FM stations in several urban markets.

The crowd swells as the second gang member, David Dinkins, leaves. He was long considered the least likely of the four to succeed and was the last to ascend the political ladder. Rumors of a possible mayoral campaign had been circulating in the community for a while. The cheers from the crowd engulfing the sidewalk suggest that Dinkins will possess unwavering black support if he challenges Koch in a quest to bring the Clubhouse its greatest victory—city hall.

Dinkins married into the Clubhouse. His father-in-law, Daniel Burrows, was an assemblyman and district leader. Up to that point, Dinkins had lost more races than he'd won, but he'd paid his Carver Club dues all the way up the Democratic Party ladder, stuffing envelopes, hanging posters, distributing flyers, and waiting his turn. When he finally graduated to elective office, redistricting had compelled him not to seek reelection to his seat in the state assembly after one term. He was appointed New York City clerk, where his most important duty was signing marriage certificates. He'd suffered two defeats for Manhattan borough president before winning. Now, as he wades through the crowd to the waiting car, shaking hands, his rising star outshines his overachieving peers.

Just behind Dinkins, standing at Sylvia's entrance, is Charles Rangel, who chats with Sylvia Woods, the restaurant owner, and Van, her enterprising son. Charlie gives Sylvia a hug, steps onto the sidewalk, flashes a smile, and waves to the onlookers—a politician's charisma on full display. The youngest of the gang, Rangel had had an inauspicious beginning, losing his first race for district leader. Thereafter, however, it was blue skies. He'd been elected to the state assembly, and then claimed a much bigger prize, winning the congressional seat from Harlem legend Adam Clayton Powell Jr.

Powell Jr. was a child of the Renaissance who had moved with his family in 1908 from Connecticut to Harlem. His father, Rev. Adam Clayton Powell Sr., had captivated many of the black newcomers to Harlem from the pulpit of his Abyssinian Baptist Church. Powell Jr. came of age during the explosive growth of the church and became Harlem's champion community activist. His "Don't Buy Where You Can't Work" movement had executed boycotts to protest the discriminatory hiring practices of Blumstein's Department Store, Harlem Hospital, and the Transit Authority. It forced Harlem drugstores to employ more black pharmacists. And Powell Jr.'s picket line at the Empire State Building had resulted in the tripling of the number of blacks working at the New York World's Fair in 1939.

By the time Powell Jr. ascended the pulpit of the church in 1937, Abyssinian had become the strongest church in Harlem, with a membership of 13,000. The church was the ideal launching pad for Powell's trailblazing political career. Powell became the first black person elected to the New York City council in 1941 and several years later the first to Congress since Reconstruction. His quarter-century career in Washington was likewise trailblazing. He sponsored bills that combated poverty, established a minimum wage, and offered aid for education.

It was also marked by controversy. He took his Harlem constituents to dine in the "whites only" congressional restaurant. He missed his own committee meetings as he traveled abroad at the public's expense. He threatened to accuse Martin Luther King Jr. of a homosexual relationship if he didn't force the cancelation of planned civil rights marches. Powell was stripped of his powerful committee chairmanship and blocked from taking his seat in the House. He broke party ranks to support President Eisenhower for reelection because the Democratic Party's civil rights platform was too weak. Throughout all of the tumult, he told his followers to "Keep the faith, baby!"

As Rangel works the crowd, bear-hugging an elderly man and kissing a baby, I reflect on his razor-thin victory over Powell in 1970. Was it the latter's flamboyant lifestyle and the consequent ethics scandal that led to his defeat? Or was it the fact that his political rise had coincided with Harlem's fall—a transi-

FIGURE 10: The Gang of Four: (*from left*) David Dinkins, Basil Paterson, Percy Sutton, Charlie Rangel

tion from Golden Age to Dark Age, when poverty, crime, drugs, homelessness, and an epidemic of dropping out, broken families, joblessness, riots, and other social ills ravaged the community? Whatever the cause, the passing of Powell and the ascent of Rangel established—more than any other circumstance—the Gang of Four's hegemony in Harlem.

The last of the gang to exit is Basil Paterson, whose Harlem roots are the deepest of the four. Paterson was born in Harlem in 1926—both his parents having emigrated from the Caribbean in Garvey's wake the decade before. Paterson's mother even served for a while as Garvey's secretary.

Paterson's political career first tacked north toward Albany as Harlem's state senator. He then lost the race for lieutenant governor in 1970 before becoming deputy mayor to Ed Koch.

Finally, there was his historic return upstate as New York's first black secretary of state, before he'd left political life for the lucrative world of labor law.

I had a further reason to be interested in the Gang of Four, since I had experienced personally the political power of the Harlem Clubhouse. When the incumbent Harlem state senator Leon Bogues died suddenly in the summer of 1985, a special election was called. To my surprise, local Republican leaders began immediately twisting my arm to run. At the time, I had no idea what a political rarity I was—a black Republican in Harlem with Ivy League credentials. So all the Ivy I dragged with me into Harlem got me into trouble again.

The leaders also liked my family heritage. My grandfather, father, and uncle had all been GOP appointees, and I could remember vividly the childhood stories of my grandfather's efforts to stem the tide of black Bostonians fleeing the Party of Lincoln for FDR, Eleanor, and their New Deal. Dad had groomed me for a political future. He saw himself as the Republican and African-American version of Joe Kennedy Sr., cultivating the electoral ground for his son that he'd never had quite enough fire in the belly to do himself. He understood that my being a Republican in Harlem would doom me forever to political purgatory. That was another fact I'd missed.

Dad had schooled me in his ideology, drawn in large part from his political favorite (and fellow famous football player with connections to upstate New York) Jack Kemp. Kemp had tried to convince Dad to return to his roots in the Finger Lakes region of New York State and run for Congress as a hometown hero, but he turned it down. "If you want to help the community," Dad would say, using his favorite Kempian maxims, "you have to build its economic base first. Handouts and welfare checks won't do it." As a congressman from Buffalo, Kemp had helped foster urban empowerment zones, where entrepreneurs received tax relief in exchange for creating economic opportunity in inner-city communities like Harlem. This policy stemmed from Kemp's belief that the greatest resources were not in the ground but in people and all that was needed was the freedom to unleash them.

"True wealth," Dad would add, paraphrasing Kemp, "is unlimited because true wealth is in each of us. The world's not a place of physical scarcity, but of human potential. There's no need to take from Peter to pay Paul. All we need to do is to empower Paul to reach Paul's potential."

When the party elders had heard me articulate these Kempian ideas, they insisted this ideological emphasis, leveraged by my youthful enthusiasm, was a formula for success at the ballot box. What was left unsaid, most importantly, was that they didn't have anybody else gullible enough to buy their argument that this was a race worth running.

To seal the deal, the operatives brought me into a meeting with Manhattan GOP leader and state senator Roy Goodman. I was finally cajoled into the race by their assertion that the Democratic choice—Basil Paterson's son, David—was "not a heavyweight like his father." Dad's best Cornell football buddy, the upstate New York businessman Jack Hemingway, would raise money and engineer the support in Albany necessary for my fledgling campaign.

Since political acumen was not an attribute I'd acquired through my highfalutin education, I failed to assess how long the odds were against my candidacy. Here I was, three years out of law school in a new and very different place, running as a black Republican in the Reagan era in the most liberal district in America.

What were you thinking?

Never mind, Mrs. Stokes. She's probably a card-carrying Clubhouse member.

I couldn't claim ignorance of my kamikaze mission, for I knew the history. More than a century before my ill-advised campaign, before there'd been a Harlem Renaissance or a Clubhouse, black America was Republican. Frederick Douglass, the great statesman and confidant of Abraham Lincoln, once exulted, "The Republican Party is the deck; all else is the sea." In 1854, the Republican Party had been founded on a pro-freedom plank and by 1863, Lincoln, the party's first leader, had issued the Emancipation Proclamation. During Reconstruction, it was the party of Lincoln that had launched America's first civil rights revolution. It had passed the Thirteenth Amendment to the constitution, which abolished slavery; the Fourteenth Amendment, which guaranteed citizenship and equal protection under the law; the Fifteenth Amendment, which prohibited denial of suffrage due to race; and in 1875, it had passed a civil rights act that barred discrimination in public places and on public carriers.

It was the Democrats who showed that progressive revolution the door, by inviting Jim Crow in. As late as the 1920s, the Republican Party included a civil rights agenda in its platform. However, it thereafter ceased to be the party of social mobility and became the party of the country club. By the late 1960s, Richard Nixon's so-called Southern Strategy had written off black America. And by the time I reached Harlem, black Republicans were as rare as snow in May, and as unpopular as the Red Sox in Yankee Stadium.

Just how steep my uphill race against Paterson was confronted me one day as I was passing out flyers outside a Harlem subway stop. A raggedy panhandler—dirty plastic container in hand—had taken up a position just a few steps away. I was annoyed by this. Now I had to compete with this vagabond for the voters' attention. I was about to shoo him away, when a discomfiting Bible verse invaded my mind.

Whatever you did for one of the least of these brothers of mine, you did for me.

I didn't need this. I glared at this bum. Jesus truly had a big heart.

I held my peace and went on campaigning. Then I flashed back to my golf-fairway vision of a man on a Harlem street begging for money. *Okay, Lord.* I decided to give the man whatever change I had in the hope that he'd be satisfied and leave. Or maybe I'd negotiate his transition.

Then he talked to me.

"What are you doing here today?"

I was surprised by his articulate use of the Queen's English. "Campaigning for political office," I responded curtly, digging in my pocket for coins.

"Which office are you running for?"

"State senate."

"Which party line are you on?"

"Republican," I growled. My patience had run out and I was upset because I had less than a dollar in change, probably not enough to bribe him to either move on or shut up.

"Republican?" he queried. I ignored him and rifled through my wallet, looking for a dollar bill. "In Harlem?"

I had four dollars and sixty-five cents in hand, and extended it to him.

"Here," he replied, refusing my donation. "You need that— and this—more than I do." He tried to hand me his penny-filled container, then dropped it and walked away.

Flabbergasted, I watched him walk off, laughing. My campaign was, indeed, laughable. The drubbing I received on Election Day vindicated his street-corner wisdom. I rejected the consolation offered by some GOP colleagues that I'd performed

FIGURE 11: At a rally for state senate in 1985. Manhattan GOP Chair, State Senator Roy Goodman, stands at the podium.

better than other Republicans in recent history by moving my percentage vote out of single digits into the teens. Paterson the son now possessed the seat that Paterson the father once held. Humbled by Harlem again, it was the first—and last—time I took on the Clubhouse.

My failed race had, however, opened a door to Albany. The positive exposure I'd received through the campaign had led to my immediate appointment as counsel and legislative director of the New York State Senate housing committee. As it turned out, I was actually on the floor of the senate chamber to greet the new Harlem state senator David Paterson on his first day in Albany. Not knowing about my appointment, he'd sent a staffer over to remind me that I'd lost the election. I approached him to explain my presence. "Maybe it's time to change registrations," he advised. "The donkey rides better in Harlem than the elephant."

The state senator–elect's tease fell on deaf ears. The truth is, neither donkey nor elephant were faring well in Harlem. The traditional politics of the Clubhouse was no match for the power of the Blight. Its political victories had not prevented the spread of crime, drugs, welfare dependency, family disintegration, abandonment, and unemployment, driving the community from Promised Land to urban wasteland.

As I rush away from Sylvia's, I think about how to explain my tardiness to Mother. I also ponder how my humble efforts—or even the rising power of the Clubhouse—could ever upend the Blight: a miasma of intractable poverty with only distant memories of inspired poetry.

FIVE

"Gone By Forty"

JUNIOR'S SLEEPING this morning. Wasn't he sleeping the last time I was here? Visiting Harlem Hospital is my least favorite thing to do these days. I'd been here the previous week for Harv, the week before that for Holmes, and it was the second time this week for Junior. I dread the thought of this routine becoming permanent.

I really don't have time for this visit. I need to prepare for court. My nonprofit took over a tenement building down the street from the shelter to create permanent housing for Harkhomes' graduates. The property is in terrible shape and city funding hasn't yet come through (one GOP friend has nicknamed me the red-lined Republican), so the existing tenants have sued to have an administrator take over the building.

Concerned about Junior, I look in the hallway for a nurse. Impatient, I scribble notes for my new business plan. My sister Lucy and I have been negotiating to take over the soul-food restaurant La Famille, which is limping through its twilight. In addition to turning the formerly homeless into dishwashers, porters, waiters, and cooks, we plan to add new programming—

FIGURE 12: At the grand opening of AMEX at the Harlem Travel Bureau

"Gospel Nights," with live music and dinner. I don't need to add another business to my overwrought entrepreneurial agenda, but I need jobs for my Harkhomes guys. With his engaging personality, Junior would be perfect as a waiter—once he gets back on his feet.

Maybe I should wake Junior up.

I'd promised Mother I'd make the staff meeting today. The month before, Harlem Travel had been burglarized. So much equipment had been taken that we'd been forced out of business for almost three weeks while we waited for the replacement computers. The timing couldn't have been worse since we'd just scheduled the grand opening of the American Express representative office at Harlem Travel. I'd wanted black AMEX bigwig Ken Chenault to cut the ribbon, but I'd been happy to get a commitment from travel division president Roger Ballou. I was relieved that we got back up and running in time to keep AMEX on board.

The burglary didn't scare off Mom, but intensified her efforts. At first, she grudgingly supported the travel agency as a part-time bookkeeper but now commuted every day from Bronxville to count the money (most of our customers paid cash) and do the banking. She was even handling customers. But having a doting, matchmaking mother around all the time had its disadvantages. My dwindling law clientele, especially the women, had to run the gauntlet of her inquiries (*Are you married?*) on the way to my office in the back of the travel agency.

As Junior breathes ever more deeply, beads of sweat curl on his forehead and run down his unshaven face. I need to find him some tissue. He's been so helpful to me, one of the key members of my posse. When drug dealers wrote threatening messages in chalk on the sidewalk in front of the Harkhomes, I started traveling to and from the shelter with at least one or preferably two shelter residents. The status of many as former drug dealers had worked to my advantage, although the current dealers had fingered me as a competitor. Every man I rescued from the street was one less customer for them. The posse hadn't been the same in the couple of weeks that Junior had been in the hospital, and the dealers knew it. My used Chevy's tires had been slashed and the windows smashed so many times I'd had to junk the car. It hadn't been worth much, but losing it meant that I would soon need a new pair of shoes.

The late 1980s crime wave had even invaded Harkhomes. Twenty dollars had gone missing, and accusations were flying. I'd been ready simply to replace the victim's cash so we didn't have to waste hours playing detective. Although some of my skills had helped me handle the nonstop crises at the shelter, Sherlock Holmes I wasn't. I would never be Shaft!

I get up from the wobbly chair, search around for tissues, paper towels, towels, wipes, spare linen, anything. I look under the counter, in the closet, the drawers, even in the bathroom. Nothing.

I sigh. Another Harlem fall from grace.

Rising in the Renaissance, Harlem Hospital had once been the black medical oasis, the one place where African Americans could find decent health care, and doctors of color were not barred from fulfilling their potential. Now uneven patient care, perennial budget shortfalls, equipment breakdowns, medicine shortages, recurrent staff cuts, and supply deficits clouded that legacy. Even the once-lovely WPA murals that adorned the lobby—symbols of community pride from black Depression-era artists—were showing bad wear-and-tear.

Reverend Calvin Butts had been right when he'd advocated for a federal takeover after a recent inspection had turned up so many problems that the hospital had been at risk of losing its Medicaid funding. I'd initially thought his calling the hospital a "cesspool" had been excessive, but I now understood that, like Powell père and fils before him, Butts had been using the big bully pulpit of the Abyssinian Baptist Church, this time to highlight the severe shortcomings I was experiencing firsthand: the fact that the hospital was a facility that, if not terminally ill, was so deficit-plagued that it needed life support. Even the hospital's leadership had been victims of Blight flight: seventeen executive directors in twenty-four years!

The journey from beginning to bottoming out had taken a hundred years. New York City officials, planning for the growth north of Central Park that would accompany the expansion of mass transit, opened Harlem Hospital in 1887 on the East River at 120th Street. In less than twenty years, a surging uptown population had compelled the establishment of a new 150-bed facility at its landmark Lenox Avenue location: for whites only, of course.

Jim Crow was evicted from Harlem Hospital during the Harlem Renaissance more quickly than it had been from other institutions, but only in part. By 1920, a direly overcrowded hospital that served (or ill-served, as some claimed) a population that was 75 percent black was run by a staff that was 100 percent white.

The Jackie Robinson of the medical profession was Harvard-to-Harlem surgeon Louis Wright. W. E. B. Du Bois and other NAACP officials forced Wright to be hired in 1919, albeit as an assistant in the outpatient unit, the lowest position in the clinic. What confronted Wright on his arrival was an infant mortality rate that was twice what it was for whites. Tuberculosis was the main culprit, killing four times as many Harlem blacks as New York City whites. Wright's pioneering presence paved the way for other African-American health professionals who maintained the unassailably high standard of care he set. By the 1930s, an irreversible policy of racial integration had been established at Harlem Hospital.

Now on a mission for Junior, I head to the restroom in search of something clean to mop up his sweat-soaked face. Do I really have time for this? I figure it's okay to be a little late. Mother's thrill at my election to the Cornell Board of Trustees has given me some grace. I'd won as a write-in candidate, a success surely helped by the fact that my four white competitors had split the non-minority vote. No doubt if Dad had still been around he'd have cheered me for winning an alum seat in Ithaca, but jeered me for losing my career in Harlem.

As I leave the room, I glance back at Junior, recalling our first encounter during a HARK street outreach on Lenox Avenue. An unemployed actor whose crack habit had landed him on a Central Park bench, Junior had been moved by "The Better Stuff," a sidewalk skit about destitution and deliverance, with me stumbling through the lead role.

Junior approached me afterward. "I'll come to your shelter," he said, smirking, "if I can give you acting lessons." We shared a laugh.

His work ethic, leadership, and sense of humor made him one of my favorites at the shelter. But my attempts to encourage him had been met by his incessant requests for cigarettes and his incurable pessimism. I feared he was a distant relative of Mrs. Stokes. One day, when I'd reproved him, Junior scoffed.

"C'mon, Rev. What ya thinkin' 'bout? Ya really think I'm gonna die in my fifties of lung cancer or somethin'? Don't worry, Rev. Just help me out with a smoke. I'll be gone by forty."

I'd first dismissed his lack of faith in the future. But after I'd read a report by Harold Freeman, the long-time director of sur-

FIGURE 13: Acting in "The Better Stuff" on Lenox Avenue

gery at Harlem Hospital, Junior's prophecy no longer seemed paranoid or hyperbolic. Freeman had authored a report for the *New England Journal of Medicine* that concluded that life expectancy for men in Harlem was shorter than that for men in Bangladesh. His research revealed that high rates of ailments common to inner cities—cancer, heart disease, measles, syphilis, anemia, mumps, hepatitis A, ear infections, gonorrhea, whooping cough—were as much the reason for the abbreviated lives as violent crime.

I'd tuned out all the chatter about black men being an "endangered species" as demagoguery. Not anymore. I knew we were in trouble. The black unemployment rate was more than twice that of white men, and the leading causes of death—homicide, accident, suicide, and close behind, AIDS—were all preventable.

The Freeman study made the Blight personal! It was no longer just a symbol of the dangers of ghetto life, but an active threat to my own well-being. I was a thirty-something black man living and working in the 'hood, walking the mean streets twenty-four–seven. My Third World surroundings now seemed like a bomb that at any moment might blow up both me and my dreams, whether I was gunned down by a drug dealer or some other unknown evil. I'd never had to confront my own mortality.

As I walk down the empty corridor to the restroom, a porter's mop on the floor of a vacant room provides me with a pleasant surprise. They do actually clean this place!

I'm reminded that I need to clean my *own* place—and find a *new* place. Carrying the financial load at the 137th Street house has almost exhausted my resources. I'd only spent one summer on Wall Street, but in Harlem I was treated as if I had downtown money. HARK was already gone from its original "ark" at 419 Convent. Likewise, supporting one another as an Acts 2:45 Christian community (*"they gave to anyone as he had need"*), which was our Harlem foundation, was passé. It may have worked

to get us out-of-towners to move to Harlem, settled and con-
nected, but changing personal and professional priorities had
proved to be strong dispersants. And almost from the beginning,
my leadership spin had been centrifugal, emphasizing outreach
over fellowship.

I pick up my pace along the corridor, remembering I'd planned
to see Walter later on today. He was on Rikers Island, unjustly
jailed for a crime he didn't commit, accused of attempted murder, an incident that allegedly happened several years ago. It was
clearly a case of mistaken identity, but the district attorney had
taken it to the grand jury. I've eschewed criminal law, but for
Walter I've dusted off my law books and boned up enough to
represent him through the grand jury proceeding. Staring at
him through the bars of the 28th Precinct holding cell the day
the cops picked him up was motivation enough. It feels like a
demonic distraction: for him to be arrested just as he's starting as
the new director of the Beth-HARK Crisis Center and continu-
ing his studies at Baruch College.

The restroom door is locked. I start metaphorically pointing
fingers. Who is to blame for the plight of Harlem Hospital? City
officials, whose commitment to care apparently waned with the
exodus of white patients and staff? Columbia University doctors, whose responsibility for quality assurance seemed to get
lost in the attention given to Columbia Presbyterian Hospital,
their favorite son by the river, rather than their bastard child in
Harlem? Or maybe responsibility lay beyond the community?
Freeman's report had compared unfavorably the federal government's response to dozens of deaths from a natural disaster to
its inaction over many more deaths in the chronic disaster area
called Harlem.

I finally get inside the restroom. It smells like cigarette

smoke—surely a patient sneaking in, just like the last time I'd
come here. I tell myself that I'm not one to blame the victim,
but I have to ask what the role of personal responsibility is in
this health-care crisis. Asthma wouldn't be such a Harlem epidemic—one of the highest rates in the nation—if we didn't
smoke so much. I've read that some researchers project that
blacks may develop heart failure at twenty times the rate of
whites. Perhaps Harlem wouldn't experience relatively higher
rates of heart disease, obesity, and other maladies if its residents
didn't excessively consume deep-fried and fatty foods. We have
enough problems without being our own worst enemies. What
would the community be like twenty years hence if Harlemites
didn't do a better job disciplining themselves and their children?
Of course, asthma would be less of a problem if particulate matter from emissions wasn't spewing forth from uptown bus depots
and waste-treatment plants. And we might smoke less and eat
better if the community wasn't bombarded by billboards and
free products that fostered and enforced bad habits.

It was a question I found myself asking over and over again:
Where was the intersection of individual and corporate responsibility? One thing was for sure: it started with better parenting. The percentage of infant deaths among blacks wouldn't be
three times the national average if pregnant mothers of color
took better care of themselves. For those babies who survived—
born poor, in overcrowded housing, with low birth weight, and
exposed to household toxins and subjected to single parent-
hood—the generational implications were unthinkable.

I spin a handful of toilet paper but then spy a whole roll on
the counter. I greedily grab it. I justify my pilfering by saying it's
for Junior's sake, and flee the secondhand smoke. I endeavor to
conceal my contraband from a passing nurse, but she's much too
preoccupied to notice. I remember her from my last visit, simi-
larly burdened, fighting back tears after losing another patient

to diabetes. My thoughts run to the sugar-laden, high-fat, cholesterol-rich diets that make diabetes-related illnesses five times higher in Harlem than elsewhere in the city. I can't get away from my belief that an ethic of personal responsibility would compel better dietary practices.

The nurse lays her hand on the shoulder of a grieving woman. *Thank God for her*, I think, and other Harlem health-care heroes—Louis Wright, Harold Freeman, and Muriel Petioni among them—who battled against the consequences of individual irresponsibility and institutional indifference.

My attention is drawn by the clamor of a stretcher being rolled into a room that's just been cleaned out. I peer past the nurses into the room to see a prostrate young black man, sedated and bandaged from shoulder to waist. I assume he's another gunshot victim up from the emergency room. The paucity of primary-care physicians in the neighborhood has left the emergency rooms overburdened with 83,000 visits a year. Patients came in suffering with everything from stabbings to cancer to migraines to colds. Since Harlem's median income of $19,000 is less than half the city's average, the ER became the first and last resort. Harlem Hospital cried out for more help, not less!

I take another look in the room. I wonder if the young man is one of the drug-dealing teens from 129th Street. I can hear the chaplain quoting the Apostle Paul: "*O Death, where is thy victory? O Grave, where is thy sting?*" I hope tomorrow's dawn won't reveal another flowery memorial spread across Harkhomes' sidewalk.

With supplies still in hand, I finally make it back to Junior's room. My satisfaction is fleeting, crushed by incredulity, indignation, and grief. The doctors and nurses are hovering over Junior's still body, a sheet pulled over his head.

Why had I lingered in the hallway so long?

My nascent headache now pounds. A nurse blocks me from moving to the bed, and places that comforting hand on my shoulder. I am sapped of speech, strength, and a sense of any fairness in the world. I stagger out. No one says a word.

I loiter in the hallway, lean against the wall, and breathe deeply. *Calm down*, I tell myself.

I try to summon the Renaissance muse. Nothing.

I try to pray. Nothing.

All I can hear is the heckling of Mrs. Stokes.

Will you be gone by forty, too?

SIX

"Let's Go! Five-O!"

YAWNING, I pace up and down near the basement front door of Bethlehem Pentecostal Assembly, another midblock Harlem brownstone church like Christ Community Church where I'd been ordained. I'd left with my homeless men in tow after a dispute with the church's leadership over the welfare of the shelter versus the worship of the church. "Is God less concerned about the woeful than the worshippers?" I'd countered, along with a litany of facts. Arson, abandonment, and decay had hounded so many people out of Harlem that 150,000 left in the decade before I arrived; a majority of those remaining were unemployed or on welfare.

The city was now Harlem's largest landlord by far, owning 65 percent of the housing stock. Yet long lines formed every night for our lousy cots. The Christ Community trustees, however, were unmoved, so Harkhomes had itself become homeless, until I'd unwittingly relocated the fledgling shelter one block north from a blighted street to the block from hell.

I glance at my watch and lean on the battered card table, which masquerades as the shelter's intake desk. I rub my eyes

FIGURE 14: Doing intake at Harkhomes

and scan the night's roster. Intake had been stressful; I'd been confronted with too many Solomonic decisions about whom to let in and whom to turn away. I want to be home in my own bed instead of lying on an unforgiving, uneven cot. I'm missing my favorite TV show, *L.A. Law*, and I'm left with the drama of figuring out how to get some sleep tonight amid the cacophony of fifteen bone-weary men.

Too wound up to sleep, I pull out my draft business plan for the combined La Famille Restaurant/Harlem Renaissance Inn, my visionary bed and breakfast development for my newest acquisition at the corner of 125th Street and Fifth Avenue. As I skim the pages, the realization sinks in: my Harlem work has morphed from silly mission to silly empire, an array of under-capitalized ventures struggling to survive. The countless rounds of trying to raise capital have been fruitless. Even meetings with business titans like Chuck Feeny, real estate moguls like Howard

Milstein, and celebrities like Bill Cosby yielded no one who was willing to share the risk of Harlem enterprises. All my Harvard-to-Harlem fellow travelers and peers had gotten married and/or obtained "real jobs." Mother incessantly reminds me of this last point.

I knew I should have kept my job in the state senate, but I'd been on the cusp of burning out, so something had to go. Commuting to Albany for a couple of days every week had been a pain, but it had provided a respite from my manic Harlem lifestyle. It had also been a strange contrast. I'd been upstate for sessions on the front end of the week as the only person of color—either elected or staff—on the GOP side of the senate. Then I'd been back in Harlem on the back end of week, where not a white person was to be found.

I stuff the business plan back into my briefcase and finger the script for my new play, *Homegrown*. Perhaps a little creative writing will chill me out after my nightmare of a day. My car had been towed for unpaid traffic tickets and I'd had to borrow money from Mother to get it back. I wanted to scream.

I get up and tiptoe down the hallway into the Fellowship Room, passing gingerly in between the narrowly spaced cots. I'm encouraged that all the men are still asleep. By the tidiness of the bookshelf and linen stacks, I can see that Walter had been the previous night's supervisor.

My smile is wiped from my face by the gaseous odor rising from Ben's bed. He's eaten too much dinner again. I pause in front of an empty cot, heartbroken that after all the progress Victor had made, he'd once again fallen short. My hope for his renewal has been dashed on the jagged rocks of his character. He'd been such a negative influence on the guys: foul-mouthed, lazy, spendthrift, and inconsistent. Maybe it was a blessing in disguise he hadn't shown up. I should've given his bed to one of the newcomers.

I feel a tug on my leg. Robert, my resident supervisor, beckons me. "You okay?" he asks.

"Just real tired," I respond. "Very long day."

"Praying for you." He extends a firm hand and I shake it. "Be encouraged." I return his smile, gratified by this little harvest from my daily sowing.

The musty smell that follows me from the Fellowship Room to the hole-in-the-wall kitchen now doesn't seem as bad. I notice the dirty dishes in the sink. Hank has neglected his turn again. Should I wake him up? I peek back into the Fellowship Room. Hank's snoring hard, and I decide to let it go. I'm still struggling to find the balance between being tough-minded and tender-hearted.

I lean on the big stack of donated clothes and canned goods that block part of the hallway. They are the fruits of my trip to Waterbury, Vermont—a journey that grew out of a telephone call out of the blue from Cornellian Will Kelly. He'd been one of my dad's peers and had read about my work in Harlem in an alumni magazine. I'd accepted an invitation to speak at his church, and had been convincing enough that the church's missions committee had commissioned an errand of mercy, gathering donated clothing and food, and driving them all the way to Harlem.

I reflect on the green trees and fresh air of my Vermont sojourn as I walk outside, struck as ever by all the nocturnal activity. Why must 129th Street at midnight be like Grand Central Station at rush hour? I block my nostrils against the toxic scent that hangs in a paralyzing pall. I cough, feeling stupid that I ever thought I'd catch a breath of fresh air here.

I move cautiously to the curb. I hear a baby crying on the stoop next door, and see a young mother, perhaps not even sixteen, hitting a crack pipe with one arm and struggling to rock her child to sleep with the other. I pause at the dilemma that faces me. I should reprove Mother Crackhead, but there are too many teenagers lurking around who could be her brother, boyfriend, pusher, or pimp. Accepting that discretion is the better part of valor, I grimace and turn away, disgusted at the sidewalk reality of children being raised in a nocturnal fog of dope.

In college I'd written a paper on President Johnson's Kerner Commission on Civil Disorders. The commission had asserted that America was disintegrating into two societies: one Negro and poor, the other white and affluent. The commission certainly reflected the realities of 129th Street. There were no whites, except for infrequent, adventuresome drug purchasers. The less than one percent of whites who did live in Harlem surely resided on Sugar Hill or Strivers' Row, galaxies away from this block.

While the Kerner Commission report had not been without its flaws, at least one of its conclusions had seemed prophetic: "Prostitution, dope addiction, and crime create an environmental 'jungle' characterized by personal insecurity and tension. Children growing up under such conditions are likely participants in civil disorder."

My anger at the irresponsibility of the teen mother turns to despair over the dismal prospects for her unsuspecting infant. Faced with weak schools, a strong drug trade, suspect parenting, and probable addiction, this child may be a future client for Mother Hale, who runs the best program in Harlem for children born addicted to drugs. But how do we stem the tide of crack babies that this Harlem heroine daily saves?

Voices across the street focus my attention. Boys are shooting hoops into a milk carton hanging from a vacant brownstone. A couple of houses down from them is a crack house masquerading as just another abandoned building. All I have to do is watch for a couple of minutes to know for sure. A man loiters; a brick is removed from the bricked-up window; the man passes money in and the crack comes out. In a moment, the man's gone and the next customer emerges from the shadows.

The consequences of this cataclysmic commerce appear as a baneful breeze rolls a faded flower at my feet—a wilted daisy astray from a cluster of candlelit curbside bouquets, left in memory of young lives vanquished by the Blight. Couldn't the police do more if their dispatchers didn't insist on issuing warnings before sending cops into "the problem block"? I'd been complaining that the government spent more time fighting crime than reforming social-welfare policies that bred the dependency that led to unlawful conduct. But time on 129th Street had changed my tune. We needed more law enforcement here, not less.

I ease east down the sidewalk, toward Fifth Avenue, and see the silhouette of the well-preserved Victorian mansion that had been built when Harlem was still a suburban village. It appears to be the only unblemished bastion on the block. Or is it really just another drug den in disguise?

The wretched realities of this block remind me of another collegiate project—my research into then-scholar, now-U.S. senator Daniel Patrick Moynihan's 1960s report "The Negro Family," about the persistent problems of the black family. I joined the critical chorus of black scholars and liberals who'd excoriated Moynihan for highlighting spiraling out-of-wedlock birth rates and the numbers of households headed by single mothers as reasons for the steepness of the poverty of the ghetto.

What a mistake that had been! Everything I was seeing vindicated the conclusions of Moynihan's study and the forewarning of President Franklin D. Roosevelt's 1935 State of the Union address, when he presaged: "Dependence on relief induces a spiritual and moral disintegration fundamentally destructive to

FIGURE 15: With other volunteers (*third from right, front row*) cleaning up the Dirty Alley

the national fiber.... [T]o dole out relief in this way is to administer a narcotic, a subtle destroyer of the human spirit." That the chief architect of big government prophesied about the deleterious details on display tonight betrays the expansion of the American welfare state in the half century since his speech, and demands a better way.

Rats rummage through the garbage near a vacant brownstone. It's easy to understand why the city's buildings department receives dozens of complaints each day about vermin. I pick up a stray soda can and fling it at the rats. They ignore my efforts to disperse them. I look down the street for possible reasons for the pest infestation. There are two. One is a vacant, trash-strewn, drug-infested lot between two dilapidated tenements, known appropriately as the Dirty Alley. The periodic clean-ups I've organized have targeted the Dirty Alley to rid it of garbage and trafficking, so far in vain. Removing the strata of debris and junk, which takes a troop of volunteers all day, only seems to signal the trash titans of 129th Street to quickly mound it up again.

As I approach the Dirty Alley, I'm struck by how surreal the lot looks, now more full of trash than it was before we'd cleaned it out a week earlier. I pinch my nose and clear my throat, less a reaction to the stench than despair over how inexhaustible this block seems in its efforts to show me its pathologies. I veer away toward the north side of the street. I remember all too well how, the week before, my shovel had become stuck in the mire. I'd finally pulled it loose, only to uncover the bodies of a cat and a rat—the latter as large as the former. It wasn't clear who had killed whom.

I look toward Lenox Avenue. Crack smoke canopies the street. I push on through the haze, drawn by the other potential rodent haven—the half-built church at the corner. It's known in the 'hood simply as "the Church." It's where the Renaissance hot spot Connie's Ballroom had stood a half century ago. Once an entertainment beacon, however, it's now a pest palace. That the hulking shell carries the name of God's holy place cuts me to the core.

To the east of the Church a stream of people are leaving No. 55, another of the block's impersonations. It's a tumbledown tenement that doubles as a drug supermarket. I've heard that No. 55 is busy twenty-four–seven. Its perverse marketing pitch is "a diff'rent high on every floor." Unsanitary plumbing, falling plaster, and broken-down stairwells add to its forbidding environment. Or so I'm told. I don't want to venture too close. Tenants and squatters have been known to direct their garbage and urine out of the windows.

Directly across the street, rounding out the Dark Corner, is No. 60, the block's most infamous edifice. It's a noisome and dilapidated hulk. Gang-coded graffiti splatters its façade, a bulletin board for the villains and madmen who rule this Gotham of a block. The true villains and madmen, however, aren't on the street. They're the drug kingpins, the slumlords, and the captains of contraband commerce who conspire with corrupt cops and officials. To me, they're soulless puppeteers, so many shadows removed from the real-life consequences of their moneymaking.

One of the most notorious of Harlem's slumlords is Antonios Morfesis, the owner of No. 60 and other innumerable hellholes. He's known to collect slums like trophies. It seems as if No. 60 has taken on his noxious spirit. I see men exit, crackheads in tow. A scream rings out from the building. It's like a scene out of a bad horror movie. Whenever possible, I enter and exit from the Fifth Avenue end, to avoid the terrors of the Dark Corner.

These abysmal conditions were recently featured for three days on the front page of the *New York Times*! The paper publicized in excruciating detail my daily wasteland in an article that followed a headline that could have come straight out of Dante: On a Harlem Block, Hope Is Swallowed by Decay. The exposé established 129th Street between Fifth and Lenox avenues as the poster child of the Blight. The block is now "the other America, the America of the black underclass":

> While the experts debate welfare reform, education and job training, generations live and die on this block, a world apart . . . increasingly violent and dispirited. . . . While the black middle class has expanded greatly in the last 30 years, a growing number of black people have also been trapped in seemingly intractable poverty.

The reporter's assertions captured my ambivalence, caught in the emotional crossfire of wanting to join my prospering peers on Wall Street yet knowing my Harkhomes men would have less hope of finding safe harbor if I abandoned ship. Helping a few homeless men seemed like a drop in the bucket amid the tsunami that was drowning tens of thousands of lives in Harlem.

I've drifted too far toward the Dark Corner. A familiar verse resounds with more relevance than ever before: *Yea, though I walk through the valley of the shadow of death, I will fear no evil, for thou art with me.* Still on edge despite the scriptural reassurance, I decide to hustle back to my refuge.

Too late! I'm almost run down by a man sprinting into the block from the Dirty Alley. Football legs, where are you?! Don't fail me now!

Accelerating like a halfback on a sweep, I scamper just ahead of the dealer, who shouts—"Let's Go! Five-O! Let's Go! Five-O! Let's Go! Five-O!" It's the battle cry of the Blight.

Fear breathes down my neck. I've learned enough street code to know that "Five-O," taken from the TV police drama *Hawaii Five-O*, means that the cops are coming. I also know that on 129th Street at midnight there are no innocent bystanders.

As I speed for the shelter, my every step seems weighed down by a stone. I lunge for the door, my escape from the war zone. Chest heaving, I slip inside, slam the door shut, and lock it. I try to catch my breath. I can't. I bury my head in my arms. I hear gunshots and lift my head for a second. Even though I've escaped the crossfire, I fear another funeral bouquet will soon bloom from the concrete.

I finally surrender to fatigue and collapse on my hallway cot, positioned so that there can be no pre-dawn escapees. My deep breathing does little to calm my nerves. I feel like a prisoner of war, a not-so-distant cousin of those outside the door, who are imprisoned by poverty, degradation, and violence.

I don't know how long I'm lying there before I hear the inevitable knock. I decide not to answer. The knocking turns to banging, and then from pounding to explosions in my ears. I fling my pillow at the door, and follow it, resolved to turn this slacker away.

"Too late. Can't come in!" I yell through the door.

"Rev, open up." It's Victor. "I can explain."

"Curfew was four hours ago."

"Give me chance t'explain."

This is the hardest part for me. I know Victor has concocted a lie. But I also know there's an empty bed and he has no place to go. I crack the door open. The stench of whiskey bends my head back. "Don't lie to me, Victor."

"Can I come in?"

"No, I'm not letting you in here tonight. I'm just extending the courtesy of hearing you out." Courtesy is the last thing I want to extend to this charlatan. But what would Jesus do?

He peers through the crack. "Y'know I went on the job interview and—"

"That was two in the afternoon!"

"It was going good 'til he asked me 'bout whether I had a record. You tol' me to tell the truth, so I tol' him the truth."

Victor clears his throat and pushes against the door. I push back. I have some doubts about Victor's account, but none about what had happened to him next. It was the same old story.

"Interview over," he sighed. "No respect. Secretary showed me to the door. Ain' want that damn messenger job no way. So upset . . ."

"You got drunk." I finish it for him.

"Sorry, Rev. I'm sorry."

I open the door slightly. The awful glare from the fluorescent light chases the shadows from his eyes. I see the tears.

"Never again, Rev. Never again."

"Promises. Promises." My patience ran out hours ago.

"I 'member your lesson this morning—Beatitudes."

Our eyes lock.

"Blessed are the merciful." His recollection of that scripture is the turning point. "Sure use some mercy right now."

His soul implores and my indignation relents. Hadn't I started Harkhomes to save the Victors, the prodigal sons of Harlem, lost in the brutal world of the Blight, never making it back home?

I open the door.

"Thank you, Rev. Thank you." Victor hugs me.

What a fool I am, letting this cussing, lying freeloader back in. I refuse to acknowledge his good night as he trudges triumphantly down the hallway. I feel like a lifeguard on the side of sharks.

I sigh, rub my forehead.

The nights are so long on 129th Street.

SECTION TWO

PLODDING

1990s

SEVEN

Find the Mentor!

I **PICK UP** the pace down West 141st Street, not wanting to be late for today's Holistic Hardware workshop. I make this trek every morning that I'm not already at Harkhomes for overnight duty. I'm never really excited about descending from the oasis of my neighborhood into "the other America."

I moved back to Sugar Hill after the HARK Fellowship evolved into Harkhomes, living a solitary existence for the first time in my Harlem history. I've been trying to fathom my ambivalence about it. It feels strange to be living apart from a community after having lived within it for so long. But I'm relieved that the men of my new community are a dozen blocks away from the floor-through brownstone apartment I'm renting on Hamilton Terrace.

Sugar Hill—the area between City College at West 140th and 155th streets, bounded by Edgecombe and Amsterdam avenues—changed in the decade since I'd relocated there from Harvard. Thirty-something professionals like me—many more yuppies than buppies—predominated among the influx of residents. Unlike me, their career choices and consequent disposable income made them players in this market, a fact of which Mother never fails to remind me.

Her killer argument is 419 Convent, the original Ark of Freedom and my first Harlem home—transformed into a magnificent art gallery replete with Romare Beardens, Jacob Lawrences, and exquisite African sculpture and oriental rugs, worth infinitely more than the $175,000 I could've bought it for during my early Harlem days.

I resolved not to tell her about the findings from my recent Hamilton Heights house tour, where I learned that Harlem had become more chic than shabby, more bright lights than dark alleys, and more trendy than tumbledown. I guess I'd been spending too much time at the shelter to notice. The white families we visited testified that they had been drawn uptown by the very low cost of housing, the well-preserved architecture, and the special sense of community. These attractions had proven strong enough to overcome crime rates that refused to go down, a paucity of retail and lifestyle amenities, and the undertow of history that deprived Harlem of half her housing stock and a third of her population in the previous thirty years.

One couple lived in a three-story limestone manse with a Renaissance Revival façade, possessing original dark mahogany mantels and staircases, stained-glass windows, and six floral tile-embellished fireplaces. They recounted how their worries about whether their school-age children would assimilate had been allayed by how the block had embraced them. I'd pondered the historical irony: how whites had resisted then taken flight as Renaissance blacks moved in, and then three-quarters of a century later, there was black receptivity to the current white incursion. What was the difference? Was it simply the passage of time? Were American race relations inherently convoluted? Was our society finally growing up? Or was it something special about the character of Harlem that I had yet to fathom?

One question weighed most heavily on my mind: Would these pioneering homesteaders help Harlem tear down the racial cordon sanitaire of 110th Street, that invisible yet impregnable barrier of the Blight that had kept Harlem a Third World colony on the most prosperous island in the world?

Walking down St. Nicholas Avenue past St. Nicholas Park, I wonder how different this park and community would have been if Robert Moses, the visionary yet controversial builder of mid-twentieth-century New York, had been less stingy toward Harlem with his public works. Of the 255 playgrounds he established in the neighborhoods around New York City, only one found its way to Harlem. How many more Harlem kids would have avoided drugs and crime, and their drastic consequences, if there had been a green space nearby in which families could stroll and play?

Turning east crosstown, I observe a strip of shabby brownstones, likely "single-room occupancies" (SROs). These houses were once single-family townhouses that were divided into rooms so their owners could rent to lodgers to make ends meet. As the economic conditions of the Blight worsened, nearly half of Harlem families were forced to engage in "lodger evil," as it was called, because so many of the roomers brought bad habits and crime into respectable homes.

Sugar Hill—where uptown life was sweetened by piles of sugar money—possessed fewer SROs than the rest of Harlem. Upwardly mobile blacks flocked to Harlem during the Renaissance and snatched up the lovely townhouses from which their white counterparts had fled. The area became the haven of W. E. B. Du Bois and his Talented Tenth. In fact, much of the leadership of the NAACP, the National Urban League, and other new civil rights organizations, though headquartered downtown, embraced this enclave of the black elite as their new home. Like the Main Line area outside of Philadelphia and Nob Hill in San Francisco, Sugar Hill signified an elevated social status.

The area possessed more pizzazz than Strivers' Row, its upscale neighbor down the hill to the east, which projected a uniformly immaculate beaux-arts design. Sugar Hill became such a debonair destination that it spawned a musical of the same name, which opened in 1931 and was a critical and commercial catastrophe. The story of young love and murder featuring successful Vaudeville actor Flournoy Miller in blackface was mercilessly reviewed by the *New York Times* as "what courtesy alone could call a musical comedy." It closed after eleven performances. Fortunately, the natty neighborhood lasted a lot longer.

Sugar Hill is not without its fallen stars, like the once-elegant, neoclassical 409 Edgecombe Avenue. Built in 1917, the thirteen-story apartment house (towering for that time) was initially home to eighty white families. Before long, the building and its commanding views became the beacon of the Renaissance, the prestigious address for the best and brightest of New York's African-American community. Among its high-profile residents were Aaron Douglass, known as the father of black American art; Roy Wilkins, the civil rights leader; Jules Bledsoe, Broadway performer and composer; William Stanley Braithwaite, poet and editor; Thurgood Marshall, NAACP lawyer and future Supreme Court Justice; Cameron White, distinguished composer and violinist; W. E. B. Du Bois; and Walter White, head of the NAACP, whose apartment became a famed gathering place known as the White House of Harlem.

The building's illustrious residents had taken flight with the rest of the black middle class as the Blight took its toll. Like most of Harlem's property, 409 Edgecombe fell into the city's hands, with 40 percent of such housing becoming vacant. Adding more tarnish to the building's legacy, a city-sponsored co-op conversion to sell 409 Edgecombe apartments to tenants for $250 was halted by a lawsuit. The tenants were suing the city for failing to remove asbestos from the roof.

I turn swiftly onto 129th Street through the Dark Corner thinking about my fifteen homeless men sleeping in an area smaller than a parlor floor on Hamilton Terrace, and the question: Had we Harlem newcomers been subject to the storms that Generation Blight had to suffer through, would we be on 129th Street instead of Sugar Hill?

I rush into the small sanctuary of Bethlehem Pentecostal Church and am pleased to see that the shelter residents are seated, awaiting my arrival. At least I wouldn't have to put them back on the mean streets first thing in the morning like I'd once had to. Our first grant from the Robin Hood Foundation provided the staff resources to keep them inside and, I hoped, on the path of progress. Recent donations from my pastor, A. R. Bernard, and other supporters had also been encouraging. But I was displeased by my coming late, because being even a second behind schedule would set the wrong example for this group. One of my guys would surely use my tardiness to justify his own future lapse.

Rasheed comes in from the shelter space downstairs and attempts to squeeze into the front row. Grumbling ensues. "Gentlemen, please, pettiness is not permitted in God's house," I instruct. "There's plenty of room for all who want progress." Rasheed is a troublemaker. I'd been forced to put him out a while back for urinating in the sanctuary. I'd let him back in after a month. I fear he's become stuck in the revolving door.

I delve into the Association Tool, today's holistic topic. I'm mindful of the time and that Mother is waiting at Harlem Travel

FIGURE 16: In the Fellowship Room (*far left*), practicing the Association Tool with the men of Harkhomes

to review business finances. We meet weekly to figure out how to keep the travel agency afloat.

I use my most stentorian voice to keep the guys, whose attention span is challenged, awake. The Association Tool imparts strategies for managing relationships so that they work for, and not against, personal progress. I'd been losing so many of my guys to bad relationship choices that I'd had to come up with some tactics for them.

It doesn't surprise me when, before I've even finished my introduction, snoring emanates from the back pew. I loudly clear my throat, to no avail. I signal to Robert, the former resident supervisor of Harkhomes, who now works on the staff of Bethel Gospel Assembly's Discipleship Ministry, another Harlem faith-based shelter, but fortunately volunteers here often. Without returning veterans like Robert, I'd be overwhelmed by the challenges these men present.

Robert employs his not-so-gentle elbow. Some snicker, as Anthony stirs, sits up, and feigns attentiveness—not as embarrassed as he should be. "Brother Anthony," I warn him, "if you fall asleep again this morning, I'm sending you downstairs to bed—not to keep sleeping but to scrub the metal frame of yours and everybody else's beds until the rust comes off."

Anthony rubs his eyes, stiffens his back against the wooden pew, and nods at me. He's gotten the message. Playing drill sergeant is unnatural for me. Walter, who's now running the Beth-HARK Crisis Center, the counseling ministry targeted at substance abusers and ex-offenders, is. I've picked up a set of people skills from him that I didn't learn in the Ivy League. I've had to. Tough love is the only way to drive these men out of homelessness.

It's been a long and winding road. The goal of my daily teaching has been to liberate with life skills minds that have long been held hostage by habits inimical to advancement. My Bible-based lessons have come a long way, evolving from the Harvard Law Black Christian Fellowship to the HARK Fellowship, from the Harkhomes Fellowship to today's Holistic Hardware class. Nonetheless, it was definitely easier dealing with the esoteric arguments of law students than with the life-and-death issues of the neediest.

The roots of these men's problems run deep, back to the Renaissance. Their grandparents—sharecroppers who were the descendants of slaves—had fled to the Promised Land of Harlem. Instead of the chains, whips, and nooses that had oppressed their forbears, these men and women found substandard housing, poor education, inadequate health care, last-hired-first-fired employment, and glass ceilings everywhere—Jim Crow in a bow tie. The unfortunate heirs of this era were my unmotivated students, the offspring of so many deferred dreams.

Harlem's devolution was so painful because the area fell from promise to despair. When the broad, clean, tree-lined, hopeful avenues of the Renaissance degenerated into Dirty Alleys and Dark Corners, when hardship and gloom evicted elegance and pride, Harlem suffered all the more. The incorrigible pessimist that she is, Mrs. Stokes had probably suffered through some of the hardships of the Blight, when Harlem became for her, as it did for most, a place "just to give up hope." Adversity no doubt turned her into an indefatigable doomsayer.

Just get over it, Mrs. Stokes. Whatever you went through, it's time to put it behind you.

I don't let my Harkhomes men listen to Mrs. Stokes. I tell them that they're not to give up hope. As far as I'm concerned, being a member of Generation Blight is no excuse for failure. It simply means working harder, being better. They're not permitted to wallow in self-pity, blame the white man, or use any perceived burden of their heritage of disadvantage as a justification for surrender. Racism—past or present—is just another barrier I endeavor to help them prepare to hurdle.

This perspective has proven hard to instill in Rasheed, Anthony, and my other students, who represent the paradox of post-Renaissance brokenness. They're products of the fateful forces that laid Harlem low but they're also human souls whose God-given dignity demands that they act responsibly, accountably, and with enterprise.

To deliver them from the bondage of the Blight, I've had to address both the structural and behavioral causes of it in their lives. The structural factors are the community's systemic, abysmal economic conditions that make it very difficult for these men to find gainful employment. The behavioral factors are personal, like a drug habit and other self-destructive choices, which cause the numbers of residents at Harkhomes to drop precipitously (sometimes to zero) every two weeks when the welfare checks—tokens of welfare-state dependency—arrive. My goal is to empower these men by restoring their sense of individual purpose and personal dignity.

So I've decided to prioritize the behavioral dimension of Generation Blight. Otherwise, my pupils might end up squandering the economic, housing, and other opportunities coming from structural initiatives. I see each individual metaphorically, as a house in disrepair, reparable if the right approach is taken. Food, clothing, and shelter, although necessary, are not sufficient. He needs nothing less than an overhaul, tearing down the worn-out value system that has plagued him, and constructing a new one in its place. He needs to supplant his old way of wrong choices with spiritual values and strategies for success.

So Harkhomes has become the social "laboratory" in which Holistic Hardware—The Tools that Build Lives—was "invented." I've worked with residents and others who came for help, and learned by trial and error that a regular spiritual diet of values, principles, and disciplines fosters moral fortitude in the same way that "three hots and a cot" sustained physical strength. Organizing these truths into a curriculum and teaching it every morning has helped me discover that the presence or absence of holistic tools in an individual's life is critical to why some escape continual crisis and others do not.

I check my watch. I need to pick up my teaching pace, since I must be at Harlem Travel by eleven a.m. I have a paying law client coming in. Then I'm meeting with Mother over finances, and then we try to reel in a potential corporate account, a large Harlem church with a group of ministers who make a lot of foreign missions trips. So I press on through the first principle of the Association Tool.

Tuck, a recovering drug addict, had been at Harkhomes for ten weeks when trouble hit. Our regimen had helped him to remain clean for thirty days. When Randy, his "get-high" buddy, had shown up, I refused to let Tuck see him. "Whatever you do, stay away from him," I advised Tuck. I explained that Randy presented too great a temptation for him to forfeit his new, sober lifestyle.

But Randy's persistence paid off. On a subsequent occasion, he'd persuaded Tuck to slip out for a birthday party. Though he'd been tempted, Tuck had been able to resist the lures of the many crack smokers at the party but had fallen victim to an unexpected police raid that had swept him up that night, along with the drug abusers. It turned out that Tuck had an outstanding warrant, so he was detained, while most of the others, including Randy, were released. Doing time derailed his progress.

"Flee the menace!" I exhort the meeting's attendees. "Who Tuck was with had more to do with his downfall than what he had done."

Fortunately, not all the guys are like Anthony, who needs another poke from Robert to open his eyes. Some understand that they won't be eligible for jobs at Harlem Travel, La Famille, or through the host of employment contacts that we have unless they pass the tests that I give them on all ten Holistic Hardware segments. So they're paying attention; some are even taking notes. I decide that now is the time to hit them with principle number two, through another crucial illustration: Jimmie.

After about seven months at Harkhomes, Jimmie had kicked his heroin habit and saved enough money from his part-time job to get his own room. I'd counseled him to limit his association with his still-homeless girlfriend, Val. Sensing that Jimmie wasn't yet strong enough to maintain his own progress while also helping her, I'd given him some information on programs for homeless women. "Don't let her move in with you under any circumstances," I'd admonished.

Jimmie rejected my advice. Val moved in and Jimmie started

using drugs again. They'd consumed all their rent money in support of their addictive lifestyle, and both ended up homeless again.

"Fence the mystery!" I explain. That's what Jimmie should have
done, keeping a safe distance from his relationship of uncertain
influence, until he was strong enough to be a positive influence
on Val. A chorus of Amens ring out. I'm gratified—some of my
listeners have found the Amen Corner and it's not even Sunday.

Before I can start my final point, J. C. Rocwell, our resident
street poet, jumps to his feet, waving his hands. "Rev. I got something, I got something."

This is not the time, J. C. Not this morning. I need to finish. But
I keep these thoughts to myself. J. C.'s train has already left the
station.

"I call this one 'Harlem Heartbeat.'" He's now on his feet, in
the aisle, his bodily groove supporting the rhythm of his words:

> For every minute there's a time
> For every time there's a minute
> A time for you, a time for me
> So open up your heart, it's your golden key.

This poem is one of his better ones. And he's grabbed the
men's attention much better than I'm doing. I just hope he
doesn't go too long.

> It's that good ol' soulful Harlem heartbeat
> It keeps you moving up on your feet
> With every little step you make
> With every little step we take
> So don't be left out, come along and join us
> Step by step walking in style and rhythm
> Keeping it moving on dis' uptown movement.

J. C. claps to the beat. Some stand, grooving along with him.
I stare at J. C., inch toward him, hoping he'll catch my signal.
In his own artistic zone, however, he misses my gestures, if not
a beat.

> We're counting our blessings and our calories, too
> Cutting down on greasy food and checking our fat!
> Step by step fighting back against sugar diabetes
> Step by step fighting back against malnutrition.

I like the personal responsibility/health-care theme of his last
beat, and he's on a roll now, but he pauses to catch his breath. I
seize the moment.

"Thank you, Brother J. C. We really have to move on. Let's
give the Lord a handclap for Brother J. C. and his poetry." J. C.
bows, basking in the applause. Several brothers offer a congratulatory hug. I would've preferred for the muse to show up through
another Harlem Renaissance poet, but with my unquenchable
thirst for verse, I'll take what I can get. I press on to preach the
conclusion of the Association Tool.

"Chester and Elisha exemplify our full association principle."

"Big Chester from D.C.?" someone asks. I nod, remembering his physique and background. "That my homeboy. What
Chester do?"

He was recently unemployed, but Chester proved to be a willing and tireless worker, and eventually took over the cooking
duties at Harkhomes. He'd gotten so good in the kitchen that
he'd also begun to volunteer with cooking chores at his church.
A deacon there had liked Chester's work ethic, had taken him
under his wing, and had recommended him for a part-time job,
first delivering food, then cooking for an elderly couple. With
the guidance and support of his deacon and others at church,
the assignment had evolved into Chester being a live-in cook,

housekeeper, gardener, shopper, and chauffeur for his aging employers.

Concluding, I modulate my voice, feeling like it's Sunday morning.

"When his mentor Elijah was about to be called home by God, Elisha found Elijah and told him, *As surely as the Lord lives and as you live, I will not leave you.* So Elisha stayed as close as possible to Elijah until Elijah was taken up to heaven.

"Find the mentor!" I punctuate my real-life and biblical illustrations. "Chester overcame both his joblessness and homelessness because he was able to . . ." I pause and nod, prompting their participation.

"Find the mentor!" they say in unison.

"And Elisha ended up with the double portion of Elijah's spirit because he was able to . . ."

"Find the mentor!!" they exclaim, more loudly than before.

"And what should you do?"

"Find the mentor!!!"

"What did you say?"

"Find the mentor!!!"

"I can't hear you!"

"FIND THE MENTOR!"

"Now shake somebody's hand and tell him what you're going to do."

As they encourage one another, I smile, savoring their enthusiasm, but only for a moment. Several men shoot their hands up in the air. The triumph of my lecture is quickly overtaken by a new challenge.

"Will you be my mentor?" one man asks.

"My hand was up first," another asserts.

I'm a victim of my own success.

"I need help the most," chimes the now wide-eyed Anthony.

"I asked him last week," fires my best student from the front row.

"Class dismissed," I announce, directing Robert to take over. I slip away, escaping these inquiries, trying now to get to Harlem Travel before noon, already thinking about the best way to handle my impatient mother.

I'm chased all the way to the office by the quandary: how can I possibly mentor all these guys and keep my clients and businesses, too?

EIGHT

A Little of Her Sunshine

I'M SITTING IN a corner of the dressing room, trying my best to focus and going over my lines again and again. I'd been warned about opening-night jitters, but how do I stop my hands from shaking? A tap on my shoulder—the hand of my mentor and producer Tunde Samuel—breaks my anxiety. I turn to his mischievous smile. "If you think you're jumpy now," he says with a smirk, "wait 'til you get out there and see your momma's big eyes staring you down from the front row."

His infectious laugh and reassuring hug mitigate my mood, if only for a moment. The thought of Mom in the front row, her knowing eyes shouting, *What in the world were you thinking, to actually go on stage?* increases my unease. What was I thinking? Mother had tried to talk me out of this acting thing, accusing me of embarking on another "silly mission." I'd accused her of aiming below the belt. She was undeterred, lambasting me as a "Spike Lee wannabe." If she'd used Denzel, it would have hurt less.

. . .

It had been a rough day. I'd had to evict a shelter resident for smoking crack in the backyard, fire an apprentice at the travel agency for cursing out a customer, deal with a fire behind the kitchen wall of the restaurant, rush back to the agency to grab another fire extinguisher, hurry back to the restaurant to put the fire out and keep the fire department from closing the place down. Just another day at the office!

La Famille had recently been robbed at gunpoint. Though no one had been hurt, the crime had exacerbated my financial precariousness, as well as the flight of customers and staff. My goal in becoming an entrepreneur had been to help build Harlem's economic base and create jobs for Harkhomes graduates and others. But there was no time to foster employment opportunities when I was focused on surviving the crime epidemic.

Tunde shouts a whisper at me and my fellow actors: "Two minutes to curtain! Showtime at NBT! Break a leg!" My edginess skyrockets. What if stage fright refuses to fade with my first lines and I ruin opening night?

NBT—short for the National Black Theatre of Harlem—is the scene of my kamikaze mission. It's a landmark theater, part of an ensemble of Harlem cultural warriors that rose during the Blight when businesses and residents were in full flight. Reflecting on their rich cultural tradition scatters my worries.

At the turn of the twentieth century, Caucasians ruled Harlem and Jim Crow reigned over Broadway. The only African-American actor on a downtown stage was Bert Williams, who made his Broadway debut in the Ziegfeld Follies in 1910. When the white cast members protested and insisted that Williams be fired, the producer Florence Ziegfeld responded, "I can replace every one of you except Williams."

Ziegfeld's decision was vindicated by Williams' popularity, which cracked open the door for other African-American entertainers to perform in Off-Broadway productions. Eugene

O'Neill's *Emperor Jones*, starring Charles Gilpin—later followed by Paul Robeson—broke the door down. *Shuffle Along*, a mega-hit in 1921, showcased Eubie Blake, who danced and sang the Charleston before big Broadway audiences, as did other African-American performers, choreographers, musicians, and producers.

But Broadway of the 1920s was closed to black theatergoers, so they went uptown to the numerous Renaissance venues and ventures such as the Crescent, Lafayette Players, Alhambra, Rose McClendon Players, and Harlem Suitcase. Orson Welles produced his singular black *Macbeth* at the Lafayette.

The Blight closed Harlem's theaters, disbanded the repertory companies, and dissipated their inspiration. Although the American Negro Theater—featuring legends such as Sidney Poitier, Harry Belafonte, Ruby Dee, Ossie Davis, Roger Furman, and Gertrude Jeannette—limped through the forties and the fifties, by 1960 it had closed, along with all the Harlem theaters. Resident and business flight conspired with the retreat of public funding, crime-induced economic malaise, the emerging media of film and television, and downtown desegregation, which opened up Broadway doors to black audiences, to shutter uptown stages. "They done took our blues and gone," summarized Langston Hughes.

Where there is no vision, the people perish.

As we take up positions on the dark stage, I press my hands tightly against my thighs to keep them from quivering. Since the opening scene reenacts wake-up time at Harkhomes, I'm pretending to sleep on a portable cot, like those onstage who are portraying homeless men. Art had met life one evening not long before, when the actors of *Homegrown* had visited the men of Harkhomes. I'd sat through the fellowship over dinner, marveling at the homeless mentoring the thespians, and enlightening them about how to move the shelter experience from its 129th

Street reality to a fictional dispensation in a 125th Street loft-theater space.

I peep at the house-lit audience and see Mother sitting next to Lucy in the front row. To survive Mother's impending critique I may have to draw on some recently cultivated goodwill. I'd been inducted into the Cornell Athletic Hall of Fame, during which I received a standing ovation. During the ceremony in Ithaca, Mother leaned toward me, rubbed my shoulder, and whispered in my ear, "Your father would have been proud of you tonight." He would also have had to acknowledge the Cornell Literacy Program, the result of my Harlem advocacy on the Cornell Board of Trustees, which had brought four Cornell students to volunteer this past summer to help Harlem kids with their literacy skills.

Mother had also beamed when Congressman Rangel had praised me when I'd been one of the honorees at a ceremony to salute Harlem entrepreneurs. He and the other Gang of Four members had been beaming since the Clubhouse gained its greatest prize: David Dinkins had become the first black mayor of New York City. When I saw the congressman lunching at La Famille with his wife Alma, I thanked him for his kind words and for including Harlem Travel when he'd showed House Speaker Richard Gephardt around the district. I made sure not to tell Congressman Rangel about my recent trip to Washington, D.C., to visit Housing and Urban Development secretary Jack Kemp and Republican National Committee chair Lee Atwater, to whom I'd pitched my Harlem community-building agenda. The jury was still out on whether support for my program would come from a local donkey or a distant elephant.

Mother had astounded me with the way she'd taken control of Harlem Travel. She was now running every aspect of the agency, and I dared not make any agency-related decision unless I checked with her. She even pulled rank on me. On a day when it had been too snowy for her to drive—her usual way to commute from the suburbs—she'd taken the Metro North train to 125th Street. It had been dark when it was time for her to leave, but she'd insisted on walking alone the two long blocks to the station, commanding me to stay in my office. I'd cut short our spat and had let her strut triumphantly out of the office unaccompanied. I'd sneaked out and stalked her at a safe distance to the train station. Some things you don't take chances with. But I'd taken a big chance taking the stage in *Homegrown*.

"If my recollection ceases to fail me, I do indeed reminiscence the half fortnight ago when we were permissible for a most protracted slumbering."

My first lines as the Professor in *Homegrown* flare in the bright lights, and a thousand eyes are upon me, extinguishing my stage fright. I thought I'd been miscast as a character whom I wrote as "a homeless man . . . nerdish, diffident—the still-hovering cloud of his troubled past characterizing his behavior. His speech is affected with a misguided eloquence, firing words and phrases like a soldier fighting a guerrilla war with bayonet tactics." What the audience is trying to figure out from my first lines is whether the Professor is affirming the complaints of his shelter mates about having to get up early for reasons yet unknown, or not. The actors and audience will soon find out that this shelter is alleged to be a crack house. And I'm going to find out that playing the Professor five performances a week will become as daunting as dealing with the real-life "professors," who live every day a stone's throw away at Harkhomes.

I'd wanted to play Minister Leroy, the reluctant hero of the drama, because I thought there'd be some sort of poetic justice in taking what I was actually trying to do in real life and realizing it in fiction. However, the director, Dwight Cook, instead had given the role to the accomplished actor-director Leon Pinkney. If I'd known that I'd end up being typecast as the Professor, I would have edited him out of the script!

I'd started writing *Homegrown* to survive the endless nights at Harkhomes. While the residents slept, I'd write, fall asleep over pen and paper, and scribble out moments that defied resolution, except for that fictional minister who with wonderful wisdom found a way out of no way. I became Minister Leroy; Harkhomes turned into the Lighthouse Shelter; eight motley men represented the real-life residents with a visiting cop, Charlie, to interrogate them; and my notes evolved into *Homegrown*, an iconoclastic whodunit that allowed an ensemble of broken men to become whole again.

"You all here are primed for exaggerastis," opines the Professor. "Officer Charles is merely a prawn in the psalms of our good doctor reverend Minister Leroy."

Oh no! I tripped up over "exaggerastis." Neither the audience nor my fellow actors seem bothered. I guess I wrote such a butchering of "exaggeration" that no one really noticed my muff, except, of course, my driven director Dwight Cook. I'm sure I'll hear about it at intermission.

I've overcome a mountain of miscues and countless rewrites on my writer's journey. I'd taken my first steps at Cornell's Africana Center, where I'd attempted to leaven Emerson, Thoreau, Melville, and O'Neill with Baldwin, Wright, Ellison, and Hansberry. Research for my senior thesis—"The Procrustean Bed of the New South: The Higher Miseducation of the American Negro"—had germinated my first play, *Cast Me Down*. I'd conceived it as a firmly historical piece about Booker T. Washington. Yet history came to life when I arrived in Harlem.

By the time of the riot of 1964, Harlem had no theatrical pres-

FIGURE 17: Barbara Ann Teer (*center, crouching*) on stage at the National Black Theater, 1970

ence, artistic vision, entertainment refuge, cultural champion, or inspiring light to provide succor and guidance to the community's spirit. Harlem's sounds, rhythms, and hopes were being drowned out by gunshots, breaking glass, and shattered dreams. Housing and people, commerce and aspirations were dying. Out of the depths, however, artistic visionaries rose to rekindle the community's spirit and help bring Harlem back to life.

Barbara Ann Teer, a successful dancer and actor both on Broadway and off, left her promising career behind and founded the National Black Theatre (NTB) in 1968. Her stated purpose was compelling: As she wrote in the *New York Times* in 1968, "We must begin building cultural centers where we can enjoy being free, open, and black," she explained, "where we can find out how talented we really are, where we can be what we were born to be." NBT went on to produce various entertainments, special events, and art exhibitions, and tour the world with its theatrical productions. Many of these Dr. Teer (as she was affectionately known) wrote and/or produced, in addition to showcasing emerging writers such as myself.

Dr. Teer was bolstered by other artistic warriors who battled through the 1960s to relight Harlem's cultural torch: Roger Furman, founder of the New Heritage Theater; Dorothy Maynor, founder of the Harlem School of the Arts; Walter Turnbull, founder of the Boys Choir of Harlem; the Studio Museum in Harlem, the first museum devoted to the art of African Americans; Arthur Mitchell, founder of the Dance Theatre of Harlem; Woodie King, founder of the New Federal Theatre; and Garland Thompson, founder of the Frank Silvera Writers' Workshop. These were some of the cultural pioneers who believed that the arts were the key to saving the soul of Harlem. They created a community-based refuge for Harlem's spirit to be renewed and sustained, to stare down the Blight and affirm, "No, we will go on."

These cultural guardians nurtured me. My passion for writing as an inner journey helped buoy my spirits in my early Harlem days, although I'd never intended that my hobby would end up onstage. *Cast Me Down* emerged from several read-throughs in the Central Park West apartment of my thespian sister, Lucy. Then came the staged readings with Garland at Frank Silvera's and with Woodie at New Federal. I'd attended workshops with Voza Rivers (Roger Furman's successor at New Heritage), exhibitions at the Studio Museum, and performances at Dance Theater and of the Harlem Boys Choir. Though I'd learned to write at Cornell and Harvard, I discovered how to make those words come to life in Harlem.

Cast Me Down had opened in 1984 at City College's Aaron

Davis Hall, down the street from my 419 Convent apartment. Dad had attended with Mother and Lucy (Lucy had coproduced it). They'd presented me with a bouquet after the show, a trophy that signified a thawing in family relations, which had been so important to me given Dad's deteriorating health.

"Splendiferal, with the exception that my anticipation with the library might be interregnum by this maltimed inquisitorial."

Laughter erupts from the audience, as my professor voices his concern—in his own twisted way—about the police investigation into the alleged drug abuse at the Lighthouse Shelter. *What's so funny? My lines aren't supposed to be funny.* My story line is the most tragic of all. Maybe I'm playing him wrong. Maybe I'll try it a different way tomorrow night. Maybe I should just let it go and trust that the audience knows best.

Cast Me Down received good reviews. (I wasn't surprised that the *Amsterdam News* liked it better than the *New York Times*.) It was nominated for six Audience Development Committee (AUDELCO) awards. It had gone on a college tour (returning to Hampton, my childhood home, was a thrill), and even had a short-lived off-Broadway run. Its success was a rare bright spot amid the gloom that encircled my Harlem life during the 1980s. Though tempted to play the Booker T. character, I'd had enough sense to stay off the stage. Indeed, church and street corner skits had been enough until *Homegrown* had come along.

As I approach the climax of my monologue, I sense rapt attention from the full house.

"There seemed to be a million white faces staring at me. One had a white hood. And was laughing."

I'm into it now. This is my moment. I remember Dwight's blocking and move forward—time to take center stage!

"They anesthetized my entire body."

FIGURE 18: On stage (*right*) at the National Black Theatre as the Professor in *Homegrown*, 1992

You could hear a pin drop in the theater. I take a beat before my next line, milking the moment.

"I felt the fingers of the Devil all over me, cutting and cutting and cutting away my manhood."

I slump to the floor to dramatize the line, and feel the audience in the palm of my hand. I know I'll never be the same again.

The climax of the play occurs when the crooked cop confesses his malfeasance and the Lighthouse's good name is cleared. The audience stands and cheers through a couple of curtain calls. Maybe this mission isn't so silly after all.

It's an NBT tradition for actors to greet the crowd after the show, and we're deluged with good wishes. I realize just how much this play is a milestone for me and how much I've changed since coming to Harlem. If anyone had told me that after ten years in Harlem that I'd be a writer/actor at a community theater, I would have agreed with my parents' response to my Harlem decision: You have surely lost your mind. I'd come to help shape Harlem, and Harlem had ended up shaping me.

A young woman comes up to me. "I loved your character," she says excitedly. "I've seen you in something on Broadway, right?"

"Me?" I'm stunned.

A male teen confesses, "I understand so much more about homelessness now. And it was funny. I'm telling my friends about this."

Next in line to congratulate me is a familiar face. Mother gives me a hug and whispers in my ear: "I want a little of her sunshine to soak into my soul. I need it."

Mom is a voracious reader of fiction—not poetry like me— and a fan of Zora Neale Hurston. Sharing this Hurston line is her literary way of patting me on the back. For me, her quoting from Hurston's prize-winning short story "Drenched in the Light" is the most amazing manifestation of the Renaissance muse. My mother: a Harlem oracle!

In this moment of poetic justice and divine favor, I know that in my small way I've joined the writers, dancers, singers, directors, painters, producers—indeed all the creators—who've sung Harlem's song, stirred her soul, and kept her flame burning, casting some light through her darkest days. For one night, the burdens of the Blight—and the words of the petulant Mrs. Stokes—have been left outside the door to stand in the cold.

NINE

From Harlem with Love

SUNSHINE BAKES 125TH Street, today free of traffic. These are ideal conditions for the second annual Harlem Ben & Jerry's Street Festival, replete with kid-friendly games, sidewalk gawkers, tie-dye T-shirts, speeches by black activists and bearded whites, and lots of free ice cream! Everybody's happy . . . well, almost everybody.

A local businessman shakes my hand. A politician pats me on the back. Anthony, the sleepy Harkhomes resident and now a Ben & Jerry's scooper—one of several test cases in this social experiment—gives me a high five. These congratulatory sentiments, however, ring hollow for me today. I have to remind myself to keep smiling.

I lost my smile during a recent conversation with Mother after another Harkhomes apprentice had failed to show up at Harlem Travel the day after payday. "Are you ready to leave Harlem?" she'd challenged me.

I couldn't tell her the truth: that I'd been ready to leave Harlem since the day I came. My Harlem career is still more deferred dream than actual accomplishment. My trekking to and fro along uptown Fifth Avenue, now with a new Ben & Jerry's stop, has worn me out. I'd not even been able to finish my Holistic Hardware class that morning, as I ran back and forth putting out fires (thankfully, metaphorical ones). I feel like a missionary waiting for my release papers to return home. Except, at this point, I don't know where home is.

Mother did not wait for an answer. "It was your decision to come to Harlem, so it's your responsibility to make it work. Getting overextended was also your choice. Focus, I keep telling you, on one business at a time. Or your law practice. Building your nonprofit. No, you want to write and act and open a pricey ice cream shop staffed by homeless men!"

Though I'm always prepared to take on Mother's tirades with the rationale, "visionary enterprise in an underserved community is a work in progress," I find it difficult to counter her disdain for my tendency to take on too much at one time. My initial enthusiasm for the Ben & Jerry's initiative had melted quickly, like some of the cones in the swelter of this summer day, in the crucible of daily operations and in the seasonality of the ice cream business.

The Harlem franchise had been my inspiration, pitched to a Ben & Jerry's executive who'd heard my sermon in Waterbury, Vermont. I'd sensed a win-win: a Harlem scoop shop that would strike a commercial blow against the community's cycles of disinvestment and unemployment and further the company's social mission. Unemployment rates in Harlem had long been more than thrice the rate of the rest of New York City, and much higher when it came to young black men.

My Vermont hosts had loved the idea of taking super-premium ice cream from bucolic New England to the heart of America's most famous ghetto. Ben Cohen, of Ben & Jerry renown, loved

FIGURE 19: With Ben Cohen outside Harlem Ben & Jerry's, planning for its opening

FIGURE 20: The *New York Post*'s write-up

the idea so much that he mentored me through the process. But it turned out to be a hard sell. Even with all the buzz that surrounded social responsibility, $1.75 for an ice cream scoop was no bargain, especially if you were collecting government assistance, which was the situation for 50 percent of my potential customers.

Sales reached fifty thousand dollars in the first month, spiked by all the hype of our opening. The media loved the idea, too. *People*, *Fortune*, *Time*, *Black Enterprise*, the *New York Times*, and the *Wall Street Journal* all ran stories, while the *Daily News* called me a "folk hero." Even the *New York Post*—with its minimalist Harlem coverage policy—did a feature.

To my surprise, the awards rolled in. I was chosen by *Crain's* magazine as one of its top forty entrepreneurs under the age of forty. I was inducted into the GTE Academic All-American Hall of Fame. I was invited to the Waldorf-Astoria Hotel to accept the

Small Business Administration's New York State Small Business Person of the Year Award. I was honored by the Municipal Arts Society, the National Association of Black Accountants, and Hampton University's Alumni Association. And I was interviewed on Japanese television, on the U.S. television show *A Current Affair*, and on a network TV special about giving back. But Tony, one of my Harkhomes guys, ended up back in jail after his photograph appeared in one of the pieces. His parole officer had seen it, visited the shelter, and arrested him for violating parole. If only he had practiced Ghost Planning, one of the holistic principles I'd taught him, the derailment of his progress might have been avoided.

Governor Mario Cuomo visited the scoop shop and later called me a "Renaissance Man," although he was probably referring to a different Renaissance than my lodestar! Legislator Michael Balboni invited me back to Albany and acknowledged my work on the assembly floor. Robert Abrams contacted me seeking my endorsement for his candidacy for the U.S. senate (I guess he hadn't checked my party affiliation). I was elected vice-president of the Harlem Business Alliance. And I was given a standing ovation when I received an honorary degree from the City University of New York's Law School.

All the media exposure led to my best Clubhouse moment. At Gracie Mansion, Mayor Dinkins presented me with his Community Service Award. At the ceremony, I sandwiched my remarks about how business had a responsibility to give back to the community between my favorite Langston Hughes poem—"What Happens to a Dream Deferred?"—and a joke: "What if, instead of Jerry Garcia, Ben and Jerry had named their cherry flavor after James Brown—Funky Cherry?" The crowd appreciated my ice cream samples more than my sense of humor.

But the hype could only sustain the shop for a few months, and revenues plunged during the winter months. The simple fact was that the market uptown for premium ice cream was weak. In my urgency to create jobs for my homeless men I'd missed the most critical factor: researching how to bring a luxury product into a poor community. Consequently, I decided that a creative, well-funded marketing strategy might give the shop a shot at survival—thus, this festival day.

I scan the crowd for Ben and resolve to break the red-ink news and explore new directions. I'm far from the only struggling Harlem businessperson. The dismal economy has hit entrepreneurs as hard as the crime. The old saying—that when downtown gets a cold, uptown catches pneumonia—seems truer than ever. I've run out of patience with all of Harlem's long-prophesied commercial saviors: the International Trade Center; cruises from a transformed Hudson River pier; big-box retail outlets in the old Washburn Wire along the East River; a 125th Street office tower; a first-class grocery store; a top-brand hotel as a hub for tourists. All of these were intended as symbols of Harlem's rebirth, although they'd mostly remained on the drawing board. The one success—an indoor incubator of rented stalls for small retailers called Mart 125—I didn't think would survive long.

The challenged Harlem entrepreneur was in fact a character as old as the Renaissance. The one great exception was Madam C. J. Walker. An orphan, she'd risen from poverty and was a widow and a washerwoman before she became the first female self-made millionaire in America. She built her beauty- and hair-care products business into the largest company owned by an African American in the nation.

A flamboyant woman who partied as hard as she worked, Madam C. J. wowed everyone with her wealth. She built a fabulous limestone mansion on West 136th Street and then an even more elaborate residence—Villa Lewaro—in exclusive Irvington-on-the-Hudson, integrating that community in exceptional style. She left an estate of $2 million—an astonishingly large sum in 1919—to her daughter A'Lelia, who made a career of spending it.

A'Lelia Walker was more than a Roarin' Twenties social butterfly; she was the Renaissance tastemaker. She transformed her mother's townhouse on West 136th Street into the loveliest place to live in Harlem. Always impeccably dressed, A'Lelia brought people from all over New York and the world to celebrate the New Negro in the black Mecca. When she wasn't buying jewels, cars, and champagne, she entertained writers, royalty, artists, actors, musicians, and racketeers—as many whites as blacks—making it fashionable and fun for anyone to come and enjoy uptown. She became a legend, not only because of her spending habits but for the Harlem Renaissance style she defined.

The commercial acumen of Madam C. J. had a shadow side. Black gangsters ran the numbers racket rather than tangle with the Jewish and Italian mobsters who controlled the Prohibition business. Playing the numbers so pervaded Harlem's culture during the Renaissance and the Blight that dozens of illegal numbers banks dotted the Harlem landscape, collecting from an impoverished citizenry countless daily bets that amounted to over 50 percent of the community's economic activity.

The "king of policy" was a numbers runner named Casper Holstein. He made his fortune in *bolita*, the name for the racket in Spanish Harlem, which yielded him apartments, a Long Island house, property in Virginia, and a fleet of cars. Holstein devised a popular betting system drawing digits from daily reports on Wall Street. His reign was cut short after he was kidnapped and ended up in jail, which left him vulnerable to up-and-coming numbers bosses like Stephanie St. Clair, Madam C. J.'s underworld foil.

Organized crime dominated other aspects of Renaissance life. The popular, whites-only nightclubs and speakeasies were run by the Italian and Jewish mafias. Dutch Schultz established his headquarters in Harlem to run New York's biggest bootleg liquor operation during Prohibition. Harlem's reputation as an underworld capital endured as the Mafioso drug distributors turned the area into a haven for heroin in the 1950s. It was a terrible irony that as white businesses and residents moved out, the white crime syndicates moved in to exploit Harlem's poverty and deepen the community's misfortune.

Harlemites had already been hard hit by the post–World War II disappearance of the jobs they'd found in the military and the Brooklyn shipyards. The rise of the welfare economy and government's easy money sidelined them in the culture of dependency, opening the door for foreign-born retailers, mostly Arabs and Koreans, to supplant the fleeing white ones.

A sprinkling of national chains—McDonald's, Burger King, and Woolworth's—failed to mitigate the dismal economic conditions. After the riots of the sixties, burned-out storefronts, a declining population, deteriorating housing, and shrinking tax rolls made Harlem even riskier for capital investment.

Even with the accessibility of legal forms of gambling like the New York State lottery, old-school Harlem gamblers were still putting their trust in local numbers bankers over the state commission. I refused to let the neighborhood runners collect bets in any of my business establishments. This stance had subjected me to periodic threats, although not as intimidating as those I received from the drug dealers of 129th Street.

I see Ben and Jerry moving through the crowd with Anita Roddick, founder of the Body Shop at 125th Street and Fifth Avenue. Ben had introduced me to Anita soon after we opened the scoop shop, encouraging me to add a Body Shop franchise to my teeming entrepreneurial plate. I first envisaged a little national retailing hub with AMEX, Ben & Jerry's, and the Body Shop as the new commercial center. Customers could pick up massage oil, ice cream, and cruise tickets within an easy stroll.

As reality set in, I instead helped Anita to establish a company-owned store that hired local residents located right across the street from the ice cream store in the National Black Theatre building. When the Body Shop opened, none of my Harkhomes referrals were hired. This was not a surprise, since my experience with the homeless scooping ice cream had convinced me it would be a leap to get them ready to sell upscale cosmetics. However, since the Body Shop had already been robbed at gunpoint and Ben & Jerry's was still untouched by crime, staffing ex-cons had at least this one advantage.

La Famille was proving to be the greatest of my business troubles. We'd recently discovered squatters in the vacant floors above the restaurant, where I planned to build the Renaissance Inn, Harlem's first upscale lodging. Initial findings of a market study had signaled that it would have to be at the lower end of the market. But meetings with Travelodge and Econo Lodge officials had gone nowhere.

The other day I'd had to stand guard to make sure a rodent didn't run into the dining room and scare away customers. Later that night, I'd come downstairs to the bar and seen Victor, a Harkhomes evictee, sitting at the bar, ordering a drink. My heart had sunk. How could I help this alcoholic kick his addiction when my establishment supported his habit? I'd refunded Victor's money and demanded that he leave, to the disdain of the bartender and customers. Before he stormed out, I invited Victor back to Harkhomes, doubtful that he'd give it yet another try.

Then I hit rock bottom. I'd been having lunch with the officials of a French tour operator in an attempt to court their much-needed business when shouts had rung out from the kitchen.

I tried to pretend that they had come from outside. But I sat mortified as one of the cooks walked into the dining room, in a daze, with egg batter all over his face. The other cook emerged directly behind him, yelling. Flustered, I mumbled apologies to my guests and then hurried the cooks back into the kitchen. I listened to their mutual accusations, spoke some meaningless chastisements, and wished I was on the far side of the moon. I lingered in the kitchen after sending one of them home. (I hadn't been sure I'd sent home the one who was actually at fault, but I had to make a snap judgment and keep one of them to finish the orders.) Too embarrassed to go back to the dining room immediately, I took several deep breaths to regain my composure. But it was too late. When I arrived at the table, the tour officials were gone.

I stand on the platform we'd put up in the middle of 125th Street and beckon Ben and Jerry to step forward so the program can begin. They wade toward me through the crowd, like the rock stars their ice cream flavors venerate.

I rehearse my remarks in my head. I could talk about the improbably tasty oasis I've created in the center of Harlem. It has a 1940s look—hanging lamps, mahogany booths, pressed-tin ceiling, ceramic tile floors, soda-fountain-style counter, and a bucolic wall of grazing Holstein cows. I'd better leave out how the novelty of the store has been wearing off, with customers walking out when they find out how much the ice cream costs.

I could describe my three interlocking goals: to employ the formerly homeless as scoopers; to return the bulk of the profits to Harkhomes; and to establish a publicity-friendly, national franchise at Harlem's commercial core, so as to spur economic development. These objectives address the structural dimension of the poverty of Generation Blight. I decide, however, that it's best not to get too philosophical, nor to mention the headaches of staffing the hard-to-employ and the long wait for profits and Perkins-like economic development to occur.

I could reflect on my training trip to Vermont. (Best perhaps not to mention what a wonderful contrast it made with Harlem life to jog amid trees every morning.) Whether in Waterbury, Stowe, or Burlington, I'd been surrounded by friendliness, laughter, and ice cream. I'd come up with my own flavor to help launch the Harlem store. As far as I was concerned, the sumptuous multi-berry concoction I called Bluesberry tasted better than Cherry Garcia, one of their best sellers. But the flavor hadn't caught on, being too fruity for the urban palate. It had been trounced by sugary new flavors like cookie dough and couldn't even compete with standards, like vanilla.

I decide that I'll definitely mention our special King Day event. Ben Cohen and I were surrounded outside the scoop shop by masses of people, black and white together, huddled against the winter chill. We'd marched down Harlem streets singing "We Shall Overcome," and then we'd crowded into the store. Unfortunately, my mood had plunged when I realized that the number of marchers exceeded the number of customers we'd had all month.

I knew that I'd have to mention how Ben and Jerry had waived the $25,000 franchise fee, and I could conclude with some of my philosophy—to instill an ethic of success and alleviate poverty, while expanding economic opportunities—and wrap up the speech with a favorite Old Testament narrative (2 Kings 4:1–7) about God's business plan.

No, best not to get too sermony.

After I tell people what a great guy he is, Ben Cohen steps up to the microphone. He's at once laid-back and passionate. How does he do that? I can't help but think of what these down-to-earth, throwback-to-the-sixties, white guys have done in fifteen

FIGURE 21: In a speckled cow hat, with Ben Cohen (*center-left, in gray wool cap, holding a megaphone*) during the King Day march

years. If they could turn an old-fashioned, rock-salt ice cream maker in a converted Burlington gas station into a $140 million business while cultivating a conscience in their capitalism that reached all the way to our black community, maybe there was hope for Harlem and me to overcome the Blight.

I see Robert, my former Harkhomes supervisor, near the platform; he's now my ice cream store manager. I'd persuaded him to leave his job as shelter director to school my hard-to-train staff in customer service and inventory control. Earlier that day, we'd discussed once more what to do about Mitch, one of our best servers, who'd refused to scoop rum raisin because it contained alcohol—although it was a negligible amount and only used for flavoring. But for Mitch, a recovering substance abuser, it was a matter of conscience, of preventing anyone from going down the path he'd been on. His compunction was inconsequential to the customer wanting the rum raisin. I lacked the Solomonic wisdom for this. I was hoping Robert might get a revelation.

At the previous day's staff meeting, Robert and I had had to confront the staff again about over-scooping the product and the fact that cash was missing from the register. Too often, the inventory was out of control and reconciling the day's cash and receipts proved elusive. I knew that with sales of this seasonal business lagging in an unconverted marketplace, subsidizing the payroll and rent out of my own pocket couldn't last much longer.

"We have come from Vermont to Harlem," Ben affirms, "not just to help you sell ice cream but to make your community a better place to live."

Ben describes the company's core values of balancing economic, product, and social missions. I've heard it all before. I tell myself to forget the warm-and-fluffy social-venture stuff for the moment. *Let's deal with how you're going to help keep the Harlem scoop shop in business.*

The program finally over, I walk with Ben off the platform and wait for the crowd to clear. An unknown woman approaches me and pulls me aside.

"Thank y'all, thank so much." She slurps ice cream as she talks. "I ain' never took my kids for ice cream 'fore."

She introduces her six school-aged kids.

"C'mon, y'all, now. Since he come so very long way here with all dis ice cream, let's all show Mistah Hollins how much we 'preciate him comin', with this special gift we got for him."

I'm still an alien in Harlem all these years later, now lumped in with these graying hippies from the north. I decide not to spoil her moment with a correction.

The children surround me, and then squeeze in with a collective hug, proclaiming in unison:

To you
From us
And Him up above
From Harlem with love.

Are you kidding me?! Though sincere, an inharmonious kids' chorus strikes me as a pretty poor surrogate for the Renaissance muse.

Feeling stickiness against my stomach, I look down at my new tie-dye T-shirt, amused the kids' gooey gratitude has turned the Ben-inspired design from hip to psychedelic. I look up to thank the children, but they're already off. The portly crew doesn't look like they need another cone, but they scramble back into line nonetheless.

What could ever be better than being anointed a sugarcoated folk hero by little fair-weather fans?

Stop laughing, Mrs. Stokes.

Where did Ben go?

TEN

No Justice, No Peace!

LIKE MANY OTHERS, I hover around the burnt-out 125th Street storefront that was Freddy's clothing store and stare, incredulous. Seven are dead in a dispute—over back rent!

Though I possess a penchant for witnessing moments of import, I could have done without having to observe the depressing details of the deadliest disaster in Harlem history, a tragedy that had turned Mrs. Stokes and other prophets of uptown doom into contemporary sages.

I was here on a political mission, to gather intelligence for my boss, Governor George Pataki. He'd appointed me state housing commissioner soon after he'd defeated Mario Cuomo. I'd become by default his chief adviser on urban issues and a putative expert on Harlem.

The news photos and TV clips have understated the magnitude of this misfortune. My gut instinct is that the governor should stay as far away from this tinderbox as possible.

Since as a Black Republican with a growing reputation for community-based enterprise I was a rare commodity, the recent rise of the GOP in New York politics had turned me from a troubled entrepreneur to trophy appointee. I'd been courted for high-profile jobs by the new Giuliani administration. After meetings with the mayor's inner circle—Peter Powers, Randy Mastro, John Dyson—I'd decided city housing commissioner was the best fit. But Rudy had chosen my Harvard-to-Harlem peer Deborah Wright, with an assist from her mentor Richard Parsons. My mentor Walter Wilson, still running the Beth-HARK Crisis Center, had not been in the loop at city hall.

I'd never expected to ride out of Harlem on a Republican wave, but with Giuliani's defeat of Dinkins and Pataki's defeat of Cuomo, both Clubhouse favorites, my stock with the Gang of Four had plummeted to new lows, even lower than during my kamikaze mission against Paterson the Son a decade earlier. I'd hoped that my rising political star might transform me from a reluctant foe to a necessary friend. With Republicans in charge at Gracie Mansion and the Statehouse, who else in Harlem was there to call?

I'd supported George Pataki as emblematic of a new generation of Republicans who pledged to resurrect the party of Lincoln by replacing the welfare state with policies that empowered individuals and fostered opportunity. Profoundly inspired by Dad's old friend Jack Kemp, this new generation of GOP politicians wanted government to encourage work, saving, and entrepreneurship through lowering taxes and fighting poverty head-on by partnering with, rather than competing against, community character-builders like Harkhomes.

My strategy had always involved restoring faith-based, local nonprofit groups like Harkhomes to their historical role as leaders in the fight against poverty and pathologies. It also meant removing government as competition for providing services and making it a partner with these worthy organizations. Instead of

FIGURE 22: Co-chair of the 1994 Pataki campaign for governor, with the candidate

building more public housing, government would invest in worthy providers of affordable housing, including nonprofit groups with a proven track record in the community.

On a philosophical level, my approach to governmental intervention rejected two extremes. On the one hand, I had no time for laissez-faire, whereby the poor were expected to pull themselves up by their bootstraps; on the other, I didn't want government aid simply given directly to the poor. As Martin Luther King Jr. had once indicated, the problem with the bootstraps admonition was that some people had no boots. The trouble with the government-solves-all approach was that money sometimes ended up in the hands of individuals whose irresponsibility resulted in dependency. It also crowded out those in the community who were already on the scene, doing good work.

Replacing these two extremes was a third way, the partnership model, which married the compassion and competence of the best community-based groups with the considerable resources of the government.

Thus, when the governor approached me to work with his incoming administration, I'd jumped at the opportunity to take what I'd learned about community development in Harlem and apply it on a broader scale. Or was such an offer an untimely distraction for my already-overflowing agenda, or perhaps an escape from my Harlem headaches and heartaches? My plan, however, was not making headway as I endeavored to navigate the choppy political waters of these deficit-busting, program-cutting times. As I maneuvered my housing agency through efforts to eliminate it altogether, I found that progress in Albany, as in Harlem, was like climbing the rough side of a mountain.

I shake my head "No!" at a pesky reporter who's recognized me and presses me for comments, as she's done other times. I try to fade back into the crowd, as I consider making a quick exit to handle some of my other priorities. But I resolve to stay at the scene while I gather sufficient information for my report. With my busy travel schedule around the state, my Harlem assignments have been few and far between. I can remember only two others.

It was the Clubhouse's finest hour since Dinkins' triumph at city hall. A press conference in the Powell State Office Building had announced Harlem's designation as an empowerment zone. This federal legislation had been sponsored by Rangel, although it stemmed from the Kempian enterprise zone—a fact that, not surprisingly, went unacknowledged. Dinkins and Sutton had basked with the congressman in his moment of glory at a political-star-studded ceremony officiated by Housing and Urban

Development official Andrew Cuomo. I was bookended in the lineup by city officials Mark Green and Ruth Messinger far from the podium, out of range of the photo op. It's a good thing state funding was involved or they might not have let me into the room.

I had also been sent to Astor Row—the fair-weather block of Harlem—to investigate why the celebrated restoration of the houses there had stalled. I strolled the singular block and observed the twenty-eight brick row houses that were a shadow of their former selves. Nonetheless, it wasn't hard to imagine the popularity of these unusual late nineteenth-century properties. They were set back twenty feet from the street, with front yards and Victorian, turned-wood, ornately spindled porches, all a uniform three stories with light courts modestly separating each pair. I thought the block might have looked more like Savannah than Manhattan; now it felt more like the edge of a war zone than the cream of Harlem housing.

For my report, I'd done research into the history of the Astor houses. Four decades after Alexander Hamilton had purchased land on Sugar Hill, John Jacob Astor, fur trader, arts patron, and the first millionaire in the United States, had bought a swath of property east of Hamilton Grange in the still pastoral but now struggling village of Harlem. William Backhouse Astor broke with the family trend of investing his grandfather's $80 million estate in midtown trophies like the Waldorf Astoria, the Apthorp, and the St. Regis. Instead, he forged uptown and developed the first speculative townhouses of Harlem's nineteenth-century real estate expansion.

The Astors were so pleased with their first real estate foray into Harlem that they commissioned the construction of a second project in 1901. Designed by Clinton & Russell, this signature apartment building at the corner of 116th Street and Seventh Avenue was named Graham Court. It rivaled 409

Edgecombe for Harlem multi-family preeminence for many years. Unfortunately, it also shared its peer's fate, falling into the city's hands in 1992.

The Astors retained ownership of Astor Row well into the Renaissance, enjoying long waiting lists for the $1,100 annual rent for each house. A 1920s *New York Times* article captured the block's appeal: It was "set back from the street with a pleasant lawn patch in front of the long porch attached to each house and shaded by good-sized trees." But there were hints of the passing of an era: " . . . the block for many years presented a picture of domestic tranquility and comfort which few other dwelling blocks in the city possessed."

The *Times* headline—"HARLEM'S ASTOR ROW FOR COLORED TENANTS"—reflected the bias of the age. The story highlighted "radical changes in 130th Street" and lamented that "a realty operator" had acquired twenty houses from the Astors and "had sold five of them to colored buyers." The story concluded on a mournful note, "Harlem's famous block . . . will soon be occupied entirely by colored residents."

What the *Times* did not report was the intense battle between the races that was raging over control of Harlem properties. With Fifth Avenue as the informal but fiercely enforced color line—the Renaissance equivalent of the "other side of the tracks"—Astor Row was one of the last lines of defense to keep blacks to the east and away from Sugar Hill, Strivers' Row, 409 Edgecombe, Mt. Morris Park, Graham Court, and other prime Harlem real estate.

White Harlemites conspired in several ways to safeguard their community. They persuaded banks to redline black buyers. They convinced realtors not to rent or sell to blacks, and made pacts among themselves to do likewise. And they bought properties to evict blacks. Black entrepreneurs and developers, Philip Payton among them, retaliated. They obtained exclusive brokerage with landlords to empty their buildings and rent only to blacks. They also purchased buildings and evicted whites, many of whom had already taken flight as soon as ownership shifted into black hands. These real estate wars raged through the first two decades of the twentieth century. But the blockbusting of Astor Row (what a surprise that the business-savvy Astors fell for this devious tactic!) proved to be the Waterloo in the battle for Harlem. The fall of Astor Row foredoomed the rest of white Harlem.

As I approached the end of the block, I looked back and observed that most of the signature porches had gone or were in serious disrepair. Not even its most-favored-block status could shield Astor Row from the storms of the Blight. The 1978 *Architect's Guide to New York City* lamented Astor Row's "restrained beauty which has been tarnished by years of economic distress." I guess it was the "beauty" of the block that compelled a 1981 designation for Astor Row as a city landmark. Why should 130th Street have gotten all the attention, when my mission field, one block south where Harkhomes was located, suffered through unrelenting dilapidation? This tale of two blocks testified to the power of legacy as a weapon against Harlem's decline.

Brooke Astor, the venerable heiress, had made a fateful visit to Astor Row in 1990. Appalled that a block bearing the family name had become "tarnished," she'd launched a public–private restoration program with a $1.7 million grant from the Vincent Astor Foundation. Perhaps she was on to something: a "block with a benefactor initiative." Was this a program to reverse the community's pervasive decline? If only other wealthy New York families would adopt a Harlem block through generous capital infusions. Was anyone interested in 129th Street?

When the first couple of porches had been restored, Brooke showed up with Mayor Dinkins to cut the ribbon. The rush to jump on the Astor Row restoration bandwagon was no surprise: the Commonwealth Fund, the New York City Landmarks Commission, the New York City Department of Housing Preservation and Development, the Historic Properties Fund, the Abyssinian Development Corporation, Chemical Bank, Morgan Guaranty, Fugi Bank, Apple Bank, East New York Savings Bank—each institution was no doubt represented at one of Brooke Astor's high-society gatherings.

I walked up to the two shabbiest townhouses, the controversial ones. Two Astor Row homeowners had been sued by the Astor's lead agency, the Landmarks Conservancy, in a nasty dispute over the pace and quality of the porch-restoration project. I asked a few questions and discovered that neighbors were rallying around the embattled residents and were critical of the Brooke initiative. I dutifully filed a report recommending that Brooke swoop in with her checkbook and pay the two men for storing the antique-porch wood supplies, which would lead to yet another restored porch. She would save the day, then Super-Brooke would be freed up for a real mission: to come one block south to 129th Street and deliver a check to Harkhomes, thus transforming this blight of a block with the power of her purse.

No action had been taken to date, and I wasn't holding my breath. Investigating the Astor Row melodrama was child's play compared with the task of assessing the Freddy's clothing store calamity. It was also imperative to give this report a historical context.

There are times when Harlem's pent-up fury bubbles to the surface; its long-suppressed frustrations over racial injustice can no longer be contained and they spill out onto the streets. Impatience over deferred dreams turns to indignant confrontation, and ultimately to violence. Perhaps Harlem's anger stemmed in part from the racist efforts to keep blacks away from

Astor Row and the Blight that followed. The terrifying rhetori-
cal question that concludes Langston Hughes' "Harlem"—"Or
does it explode?"—has been answered in the affirmative again
and again. The Harlem explosion—unpredictable but cata-
strophic—has taken on historical inevitability. The tragedy at
Freddy's was one of those times.

As was March 19, 1935. The riot that started that day was not
really about Lino Rivera, a black teenager accused of shoplift-
ing a knife and taken to the department-store basement to be
beaten. It actually had little to do with the false rumors that
the police had killed the sixteen-year-old. The true culprits were
the Great Depression, which stoked Harlem's poverty; soar-
ing unemployment; endless soup lines; escalating disease rates;
deteriorating housing—far beyond what the white community
suffered; and the failure of New Deal programs to reach to the
depths of Harlem's plight.

Discrimination plagued all aspects of Renaissance life, but
nowhere was the impact starker than in the difference between
housing costs. In Harlem in the 1920s and 1930s, single blacks
paid three times more in rent than did their white counterparts.
The average black family paid $9.50 per room per month, but
the average white household paid $6.67 for similar space. Such
price-gouging no doubt brought the ire of community residents
to a boil. Since it was increasingly clear that Jim Crow was no
longer only south of the Mason-Dixon line, thousands took
to the streets on that fateful day. Three were killed, hundreds
injured, and six hundred stores were looted, which caused
millions of dollars in property damage. The rioters vented their
rage against the large number of white-owned establishments.

The Harlem Renaissance, one of the greatest movements in
African-American history, was knocked to its knees. The white
patrons of Harlem's social and entertainment scene slowed to
a trickle. The march of the black masses to their new Mecca

ground to a crawl. A reverse diaspora threatened. The flowering of black culture began to wilt.

August 1, 1943 was also one of those times. Eight thousand New York State guardsmen and fifteen hundred civilian volunteers joined 6,600 police officers to quell the street violence provoked by another false rumor: a white policeman had shot and killed a black soldier, with the soldier's mother watching!

What actually happened (the black soldier was slightly wounded by the cop for interfering in the arrest of a black woman) was inconsequential to the hordes of young blacks who threw bottles and stones at the wounded soldier's hospital before they marauded through the community. In their wake were six dead, four hundred injured, hundreds of businesses looted and burned, and five hundred arrests. All of the arrested were black; one hundred of them were women. New York mayor Fiorello H. LaGuardia suspended the wartime dim-out so the tumultuous streets could be illuminated. What bitter irony for Harlem! Those bright lights meant that her Golden Age had finally gone dark.

The mayor also imposed a curfew, closed all liquor stores and bars, and halted traffic, except for guarded food trucks and trolley cars. The riot of 1943 did more than shut Harlem down for a few days. It put the final nails in the coffin of the Renaissance.

July 19, 1964 was also one of those times. Martin Luther King's speech during the March on Washington the summer before had extended to the utmost the rising expectations spawned by the civil rights movement. This movement had penetrated Harlem before other northern cities, but the Congress of Racial Equality (CORE) employed different strategies than King's Southern Christian Leadership Conference (SCLC). Instead of the SCLC's bus boycotts, sit-ins, and freedom rides, CORE implemented rent strikes against unscrupulous landlords and pressed for civilian review boards to consider complaints about police abuse.

Such activism apparently did nothing to defuse Harlem's growing frustration over decades of the Blight. By this stage, the drug-addiction rate was ten times that of New York City in general. Murders in Harlem occurred at six times the city average. Half of Harlem's children were being raised by a single parent, or none at all. Yet no one could have predicted or imagined that another angry day in Harlem would ignite summers of urban unrest all across America.

The precipitating incident on that fateful day was Thomas Gilligan, a white off-duty police officer, shooting and killing James Powell, a fifteen-year-old African American. Several days of peaceful protests erupted on 125th Street into a community-wide uprising. Bottles were thrown, guns fired, bricks hurled, storefront windows smashed, garbage cans set ablaze, and stores looted as youths ran wild. Although city hall declared a state of emergency in Harlem, the turbulence lasted five days. The outcome was devastating. One person was killed, a hundred injured, 520 arrested, and untold millions of dollars were incurred in property damage.

In the 1920s, Harlem had led Black America in a cultural uprising. In the 1960s Harlem's symbolic place as the black capital had the opposite effect: it ignited urban upheaval. The riot of 1964 sparked a nationwide conflagration of inner-city violence that raged for five consecutive years, the longest period of American domestic strife since the Civil War.

In a real sense the reverberating unrest was the Civil War reborn a century later. The combatants changed. The conflict between North and South was now a battle between black and white. The de jure slavery of the plantation had been succeeded by the slavish conditions of the ghetto. African Americans burned inner cities as if on General Sherman's march through

Southern cities. LBJ's civil- and voting-rights legislation echoed Lincoln's Emancipation Proclamation.

The radicals rose over the reformers, preaching revolution. Stokely Carmichael's confrontational shout of "Black Power!" drowned out Martin Luther King Jr.'s conciliatory song, "We Shall Overcome." The violence spread slowly at first, erupting in Bedford-Stuyvesant in Brooklyn days after Harlem. It spread like wildfire a year later.

The summer of 1965 witnessed the flames of unrest jumping from the East to West Coast. Thirty-four died, thousands were injured, and scores of buildings lay in ashes in the Watts district of Los Angeles. The summer of 1966 multiplied the riots across America's ghettos; firebombing and looting became pastimes for urban youth. During the summer of 1967, dozens of inner-city war zones raged, but Newark and Detroit flared most fiercely. National guardsmen besieged New Jersey's largest city for three days, while Motown saw 7,200 of its residents arrested.

April 4, 1968 was also one of those times. When Martin Luther King Jr. was cut down by an assassin's bullet on the balcony of the Lorraine Hotel in Memphis, Harlem erupted again, but this time in concert with civil disorder that seemed to plague every U.S. inner city. The two deaths, numerous injured, and burning buildings from the rioting in Harlem compelled New York mayor John Lindsay to march up Lenox Avenue through a hail of bricks to urge the masses to go home.

It would take a while for the Harlems of America to calm down after King's death. With the dream of economic opportunity, the hope of racial justice, and the ideal of ethnic harmony having fallen with King's body, it would take generations for America's social fabric to begin to heal.

• • •

Harlem was still healing as the circumstances leading to Freddy's tragedy began to take shape. I sensed that, as I walked 125th Street, one of those times in Harlem might be imminent. I heard the signature chant of the post-Renaissance protest movement—"No Justice, No Peace! No Justice, No Peace!"—with ever-increasing intensity. A generous complement of police officers flanked the protesters, who were being rallied by the Rev. Al Sharpton.

Maybe Harlem was still angry over Dinkins' reelection loss to Giuliani in 1993. It had been a devastating defeat for the Clubhouse, sparking rumors of its demise. The ascendancy of Carl McCall (another Clubhouse stalwart) to state comptroller, the first black man elected to statewide office in New York, quelled such speculation, but hardly tempered the mounting community tensions.

Mayor Giuliani's refusal to meet with black elected officials and activists further stoked Harlem's anger, as did his crackdown on vendors on 125th Street. His plan to remove them to an alternative open-air market on 116th attracted tepid support from the thousand or so unlicensed entrepreneurs, who'd been an uncontroversial fixture on the community's main thoroughfare for many years.

From my Ben & Jerry's store I watched with ambivalence as a plethora of cops, many on horseback, blocked the peddlers from their normal commercial activity. Though they weren't direct competitors with me—none sold ice cream—I knew fellow storeowners who strongly believed their business suffered because of the vendors' competition, congestion, and debris. But I also knew several street vendors, including some men from Harkhomes, whose livelihoods would be more difficult because of this enforced eviction.

Worst of all for me, all of the commotion on 125th Street was keeping direly needed patrons away from Ben & Jerry's, La

Famille, and Harlem Travel. Combined with the never-ending fact of crime, this continuation of Harlem's commercial upheaval was shrinking the customer base to untenable levels.

Even after the vendors' removal, the picketers persisted. They urged a boycott of businesses that weren't black owned. Though I was spared the angry calls in front of my scoop shop, sales continued to suffer as confused shoppers stayed away. Reverend Sharpton held a press conference about two lawsuits against city hall: to overturn the ouster of the vendors and to reverse his arrest for selling Bibles on the street in front of his office. Among the dozens of arrests for disorderly conduct were two noteworthy detainees: Morris Powell, the incendiary head of the 125th Street Vendors Association, and Roland Smith, a purveyor of African jewelry and books.

Less than a year later, Smith joined Powell, Sharpton, and others in a new series of protests. Sikhulu Shange, a black record store owner, was locked in an epic lease battle with Fred Harari, a Jewish businessman. Harari had leased the 125th Street retail space for his business, Freddy's Fashions, from the United House of Prayer for All People, the owner of the building that Daddy Grace had bought from Father Divine during the Renaissance. Harari subleased part of his space to Shange but refused to give the long-standing, popular businessman a new lease.

With street sentiment still raw from the vendors' ouster, the masses rallied to Shange's support. They seized the opportunity to vent frustration over the chronic deficit of African-American commercial clout in America's black capital. Harari's intransigence, the church's inattention, city hall's insensitivity, and local leaders' lack of intervention aggravated Harlem's anger.

On December 8, 1995, an everyday morning in Harlem, Ronald Smith walked into Freddy's Fashions with a handgun and a canister of flammable liquid. He shot and wounded four people, then splashed paint thinner over the clothing in the store and set it on fire. Smith shot himself and died in the blaze, along with seven employees.

Outrage poured in from all quarters. To stem the flood of criticism, Mayor Giuliani went Christmas shopping in Harlem and was confronted with the question, "Why did it take a fire for you to come to 125th Street?" A much more important question, which climaxed my report, that I wish the mayor—or somebody—had answered was—Will American social progress ever obviate Harlem's violent outbursts; or is the next explosion as inevitable as a summer thunderstorm?

ELEVEN

What's This Guy Doing on 129th Street?

As I end one of my now-rare visits to Harkhomes, my persevering shelter, I reflect on one of my best days as state housing commissioner. I'd toured several northern Manhattan housing sites with applications pending for state funding. I'd conducted a staff meeting in my Powell Office Building district office. And I'd presented grant awards to worthy community-based groups.

My tenure as housing commissioner had been testy. While I'd been fending off attempts to eliminate or consolidate my agency from nameless upstate detractors, unknown downstate adversaries were using the media to publicize my "near-bankrupt businesses" as ubiquitous rumors circulated of my political demise.

I shouldn't have been surprised at this battlefield. Dad had schooled me in the treacherous pathway of politics, which is why he steered clear, except for his Swedish sojourn. He would've been vexed by my first career road out of Harlem, meandering north to the state capitol instead of south to the financial one.

By spending half of my week in Albany and traveling the state much of the rest of my time, I had little time for grassroots activ-

FIGURE 23: As state housing commissioner, presenting a grant award to a community-based group

ity. To sustain Harkhomes, I'd videotaped my Holistic Hardware teachings so they could be shown daily to the residents. Enough Holistic Hardware graduates had committed to help at the shelter to create a strong core of volunteer veterans who, supported by staff, could keep the program going.

I'd been delighted to put on my jeans, sweatshirt, and sneakers to help with the evening's shelter cleanup. It was just like old times, with one wonderful exception. I used to be at Harkhomes for the night. But now I was domesticated—married with a baby daughter—so I was on my way home to Sugar Hill.

Harkhomes had fared better than my other Harlem ventures. Harlem Travel was relatively stable compared with Ben & Jerry's and La Famille. When I'd taken the state job and become an Albany-bound, absentee entrepreneur, I'd hoped that the economic tide of the Harlem marketplace would finally turn. I'd also hoped that the capable managers I'd left in charge of my businesses would keep the latter afloat long enough for the swelling streams of uptown commerce to sweep them to solvency, if not prosperity.

That was more wishful thinking. The recent protests had lowered pedestrian traffic and pushed all my businesses to the brink. Crime seemed to be down, but the chaotic climate on 125th Street in the run-up to and aftermath of the Freddy's tragedy had led to a net loss of customers. I'd lost the irreplaceable Robert at Ben & Jerry's to a better job, and with him had gone the scoop shop's operational stability. Tourism had kept the languishing La Famille afloat as local patronage has dwindled.

Harlem Travel remained the oasis in my entrepreneurial wasteland because of the valiant management of my mother. I thought we'd have to close the business when I accepted the gubernatorial appointment. Why would Mother keep making the suburban commute without having her son in the office to boss around daily? Much to my surprise, she never missed a beat. The biggest threat Harlem Travel now faced had little to do with maternal whims or the ongoing challenges of the Blight. Internet-based travel services were shrinking our customer base.

The truth is that all my businesses had turned out to be more charitable than profitable, more jobs programs for the homeless

than self-sustaining enterprises. My plans for the money-mak-
ing ventures to produce enough profit to support my nonprofits
had been frustrated by the inhospitable Harlem climate and my
own suspect decision-making, such as the fact that I went into
politics and left these nascent companies in the hands of others.
Mother had been too busy with Harlem Travel to harangue me.

The one bright spot had been my writing. Though *Homegrown*
had not become a big enough hit to move venues, it had been
popular enough to be extended twice and brought back for
another run at NBT. My producer Tunde believed that the play's
future would be as a musical. So I'd been spending much of my
travel time revisioning my characters in a Broadway musical,
hoping that this wasn't just another one of my forever-deferred
dreams.

I finish with the cleanup and check my watch. I hurry through
my goodbyes and run to the door, pleased that I can still make it
home in time to try to rock my toddler Shelby to sleep. My grin
broadens as I hit 129th Street. It appears quieter than I remember it. By this time a few years ago, the block would have been
packed, and getting busier as midnight approached. Now, hardly
anybody was hanging out.

I pause on the sidewalk and look up and down both sides of
the street. I can see no crack lines, though I've heard that the
drug traffic has been forced inside. I look west again, double-
checking the Dirty Alley and the Dark Corner. No crackheads
are exiting No. 60, no drug dealers are running from the alley,
no rodents are scampering around. And there are no sidewalk-
memorial bouquets. These are good signs.

My strut, however, never catches a rhythm. My smile vanishes as two burly men jump out of a parked car and rush at

me. Startled and thinking I'm about to be robbed, I start to run—believing I've got something left in my football legs—and glance back. I see that both men are white, and that one of them is young enough to be a rookie cop. I freeze. Could this really be happening to me?

Images of James Powell and Eleanor Bumpers and Rodney King flood my mind. I remember the time when two white troopers pulled me over on the New Jersey Turnpike. I knew I hadn't been speeding, but the officers held me for an hour and gave a ticket anyway. I know the drill. I've heard about it many times. I'd never had to use it, until now.

I quickly throw my hands high above my head. "Hey, I'm clean. I'm clean."

Hands slam into my shoulder and back, taking my breath away. The cops push me hard against the wall of a building, their fingers running up and down my arms and legs, digging into my flesh. I clench my teeth and stifle my anger to push out the words.

"Listen to me, you got the wrong guy," I assert, my voice trembling. "I work for Governor Pataki."

"Yeah right," chuckles one cop. "And my boss is Peter Pan."

"Don't even try it," exhorts the other. "We saw you looking for your gang!"

"I'm the state housing—"

"Shut the hell up!" threatens the other.

I'm about to lose my temper and give the officer a piece of my mind. Instead, I pray, and reach for a piece of scripture to stem indignation's tide: *Blessed are those who are persecuted because of righteousness' sake, for theirs is the kingdom of heaven.*

It's not working. I'm still at the boiling point.

I intensify my inner journey. The Renaissance muse comes to me:

Let us forgive Ty Kendricks
The place was Darktown. He was young.
His nerves were jittery. The day was hot.
The Negro ran out of the alley.
And so Ty shot.

Let us understand Ty Kendricks
The Negro must have been dangerous,
Because he ran;
And here was a rookie with a chance
To prove himself a man.

The officers empty my pockets, handcuff me, and lead me to their unmarked car. I'm aware that "stop and frisk" means that cops detain crime suspects, pat them down, find nothing, and let them go after a short time. This stop-and-frisk tactic has been recently escalated as part of a policing approach emphasizing preventative measures against lawbreaking. That it disproportionately singles out blacks and Hispanics has not slowed its aggressive implementation.

I know the law. The Supreme Court has ruled that for police officers to stop me they must have a reasonable suspicion for a crime. There's also a higher standard for them to frisk me—a reasonable belief that I'm armed and dangerous. What were my "furtive movements"—looking one way, then the other? I open my mouth to explain that they have no legitimate basis to stop me; to complain that I'm being mistreated because of the color of my skin. But I catch myself, remembering where I am. Cops have always had carte blanche on 129th Street.

I dredge up more of Sterling Brown's "Southern Cop." I must give some perspective to my rage, focus on what's most important—coming out of this alive!

Let us condone Ty Kendricks
If we cannot decorate.
When he found what the Negro was running for,
It was all too late;
And all we can say for the Negro is
It was unfortunate.

Let us pity Ty Kendricks
He has been through enough,
Standing there, his big gun smoking,
Rabbit-scared, alone,
Having to hear the wenches wail
And the dying Negro moan.

I'd heard about the aggressive policing policy implemented by police commissioner William Bratton with "stop and frisk" as a cornerstone of his efforts to combat crime. The decline in crime had made Bratton something of a poster boy. He'd been on magazine covers, TV shows, a European speaking tour, and been compared to Teddy Roosevelt, who'd famously fought crime in New York City a century before. The homicide rate was finally falling in Harlem, even faster than in the city as a whole. Bratton's visibility, though, had infuriated Mayor Giuliani. Not one to be outshone, Rudy had decided it was time to cut Bratton down to size, and so had halved his press staff.

Crime rates had fallen faster in New York City than at any time since the end of Prohibition. They signified the first major blow against the Blight and the destruction wrought by the influx of heroin in the 1950s and crack cocaine in the 1980s. The get-tough policy was a welcome change to the culture of permissiveness that had equated criminals with their victims— an example of misconceived governmental policy that failed in its principle job of protecting the lives and the safety of its citizens. As criminals cycled in and out of society, they'd torn into Harlem, its businesses, and its people, leaving those who couldn't flee more terrorized and vulnerable than ever. Yet, how to balance effective law enforcement with the fair treatment of individuals had been an elusive goal. I was now experiencing the outcome of failing to realize that.

I'd been in favor of stronger local law enforcement—especially on 129th Street. Mayor Dinkins had begun the police's assault on violent crime. Near the end of his one term in office, he'd enlarged the force and empowered the precincts with increased patrols. I'd worked with these officers because all my businesses had been burglarized except Ben & Jerry's. The ex-cons behind the counter worked better than any burglar alarm or cops on the corner.

It was a tough sell. Harlem had long harbored suspicions about the police and the practices of the NYPD. The goodwill that had been generated by the appointment of Lloyd Sealy in 1963 as the first black officer to command a police station—Harlem's 28th Precinct—had been fleeting. The police brutality that provoked the 1964 riot had led to demands in the community to rectify the ratio of one black for every six white cops across Harlem's three precincts. More recently, endless allegations of corruption and brutality surrounding the "Dirty Thirty"—police officers in Harlem's 30th Precinct who'd been accused of selling cocaine, taking payoffs, and robbing drug dealers—had left relations between Harlem and the NYPD even more strained.

Mayor Giuliani had gone further than Dinkins by focusing on quality-of-life crimes. This had meant stopping guys with dirty squeegees from "cleaning" your car at intersections and then demanding money, to smoking marijuana and urinating in public. There'd been more arrests of drug dealers, but also more I.D. checks and pat-downs. This strategy, combined with the deadly toll of the Blight on young black men, diminished the crack trade.

The officers shove me onto the back seat of their vehicle. My indignation rages. I fall prey to my long-festering (if much-cherished) conspiracy theory. Just as the Clubhouse has been plotting to remove me from my position in Albany, so they're now exacting revenge for my refusal to become a Democrat.

I stew as the cops talk between themselves. Statistics flood my mind: African Americans constitute 50 percent of the nation's prisoners but only 13 percent of the population. We are eight times more likely to be in jail than whites. More black men are behind bars than in college. . . . But . . . Harlem's murder rate, down 68 percent; robbery, down 60 percent; rape, down 70 percent; burglary, down 81 percent; total crime complaints, down 62 percent. . . .

The police search my wallet. I hope they quickly discover my state I.D. I see them studying something. I lean close to eavesdrop on the conversation.

"Not good," says one cop.

"What's this guy doing on 129th Street?" questions the other.

There's silence up front. Though still irate, I feel vindicated, and expect immediate deliverance. Their several phone calls exacerbate my impatience. These idiots don't know what to do with me.

Finally, they get out, pull me out of the car, and remove my handcuffs.

"You're free to go."

"Accosting innocent citizens because of their skin color is not in your job description," I fire at them. "I want your names and badge numbers." But before I can finish the sentence, they jump in their unmarked car and drive off.

I stand and watch them go, frozen in the cruel irony of the moment. The very force that has proved a fundamental step toward Harlem's revival has had a human cost: innocent people at best jostled and at worst brutalized, a terrible trade-off that has trampled me tonight.

But was it a necessary trade-off? Could the dramatic plunge in crime have somehow been achieved without the housing commissioner being treated like a drug lord?

I walk off, feeling pain in my shoulder for the first time. Too anguished and agitated to drive, I sit in my parked car for I don't know how long, breathing from the abdomen to calm my nerves. I rub my forehead and mop my sweaty brow. I turn the steering wheel back and forth, even though I'm still parked. Finally, I pull off, checking my rearview mirror for cop cars, braking for sirens, and keeping my throbbing shoulder still. Halfway home, I pull over. My hands are shaking too much for me to keep driving.

I hang my head. Harlem's best friend in her ride to a new renaissance had suddenly acted like my worst enemy. How long will my being a black man in America—whatever my status—subject me to the indignity of collective miscasting?

I hate to say I told you so, but I told—

SHUT UP, Mrs. Stokes!

TWELVE

Look Out!

I'M BONE TIRED. I plod out of 333 Convent Avenue, yawning and checking my watch, my Saturday honey-do list in hand. I've already started a load of laundry, weeded the backyard, changed a couple of diapers, tried—unsuccessfully—to fix a leaky faucet, run to the neighborhood store because we were out of diapers and wipes, mopped the kitchen floor, and moved the car to avoid a parking ticket. A toddler and pregnant wife in a late-nineteenth-century brownstone means there's always too much to do.

So I need to make this a quick trip. I promised Mother I'd get the banking done this week to give her some well-deserved time off. Harlem Travel soldiers on because Laura the Lionhearted refuses to give up her command. At first she wouldn't come to Harlem; now she won't leave. Mrs. Tentative has become Mrs. Tenacious. I laugh every time I think about it. I love God's sense of humor.

My mother's commitment to the travel agency—my last Harlem business standing—betrays the kind of transformation

I've been waiting to see in some of the homeless men I've been working with for what seems like centuries.

Closing La Famille and Ben & Jerry's had been inevitable. They'd never recovered after the street-vendor protests and the Freddy's tragedy. I'd suffered when Harkhomes closed, but my encounter with the police had made it simply too difficult to return to 129th Street. There'd also been a decreasing demand for beds—we'd been less than half full most of the time. It was a far cry from the lines waiting to get in just a decade ago. I'd like to think we helped change the neighborhood enough to put ourselves out of business.

Wishful thinking.

I know, Mrs. Stokes, I know.

But Harkhomes continues, through *Holistic Hardware.* I created a self-help video series from the life skills I'd taught daily at the shelter, featuring ten holistic tools: vision, responsibility, self-esteem, faith, discipline, association, planning, work, wealth, and love. The videos featured me teaching the principles, illustrating them with dramatic sketches that I'd written and directed,

FIGURE 24: Illustrating one of the life skills in the *Holistic Hardware* video

and providing inspirational testimonies from Holistic Hardware graduates about how the program had fostered progress in their lives. After Mother had seen one of the tapes, I never heard her utter the words "silly mission" again.

With the support of Here's Life Inner City, a nationwide ministry that empowers churches to work with the urban poor, I'd designed these materials for ministers, counselors, social workers, and volunteers—anyone who wanted to help people help themselves overcome life-destabilizing crises like homelessness, addiction, or chronic unemployment. The American Bible Society was so impressed with the curriculum that it published a special-edition Holistic Hardware Bible to support my workshops. My test marketing of the video among Harkhomes alumni had revealed the Responsibility Tool as the favorite for its dramatic adaptation of Jesus' house-built-on-rock versus house-built-on-sand parable.

I lumber to the car, which is holding up well under the burden of my daily reverse commute—although to White Plains and not to Albany. I'd left state government and joined Wilson, Elser, the corporate law firm specializing in insurance defense work, but with an Albany lobbying arm, shepherded there by my fellow Cornell trustee and political mentor Jerry Ruderman. Though I appreciated the irony of rejecting a Wall Street firm just out of law school and ending up with a White Plains firm many years later, I treasured the suburban retreat from the urban and upstate battlegrounds. I might have been the only lawyer in the history of humankind commuting from the black cultural capital to the seat of one of the wealthiest counties in America.

First I thought it would be Albany, but would White Plains instead be the one-way ticket out of Harlem I'd been waiting for all these years?

. . .

Starting up our Galant, I stretch through another yawn. Shelby had slept less than usual the previous night, and her sleeplessness exacerbated my insomnia, which had plagued me since my run-in with the police. I'd decided against publicizing the incident; I didn't want any more tabloid headlines. Instead, I'd used it as my rationale for taking a breather—from politics, from my enterprises, from Harlem, from everything!

I carried the sleepless Shelby down the stairs to get her a bottle, and rocked her as I channel-surfed before stopping on *Showtime at the Apollo*. I've never seen *Showtime*. Being an early churchgoer on Sunday mornings had precluded any late-night TV. But the *Showtime* act was so banal that I tuned it out, and instead let my mind drift to the history of the theater.

Harlem possessed no greater symbol than the Apollo Theater on 125th Street. Its landmark marquee was Harlem's signature, a trademark of artistic excellence and community pride that was known around the world. It had been the sign I'd seen in my fairway vision of Harlem so long ago, beckoning me to the community. If I'd known that the Apollo was actually closed at that time, would I have considered the signification any less divine?

The Apollo had come to life during the Roarin' Twenties, when Harlem's nightlife was hotter even than that of Broadway itself. Whites stormed uptown (some even taking the A train), and congregated at Seventh Avenue and 131st Street, known alternately as the Boulevard of Dreams, the Stroll, or simply the Corner. There, legends Duke Ellington, Bill Bojangles Robinson, Bessie Smith, Lead Belly, and Billie Holliday touched the lucky wishing elm dubbed the Tree of Hope, which was flanked by the Lafayette Theater and Connie's Inn. "Slummin'" Caucasians partied at upscale whites-only joints like Small's Paradise and the Cotton Club. How ironic it was that, because

Jim Crow ruled, blacks were excluded from experiencing live the amazing artistry that was being created by members of their own community.

More adventuresome whites frequented the speakeasies and gin mills—Glory Hole, Sugar Cane, Little Savoy. Even the restaurants—Tabb's, the Marguerite, and Johnny Jackson's—were destinations for the downtown crowd. One might say that a significant marker of progress in American race relations was laid in the cabarets of the Renaissance, where whites were exposed to a new and different milieu, rhythm, feel, and language that not only expanded their cultural horizons but opened them to new social possibilities.

I've witnessed this dimension of Renaissance racial experience in a much different way. The legacy of whites flowing uptown has continued, as a new renaissance has emerged. This time, they're not going to cabarets and clubs but homes and neighborhoods. The fact that whites had come, even in the face of the Blight and racially tinged street protests, spoke volumes about Harlem's unique character.

For the locals and black visitors of the Renaissance, cellars, lounges, rib joints, supper clubs, taverns, cafes, bars, and grills were places where they could enjoy themselves without worrying about white folks—hotspots like the Renaissance Ballroom, the Alhambra, and the Savoy Ballroom. The last featured swing dancing and was celebrated in one of the era's hit songs, "Stompin' at the Savoy." Rent parties were also popular among Harlemites. These informal gatherings served their liquor bootleg and their jazz hot. They also provided economic lifelines to tenants, who'd charge neighbors admission.

The Apollo itself grew out of Hurtig and Seamon's Music Hall on 125th Street, which featured burlesque for whites only. In 1934, two Jewish businessmen, Frank Schiffman and Leo Brecher, acquired the hall and renamed it the Apollo Theater.

They soon established it as the best place to showcase black talent—"where stars are born and legends are made." It lived up to this billing, becoming world-renowned for helping to launch the careers of Diana Ross & the Supremes, Aretha Franklin, Stevie Wonder, Marvin Gaye, Sarah Vaughan, Patti Labelle, The Isley Brothers, Lauryn Hill, and Mariah Carey. Amateur Night–winners included Luther Vandross, the Jackson Five, Gloria Lynne, Dionne Warwick, and Gladys Knight, though James Brown flopped there in 1952.

The Apollo was the only entertainment venue to endure long into the post-Renaissance, ironically helped by Jim Crow. As Harlem's theaters, clubs, and halls were closing during the 1940s and 1950s, the Apollo attracted new talent and top acts, trading on the fact that leading downtown venues like Radio City Music Hall and Madison Square Garden were closed to African-American entertainers. But not even the Apollo could survive the riots of the sixties, becoming the ultimate reminder that something was desperately wrong with Harlem. The Blight had claimed its greatest prize.

To its credit, the Clubhouse revived the Apollo. In 1981, four years after his failed bid for mayor, Percy Sutton discovered a higher calling than Harlem politics—saving the neighborhood's culture. He organized an investment group to acquire the Apollo at a bankruptcy sale, then deployed his political resources to garner landmark status and public funds. He later recruited his Clubhouse comrade Charlie Rangel to chair the affiliated foundation, and capitalized on the Apollo brand by starting the nationally syndicated new-talent, variety show *Showtime*.

Since *Showtime* was putting me to sleep like Shelby, we headed back upstairs. She slept through the rest of the night, which is why my eyes are only half-closed right now.

· · ·

Heading down Convent Avenue, I remember to avoid Lenox Avenue and 118th Street, the site of this afternoon's so-called Million Youth March. Patterned after Louis Farrakhan's Million Man March of several years ago in Washington, D.C., this rally was really more hype than substance. Khalid Muhammad, the demagogic organizer, was a Farrakhan acolyte, but without his mentor's stature or following. I'm upset that he's chosen to stage the march in Harlem, exploiting the stature Harlem has held since Garvey's days as an enduring symbol of black nationalism and pride.

There is, I suppose, a historical continuity. Black nationalism—the worldview that black people share a common perspective, culture, and destiny—has deep roots in America as a response to the reality of racism. In the early nineteenth century, Paul Cuffee sought to take a convoy of blacks to Africa. Several decades later, Martin Delaney offered the rallying cry "Africa for the Africans." His contemporary, Henry McNeal Turner, had a program of repatriation. All these men paved the way for Garvey's plan to establish Harlem as the center of Afrocentric consciousness and activism, from which one could establish a homeland in Africa for 400 million black people. But by Garvey's death in 1940, the back-to-Africa clarion had been reduced to a whisper.

Nevertheless, the central themes of this radical doctrine—distrust of the white man and his racist systems, and promotion of black entrepreneurship to protect and advance collective interests—persisted in the Pan-Africanist writings of Du Bois, the fiery oratory of Malcolm X, and the hate speech of Louis Farrakhan and his apprentice Khalid Muhammad. Unfortunately, among the black nationalistic leaders of this era, the racialist strain of distrust was overshadowing the economic dimension of creating businesses and jobs in underprivileged communities. For me, Khalid Muhammad exemplified this regressive trend.

Malcolm X was Harlem's most famous nationalist. Though his work in Harlem spanned a relatively short period (from his selection to lead Temple Number Seven in 1954 to his break with the Nation of Islam ten years later), Malcolm's impact was epochal. He exhorted and organized Harlemites—especially men—to work on themselves, their businesses, and their community, so they could take pride in themselves and their accomplishments.

Whenever I heard my mentor Walter Wilson preach, I imagined him as a modern-day Malcolm X, and his fiery sermons and ardent commitment to uplift black men reminded me of the legendary leader. Now an ordained minister on staff at Bethel Gospel Assembly, Walter was executive director of Beth-HARK Crisis Center, which had lasted the longest of all my institutional offshoots. Though we were both Bethel members, I didn't see him much these days. He'd apparently been spending a lot of time speaking outside the church, motivating individuals and groups in circumstances similar to the ones he overcame.

The report I'm hearing over the car radio—Khalid's latest sound bite, which attacks Harlem leaders as "sissified" and "boot-licking"—smacks of Malcolm's incendiary, counterproductive rhetoric. One of Malcolm's more memorable declarations was when he called the 1963 March on Washington "the farce on Washington." Blacks shouldn't get excited over a demonstration, he said, that was "run by whites in front of a statute of a president who had been dead for a hundred years and who didn't like us when he was alive." Nonetheless, Malcolm X changed after he left the Nation of Islam and made his pilgrimages to Mecca; he eschewed hate speech. Didn't Khalid know his history?!

Apparently not, for Khalid was also influenced by the reckless rhetoric of the Black Panther movement of the 1960s. Any speaker who foments violence as a means of change is the worst kind of leader. He couches pressing problems like the empowerment of black youth in terms so rabble-rousing that he alienates meaningful support, even from those in his own community. That Khalid has any support at all testifies to the festering legacy of slavery and segregation on the African-American psyche.

Why is traffic moving so slowly? On a Saturday?! Oh no! What's a police barricade doing all the way over here? Look at all the cops. You got to be kidding me! You'd think the pope or president was coming to Harlem.

I know Mayor Giuliani wants to prevent another Harlem riot or Freddy's Clothing Store tragedy, but does he really need countless police patrols, police in riot gear, police on horseback and in police cars, paddy wagons, buses, vans, motorcycles, and tractor-trailer trucks? For a rally of a few thousand orchestrated by an extremist whom the vast majority of the African-American community has already marginalized? How am I supposed to get across town?

This travesty had been brewing in months of quarreling between the two provocateurs—Khalid and Mayor Rudy. Khalid's anti-white statements led Rudy to denounce the "hate march." The unintended outcome was approaching absurdity: more cops on the streets than protesters.

A yellow "POLICE LINE—DO NOT CROSS" ribbon extends across the entrance to the 116th Street subway. Khalid's race-baiting has now apparently made public transportation unsafe. Khalid strikes me as someone who feigns anger as a weapon to rile people up, highlighting the difference between a genuinely

angry man and a sociopath projecting anger for his own purposes.

The mayor denied Khalid a permit to rally in Harlem on
Labor Day weekend while decrying his adversary as a hate mon-
ger. Not surprisingly, this not only exacerbated tensions but led
to a parade of tabloid headlines and a subsequent court battle
that defended Khalid's rally as a statement about free speech.
The litigation went all the way to the second circuit of the
Federal Court of Appeals. The three-judge panel had upheld
the rights of the rallyers but circumscribed Khalid's free speech
rights, limiting the march's area from twenty-nine blocks to six
and its time frame from twelve hours to four.

The deliberately incendiary pronouncements of Khalid notwithstanding, the threat to public safety was way overblown.
Even if city hall factored in the past history of Harlem with
sparks that open wounds and trigger riots, a firm but much
lower-key police presence was the way to go, thus avoiding the
extremes of minimal presence or ridiculous overkill, which, I
feared, would be the real threat to peace today.

My frustration intensifies as I direct the car southward, forced
to cross to the east side at 96th Street. One of my favorite verses
from Proverbs comes to mind: *It is to a man's honor to avoid strife,
but every fool is quick to quarrel.* Since I can't park anywhere near
my office, I'm now hustling on foot, trying to make up for lost
time. I'm stopped in my tracks by a remarkable sight: street vendors hawking their wares (black pride T-shirts; bean pies; and
black, green, and red flags, the Pan-African colors) in the midst
of police who are ready for a riot. Given the mayor's animus
toward the street vendors, it appears that his orders to focus on
Khalid have given his erstwhile nemeses a reprieve, and they're
making the most of it.

I see the devoted, young and old, making their way through

the maze of police to the site of the march. I'm tempted to follow just to check it out, but I'm disgusted at the spectacle of it all. I feel that the cause of black empowerment is too great to be cheapened by the media circus that circles the clown in charge. What Harlem needs is more love, not a loudmouthed hater masquerading as the latest hero of the dispossessed.

On my walk back to my car, I hear a loud noise from above. I look around, then hear somebody yell "Look out!" I turn to see a police helicopter swooping low over the Harlem rooftops, heading toward Lenox Avenue. Like everyone else, my reflex makes me duck. In its incessant whirr, I hear the snicker of the inescapable Mrs. Stokes.

The chopper arrives to witness Khalid, wearing his signature dark suit accented by a black, green, and red sash, close the rally. As the minutes tick down, he makes his inflammatory points: "We came in peace, we came in unity, we came in love," he exclaims. "They changed all the rules. And stop asking me about the Jews being the bloodsuckers of the black nation. They are the bloodsuckers of the black community."

Not one to turn the other cheek, Khalid concludes by urging the crowd to resist any police confrontation, firing one final salvo at the mayor: "We'll mop these streets with you today." He then offers, without apparent irony: "Go in the way of love, go in the way of peace." Right on cue, the surrounding police surge toward the stage. Khalid flees, with the cash his associates collected in plastic buckets from the crowd. Was it really all about the money?

The police mount the stage, the helicopter swoops in, and— no surprise—the masses react, flinging bottles, chairs, and expletives at the cops. The officers push into the crowd, firing pepper spray. There's one arrest, a few injuries, and lots of recriminations. With no cooler heads prevailing, the Khalid–Rudy encounter has raised some unnecessary Harlem unrest. Today has turned out to be one of those indignant times in Harlem, when it didn't have to be.

I arrive home, only to be dispatched on additional errands, right back out to the indifferent Harlem streets. It's not a good day for me, or for Harlem.

How long, I wonder, will the antics of irresponsible men keep getting in our way?

SECTION THREE

PROVIDENCE

2000s

THIRTEEN

We Love Bill!

Curious about the commotion at the window, my client and I join other patrons looking out from the second-floor dining room of Bayou restaurant. A stream of people is crossing Lenox Avenue at 125th Street. A middle-aged African-American woman in the group exclaims, "It's Bill!" and scampers out in pursuit of the crowd. No further identification is needed. William Jefferson Clinton, the forty-second President of the United States, is in Harlem to celebrate the opening of his uptown office.

President Clinton is indeed an accidental Harlem hero. Moving his post-presidential office to Harlem was Plan B, since Carnegie Hall Towers on West 57th Street—a midtown Manhattan status symbol—had been Bill's first choice. But controversy over taxpayers paying exorbitantly to accommodate an ex-president had forced him to look for cheaper space. Clinton's Harlem advent was transformative. He became the presumptive champion of the black community's concerns rather than a refugee from an overturned lease deal.

I'd been traveling so much that I'd missed the media run-up to this event. I'd left the Wilson, Elser law firm to become the spokesman for the Life's Playbook program, the brainchild of fellow Cornell trustee and GTE chairman Chuck Lee. GTE sponsored the Academic All-America Hall of Fame, of which I was a member, and Chuck decided to draft me and other Hall-of-Famers as role models for the nation's youth. My motivational speaking tour to middle and high school students had taken me from Nashua, New Hampshire to Tulsa, Oklahoma to Spokane, Washington—visiting over 150 schools in twenty states. I'd adapted my interactive talk—the "Seven Ps of Success (Perseverance, Picture, Passion, Pick, Pain, Probity, Providence)"—from Holistic Hardware. I'd transformed the remedial principles developed for the homeless into precepts for young adults that would prevent them from getting into the

FIGURE 25: Interacting with some high-school students following one of my motivational talks

kind of trouble into which too many of the Harlem down-and-out had fallen.

In Cheyenne, a group of female students had been so inspired by my talk that they'd approached the podium afterward to greet me. As one student leaned in to thank me, the others joined in for a collective hug. Reminded of the 125th Street ice cream–smeared embrace of years ago, I hugged them back, and said, "From Harlem with Love." Surprised, the students lingered, smiled, and asked questions about my experience in a galaxy far, far away.

Holistic Hardware itself had also put me on the road. I'd consulted with faith-based organizations, social-service nonprofits, and governmental welfare-to-work programs, helping them shape effective outreach and uplift programming for homeless, hard-to-employ, drug-addicted, and other distressed populations. I'd been to Atlanta, Los Angeles, New Orleans, Ithaca, Chicago, St. Louis, Indianapolis, Birmingham, and Minneapolis with my video-based workshops. *Holistic Hardware: Tools That Build Lives*, the video format of my Harkhomes curriculum, was being used by dozens of groups across the nation as an empowerment tool for individuals struggling through personal crisis.

Leaving the restaurant, I wonder whether to detour on my way back to my Sugar Hill office to sneak a peek at Bill's welcoming ceremony in the Powell Building plaza. I decide to follow the Clinton crowd, since it is an historic moment of sorts. Harlem has never had a post-presidency before, and this one has the potential to help her cast off her negative reputation.

I pass Harlem's first Starbucks coffeehouse, sparkling on the corner of 125th and Lenox, and marvel at the eclectic scene inside: blue-collar blacks, young whites, Hispanic professionals, and European tourists, in line for lattes costing $3.50. It hadn't been that long ago that I couldn't sell an ice cream cone for half that price.

The thought of ice cream reminds me of how, before Clinton had come to Harlem, Harlem had come to Clinton. During his first year in office, I'd been invited to a ceremony at the White House celebrating community-banking legislation. My Ben & Jerry's shop had been partly financed by Community Capital Bank, a prototype for a new federal program Clinton was proposing.

I decided to surprise the president with his favorite flavor: Chunky Monkey. So I packed a couple of pints in dry ice and threw in a pint of our signature flavor, Bluesberry, and set off to Washington, D.C., with great expectations and lots of calories.

My dry ice was removed at airport check-in, my pleas about preserving the president's favorite ice cream having fallen on deaf ears. I'd persevered, figuring that melted Monkey was better than none at all.

My mission survived the first White House checkpoint, but met its match in a portly guard at the second gate. My protests about the exalted destination of the gift had provoked a yawn, and the guard had confiscated my still-chilled container, promising to send it on as soon as it was sanctioned. Once in the Oval Office, I'd told President Clinton and Vice-President Gore about my ice cream travails. Though I discerned a smirk on Al's face, Bill wasn't amused, sending an aide scurrying in search of the contraband, which—no surprise to me—was nowhere to be found. The mystery of the missing Monkey was never solved!

I cross Lenox Avenue and gaze back east down 125th Street, looking past the shuttered, deteriorating four-story building that once housed two of my businesses, Ben & Jerry's and La Famille. Mother had continued to run Harlem Travel after my professional transitions had led elsewhere, but she'd tired of putting out operational and fiscal fires without my hands-on support. I'd finally convinced Mother that we should sell Harlem Travel—at a loss. She hadn't been a happy camper, but I knew she was better for the experience because I'd only had to endure one of her gentler tirades.

A couple of blocks beyond these bittersweet memories, I could discern in the distance the institutional counterpart to Clinton's arrival, the new Harlem Pathmark. The enduring Clubhouse influence had seeded it. Dinkins' city hall had proposed transforming the vacant lot at the southeast corner of Lexington Avenue and 125th Street into a superstore in 1991. Big supermarket companies had kept out of Harlem since the contraband and welfare economies of the Blight had compelled 70 percent of Harlem residents to shop outside of the community. National retailers figured that the remaining 30 percent were mostly on food stamps, and so stayed away. Of course, fast-food chains like McDonald's, Burger King, KFC, and Popeye's saw a market. They joined the superfluity of greasy local eateries, ensuring a steady flow of diet-plagued patients to Harlem Hospital and other health-care facilities.

A recent family trip to the new Pathmark proved to be a welcome alternative to maneuvering through traffic on the George Washington Bridge on shopping incursions to New Jersey, or protracted rides to get groceries in Yonkers, or the less painful but insufficient forays to the Fairway at 132nd Street on the Hudson. I'd been struck by the crowd waiting to recycle their cans and bottles, and the long line of shoppers laden with bags of groceries and looking out for gypsy cabs. Harlem in her inimitable way had already put its stamp on the community's first national chain supermarket and large retail development to be built since the riots of the sixties. Had it really taken Harlem over thirty-five years to recover from those fiery summer days?

The Pathmark chain had proven to be an exception to inner-city commercial avoidance. It had opened stores in the Bronx in the 1960s and Bedford-Stuyvesant in the 1970s, and cracked a very tough nut, Newark's Central Ward, in 1990. With this trailblazing track record, Pathmark had taken on Harlem and encountered unprecedented ethnic strife, albeit of a different kind than the Khalid–Rudy scrap. This fight had a longer build-up and less grandstanding with none of the traditional white-versus-black hostilities. Instead, minority groups were at war.

Throughout the Blight, the African Americans of Central Harlem and the Hispanics of East Harlem found themselves on the same side of the community battlefield, pitted against a wary white establishment. But the demands of financing a $15 million project forced city hall to jettison the original Hispanic developers. City officials claimed that a subsequent search failed to discover a suitable Latino replacement. To the consternation of East Harlem leaders and their constituents, a Central Harlem mainstay was selected. No black Harlem institution could have irked Spanish Harlem more than the Abyssinian Development Corporation. ADC, as it's known uptown, is the development arm of the Abyssinian Baptist Church, with a tradition of Harlem activism established by the Powells decades earlier.

Rev. Calvin Butts had launched ADC in 1989 to address the Blight. First, ADC developed senior housing and then organized the Central Harlem Local Development Corporation to foster neighborhood businesses. Educational programs had followed but controversy had struck when ADC had stepped in as the Pathmark developer. It was a move that had so angered the politicians, merchants, and residents of East Harlem that they'd organized to block the project. Giuliani's city hall had brokered a compromise: 51 percent ownership to the ADC-led group; 49 percent retained by the city to be turned over to Hispanic community-based developers. And Pathmark stepped up with a last-minute pledge to fund some economic-development projects in East Harlem.

Charges of "anti-Hispanic bias" and countercharges of race baiting had continued to fly. What had enraged the Latino opposition was what they perceived to be the unfair advantage that millions of dollars of government grants, loans, and tax abatements had created for Pathmark over neighboring bodegas. But with Harlem's unemployment remaining in double digits, over 30 percent of the population living in poverty, and private investment dollars less common than white residents, the uptown powers-that-be had pressed on.

Because city-owned land was involved, Pathmark's fate had come down to a single vote before the Manhattan borough board, which was composed of the Manhattan borough president, city council, and community board members. The project looked like it was heading for defeat, but an eleventh-hour change of position by Guillermo Linares, a Dominican councilman, had saved the day for Pathmark. The Hispanic independent storeowners had received a consolation prize, a $12 million Chase Bank loan program targeted for midsize markets.

If only my businesses had still been open, only two blocks away from all the new Pathmark activity, I'd have surely met my break-even numbers, even with just a modest spillover. It was no consolation that I'd been just ahead of the market.

I glance down into the subway station on the corner of 125th Street and Lenox Avenue, and observe a racially mixed group of straphangers heading up to the street. Is Clinton's presence a signal to white riders not to flee the train before it reaches Harlem? Will the racial composition of those on the Harlem Metro North platform be changing, too?

As I maneuver along 125th Street, I notice the face-lift being given to the venerable Studio Museum in Harlem, as if the old guard were sprucing up for the new guy. I'm struck by the abundance of flyers, fans, and buttons bearing Bill's face. The fact that thousands of people are on Harlem's Main Street for a reception rather than a riot enthralls me. It feels strange, for the one basking in the ebony sunshine is a white man—one, moreover, who was impeached and whose eleventh-hour pardons sparked controversy. Nonetheless, the clouds over his presidency are being blown away by the winds of this new day in Harlem.

Clinton's popularity among African Americans was always based more on emotion than on policies or programs. The black community's loyalty stemmed not only from the president's open-armed, down-home political embrace but also smacked of long-standing American role-playing: that of the fealty of blacks to a white man plagued by a status quo that had also persecuted them. That Clinton's self-inflicted misfortune didn't fit this archetype well seems lost on Harlem this afternoon.

Serenaded by a violin rendition of "We Shall Overcome," Clinton mounts the dais, beaming from ear to ear. Cicely Tyson is at his side, the Clubhouse all around him, and William Jefferson Clinton Day is proclaimed. "You were always there for me," Bill exults. "I'll try to be there for you." I feel alone in my skepticism, sensing that Clinton's promises to Harlem will benefit the newcomers more than the old-timers acclaiming him this afternoon.

Congressman Rangel orchestrates the scene, gleeful that his shepherding of Hillary's recent senate victory has yielded a second prize—an ex-president in his district. Rangel lifts Clinton's hand high in triumph. They sing, leading all—even me!—in an inspirational version of "Stand by Me." The masses cheer and chant. It's a clamor that is strikingly different from Harlem's angry days: from "No justice, No peace!" to "We love Bill! We love Bill!" In the refrain, I also hear a requiem for the Blight—part plea, part promise that Harlem's Dark Age might be over and a New Renaissance will begin. Will the president's advent be a green light to white America, which decades ago abandoned the Harlems of the nation to impoverished people of color—a message that it's okay to come back? Is this to be the day when the 110th Street wall fell?

Not everyone's happy with Clinton's new role as welcome-mat-in-chief. Members of the New Black Panther Party are upset that America's black capital has so quickly turned from black pride to white adoration. "Go home! Go home!" they shout, followed by "Whose streets? Our streets!" Dressed in black paramilitary uniforms, these black nationalists are led by Malik Zulu Shabazz, adorned in Garvey-evoking red-and-green piping and a five-star collar. I hear one of his disciples admonish a Clinton devotee: "What would Malcolm say about this?"

I'm not surprised at the mention of Malcolm X. His intelligence, charisma, and confrontational style ("If someone puts his hand on you, send him to the cemetery") made him a compelling alternative to the more moderate voices of the civil rights movement. They also made him a target of FBI probes and ostracism from the Black Muslim hierarchy, which conspired in his downfall. Nothing testifies more to the ideological distance that Harlem—and America—has traveled the last three-quarters of a century than the choices of today's crowd. Whether it was Garvey's pomposity, Malcolm X's acerbity, or Clinton's New Harlem gamesmanship, the Harlem political rock star had always been protean, changing from populist to provocative to post-presidential. I pray it spells progress.

The Garvey-like New Black Panther general signals his troops to shout more loudly about advancing gentrification and retreating community identity. But they have no hope of competing with the din of the enthusiastic audience. Still at the mike, Clinton, ever the ebullient crowd-pleaser, jokes about playing his sax at the Apollo, which is itself using the occasion to market its new programming. Flyers are being passed out promoting the upcoming Apollo showcase *Harlem Song*, George C. Wolfe's musical revue that celebrates Renaissance and modern Harlem in song, dance, and multimedia.

Clinton's depiction of Harlem as a place "where there's rhythm to life and a song in the heart," as "human and alive," recalls the Renaissance surge of whites endeavoring to be in touch with their true selves by coming uptown. The president would no doubt have been one of them, slummin' it in Renaissance cabarets. Whether he will hang out in the New Harlem is yet to be seen.

"I want to make sure I'm a good neighbor in Harlem," Clinton continues. "I'm glad property values are going up, but I don't want small-business people to be run out because I'm coming in."

I just can't continue to feign applause. Of course, Clinton will become the new face of Harlem gentrification, and increase the risks for the community's old guard. My hollow feeling deepens with each effusion. How will he deal with the powerlessness that results when people see change they believe isn't meant to benefit them?

Clinton touts the Clubhouse's greatest blow against the Blight—the Upper Manhattan Empowerment Zone, aka UMEZ—a Kempian concept realized under Clintonian rule. UMEZ fueled growth in retail outlets in Harlem through a federal, state, and city fund of $300 million to invest in projects that foster economic development. These public dollars leveraged, as the president reminds us, $600 million in private investment. He also notes the initiative's star power: it had been orchestrated by Clubhouse member Rangel, chaired by corporate bigwig Richard Parsons, and advised by celebrity lawyer Johnnie Cochran.

Clinton descends the platform to shake hands and dispense hugs to fans, reminiscent of Ben's red-carpetlike stroll along 125th Street during the ice cream festival almost a decade before. I walk away, frustrated about the protracted festivities. I would have preferred a different symbol for the rebirth of Harlem:

someone like a more moderate Malcolm X, charismatic, caring, but also community-rooted, rather than a white Southerner who'd relocated and was himself in need of redemption.

I've got to stop listening to Mrs. Stokes. He could live up to the hype.

By their fruit you will know them.

An empathetic ex-president is not a bad consolation prize. Plus, he adds value for us forever-fledging entrepreneurs. The message rings loud and clear that now that Clinton has come, anybody can come—Harlem is safe and open for business. Maybe I'd feel differently if I still had a boat in the water. I try to resist the taste of sour grapes: the guys selling Clinton buttons and T-shirts are making a fortune.

I glance back at the overflowing press corps and imagine tomorrow's headline: THE COMEBACK KID BECOMES HARLEM'S RENAISSANCE MAN. He'll be crowned King of the Renaissance II. When they hear of all the good things going on in Harlem, people all over the world will respond, "Thanks to Bill." The truth is that Harlem has saved Clinton, not the other way around—burnishing his image as "America's first black president," in the famous words of Toni Morrison, and pushing him beyond his post-presidential blues. My hope is that he'll show Harlem some love by completing his unfinished presidential business in redressing racial injustice and providing the long-awaited and much-needed leadership required to address the poverty and pathology of the urban underclass.

As far as I'm concerned, it's the least he can do, now that the world's most famous black community will be perceived as having a white savior.

Are you surprised?

Never mind, Mrs. Stokes.

FOURTEEN

Into the Marvelous Light

"YOU WANT ME to swing the block to Twenty-Six or drop you at the corner?" the cabbie asks as we ride down Lenox Avenue.

I hesitate, surprised by the question. Cabbies never used to drive onto 129th Street—let alone pick up and drop off inside the problem block. At least, they never did it for me; one had to be a drug dealer for that privilege. Now I have the option of being driven straight to my destination. I wonder if newspapers, flowers, and pizzas are being delivered to the block, too.

"Take me to Twenty-Six," I say diffidently, unconvinced that things on 129th Street have really changed. It's my first time back on the block since my law-enforcement encounter—Why am I still euphemizing it?

Before the cabbie turns, I glance down Lenox toward 125th Street, and admire the Harlem Center, a new ten-story office tower with Staples, CVS, and Marshalls at street level. Fresh off its Pathmark victory, ADC had joined forces with the major developer Forest City Ratner to build this commercial project, with state agencies above its national-brand retail base and Blockbuster and H&M a stone's throw away. As crime had dropped and more residents with greater disposable income had moved in, the public–private strategic policy-making had accelerated the commercial renaissance of Harlem.

The new Pathmark, so long in its genesis, had already spawned development. Across the street two shopping centers are emerging: Gateway, featuring Seaman's Furniture and Duane Reade; and Gotham, sporting Foot Action, Children's Place, AT&T, Rockaway Bedding, and Payless Shoes, with a Department of Motor Vehicles office upstairs. Several blocks to the west along 125th Street a Magic Johnson movie theater, Disney Store, Old Navy, Modell's, HMV Records, and New York Sports Club populate Harlem USA, the community's first shopping mall. The clamor of the advancing chains drowns out any outcry from long-standing neighborhood stores and their activists, confounded by the surging national brands that are suddenly deluging Harlem's commercial landscape.

It's clear to me that Harlem's commercial rivers have finally begun to flow again, and mightily so. The priorities of livelihood and family had pushed me out of the streams of entrepreneurial endeavor. I was downsized out of my motivational-speaking assignment when GTE merged with Bell Atlantic to form Verizon, so I went back to practicing Harlem law, advising companies, churches, and other nonprofits on business and real estate matters. And I'd moved my growing family to Yonkers. I was ambivalent about leaving Harlem after two decades, but the Blight, working through the city-owned brownstone next door to our 333 Convent home, had forced the issue. Crack stems and then used condoms had started showing up in our backyard, evidence that business for the pimp who operated out of the third floor of the city house was picking up—a precarious circumstance for my three young kids who loved to play out there. My efforts to get the creep evicted had failed.

So the odyssey continued. First, my office moved to the suburbs and my residence remained; now my residence had moved to the suburbs and my office had returned to Harlem. I won't even hazard a guess about the next turn on my Harlem rollercoaster ride.

As the cabbie enters the block, my head swivels this way and that. I see no crack queues blocking the sidewalk; no unsupervised, truant children are playing in the street; no gunshots ring out in the distance. But then, I tell myself, it's only midafternoon. Then, just to nip any optimism in the bud, like a ghost from the past, a teenage mom pushes a baby stroller past. I roll down my window for a closer look, relieved to see that she's not smoking crack or anything else.

I get out of the cab and look for Ralph Acosta, the "Mayor of 129th Street." His daily perch—the rusty metal-frame chair in front of Building Number 26—is empty. I hope he's okay. He's had his share of health challenges; besides, life has always been a lot more fragile around here.

I turn, lured by the clamor of construction crews working (at a quick count) on a dozen buildings that are either being rehabbed or developed. I move, with just a bit of caution, toward the Dark Corner to take a quick look at my old nemesis the Dirty Alley—that vacant, trash-strewn, drug-infested lot between the two dilapidated tenements that we could never keep clean. In its place, I see a courtyard. A courtyard? I pirouette, thinking my sense of direction has temporarily failed. No, this is it.

I push against a locked gate, and peer through the filigreed iron bars. Inside are freshly painted, renovated buildings, sitting behind a green, newly mown lawn. The plaza comes complete with a flower garden and a gaily colored gazebo. The Dirty Alley has become a manicured courtyard in a gated community. On the block from hell?! Had Brooke Astor's foundation decided after all to swoop one block south and transform "the other America" into an urban paradise? Or had aliens landed in Harlem and conquered 129th Street?

I turn away, seeking to reassure myself with a familiar frame of reference. But even Bethlehem Church, the former home of Harkhomes, now boasts a bold new sign. I peek through the windows and see desks with computers instead of rows of cots. The homeless have been replaced by hardware. Now I'm convinced of the sea change.

"Joe!" Ralph, now back on his perch, beckons me. I lean down to receive the hearty greeting he offers to all. The bloodshot eyes in his grizzled face reveal the toll of his debilitating diabetes, but the spirit of this gregarious senior citizen remains unquenchable. "Thanks for coming. Sure took you a while to respond," he chirps.

I hesitate.

"How ya been?" he continues. "You ain' been round here since your shelter closed. How long that been?"

"Too long," I state. Not long enough, I'm thinking. I know to the hour how long ago it was when I was accosted by the police, but a detail like that could stir up emotions I'd rather leave dormant. I check my hands; they're not quivering. My hope today is that time has healed the wound and buried those memories in the graveyard of the Old Harlem.

I kneel down next to Ralph and change the topic, waving my hands in both directions. "You're the man, Ralph," I say, pointing toward the transformed lot. "Lots of progress going on around here. Look at all the building, and what happened to the Dirty Alley?"

"Just Pascal," he says disdainfully. "He put crazy colors outside and smooth jazz inside to attract white tenants while booting our folks off their stoops."

I've only heard positive things about Pascal. "He can't be all bad, Ralph. Let's not quibble over color scheme when we've got new housing and a better environment."

Pascal is Gregory Pascal, the driven developer of West Indian descent who's become the baron of 129th Street. Ralph explains Pascal's ascendancy through a city program that transfers distressed properties to minority builders to repair, own, and manage. In this and other initiatives, the city has unloaded some of the hundreds of Harlem buildings and lots that the Blight had put into its hands. In return, Pascal is to maintain low-income rentals for fifteen years.

Sensing Ralph's petulance, I cloak a smile of gratification that my efforts to highlight the block's need for public funding while I was in government eventually bore some fruit.

"Y'know, he's trying to sell one of his shells for a million bucks," Ralph growls, as if he's heard nothing I said in Pascal's defense. I'd better be careful. I'm a wannabe developer and Ralph sounds like the kind of guy who wants to throw all developers under the bus.

"He won't get that much for it," I respond diffidently, thinking about the shell I could've picked up for $35,000 a decade ago. Harlem property values have increased exponentially in the last few years. Mother's recent lecture on my missed opportunities was as annoying as ever.

Pascal's empire includes seven buildings on 129th Street, which is about a third of his holdings over five Harlem blocks. To Ralph's dismay, Pascal's strategy of putting working, rent-paying tenants, regardless of color, in his buildings is gentrifying the block—in a hurry.

"Y'know, Pascal's as bad as Lars," he continues, indignation rising with every word.

I had met Lars Westvind, the Swedish-born artist turned landlord, when I started Harkhomes in the stormy eighties, which, as I continue to survey the scene, seems like a century ago. Lars had renovated an Astor Row shell and raised his family there while he transformed abandoned buildings on 129th Street into rooming houses. As many whites as blacks now populated his buildings, including Gulsen Calik, his Turkish-born wife, and Gulsun Erbil, the Turkish artist who'd started Gallery X as a live-work studio in one of his buildings.

Old School Harlemites like Ralph despised the New Harlem housing opportunities for whites that were created by Pascal and Westvind. This vanguard represented the racial flip side of the residential pathways forged by Philip Payton. During the Renaissance era, the father of "Colored Harlem," opened the uptown door for blacks as whites left; in the New Renaissance, the trailblazing developers were unlocking the entry for whites. However, I didn't get the impression that blacks were leaving. The question was whether we'd see a throwback to the race wars of the old century or leap into a future marked by racial reconciliation.

Ralph presses his point about the block's racial transition. "They really been coming since the front-page articles." He sees my inquiring look. "Y'know we famous now."

"*Amsterdam News?*" I query. It's the city's oldest and best-known black newspaper—a Harlem institution. Though profitable, the weekly faces criticism that it's too "bourgeois," with society coverage overshadowing substantive issues. The mantle of publisher had recently passed from Wilbert Tatum to his daughter Elinor. Some were saying the transition was long overdue.

"You know better," he laughs. "Wait here a minute. You're gonna love this." He saunters into the brownstone behind him.

I study the block. The road has been repaved; trees are growing. I can see that a preschool has opened, and construction work is everywhere. I notice a pregnant teen accompanied by a note-taking, middle-aged woman, and a twenty-something white guy—clean-cut, suit and tie, briefcase in hand—striding off the block, no doubt headed to a business appointment. White social workers and white-collar residents? Aliens have indeed landed on 129th Street.

"We gotta whole bunch now just like him." Ralph returns in time to point disdainfully at the man. "He lives in the burbs, where all of them live."

By "burbs" (i.e., the white side), Ralph's referring to the fresher facades of the east end of the block, near Fifth Avenue, where the bulk of the townhouses are. The less "upscale" region—the Lenox Avenue end—is called the "city" (i.e., the black side), the locus of the tenements. I'm fascinated by the tenacity of America's class and racial mores, and how they move from the abstractions of arm-chair academics into realities in a recovering ghetto.

Ralph hands me a file chock full of dog-eared newspapers. I scan the front-page headlines of three *New York Times* articles about 129th Street: IN HARLEM'S RAVAGED HEART, REVIVAL . . . BENEATH NEW SURFACE, AN UNDERTOW . . . LINES THAT DIVIDE, TIES THAT BIND.

How did I miss this?

I realize that the wounds of my encounter with the police had blinded me to the profound changes taking place on my old street. I scan the news clips, focusing on the highlights: unprec-edented economic growth; a startling decrease in crime; the ebb of crack; the remaking of welfare; an influx of immigrants; a city drive to redevelop the housing stock; the rise of neighborhood organizations focused on restoration. Was it that long ago that the *New York Times* reported on the block's drugs, dilapidation, and despair?

A quote from a resident jumps off the page at me: the block

has "moved from the darkness into the marvelous light." The comment probably came from one of the Bible-toting, bonnet-wearing church ladies I used to see praying for the block. I recite to myself the biblical basis for her cheery conclusion: *That ye should show forth the praises of him who hath called you out of the darkness into his marvelous light,* encouraged that the brightening of this block vindicates my prayers as well.

I pause at another riveting statement: the "remarkable" evolution of 129th Street has transformed the block from the "isolation" and "deprivation" of "another America" to "just an American block."

Take that, Mrs. Stokes.

I excitedly congratulate Ralph.

He laughs. "If we believed our press, you'd think Donald Trump was ready to move in." He directs my attention toward the Dark Corner. "Didn't you read the part about the 'under-tow'?" I confess that was the part I skipped over.

"Keep watching," he instructs me.

FIGURE 26: "The Church" flanked at the far right by the infamous "No. 60" at the Dark Corner

I see some boarded-up windows at the ominous No. 55, the immovable eyesore of the church next to it. Across the street is the infamous No. 60. I ease down the street a little ways to improve my view. I'm not watching long when out from No. 60 hustle young black men, crackheads in tow. I glance at Ralph. Our eyes lock in a moment of shared understanding, tempering my great expectations. I rub my forehead: the traditions of the Blight die hard.

"And the wars rage on," Ralph adds. We both know he's talking about turf wars between drug gangs: the Lenox gang, which moves around the Dark Corner like they own it, versus the St. Nick gang, composed of the bad boys one block west coming out of the St. Nicholas Houses, the housing project where Walter Wilson and I volunteered our time in the eighties. The problems back then—broken windows, defective elevators, and leaky roofs—pale in comparison with the random bullets of gang warfare.

A dark-skin, sandaled man in a multicolored robe approaches, and greets us with an almost unintelligible French accent. Ralph introduces me to Michel, a Senegalese immigrant who's driving a cab and starting an auto-body shop. He's one of a growing number of Harlem residents from Africa, who, when combined with Caribbean immigrants, comprise 15 percent of Harlem's black population.

"I'm teaching him English, not Ebonics," Ralph announces, wearing his pride prominently.

"How's that Senegalese restaurant that opened recently on 116th Street?" I query.

"Good." Michel passes me a card. "I wait tables there some nights and weekends."

Upwardly mobile Africans, part of Harlem's new generation

of strivers, were a recent phenomenon. Harlem was now a magnet for thousands of West Africans, who constituted the largest
foreign influx into Harlem since the masses arrived from the
Caribbean during the Renaissance. These new immigrants—
from Nigeria, Mali, Liberia, Ghana, Senegal, and elsewhere—
had taken full advantage of the State Department's policy in the
1990s of greater visa availability.

Some, like Amadou Diallo, who'd been shot forty-one times
by police, had not survived. Most, however, were like Michel,
whose success had many fathers. Liberals could take credit for
lowering the bar for immigrants to come to the United States.
Conservatives could trumpet the aggressive policing that had
turned 129th Street into a safe haven for dozens of Michels to
live and climb the ladder of success. Democrats could underscore
the importance of government programs such as the Community
Reinvestment Act and the Empowerment Zone as resources for
Michel's new business, while Republicans could credit the advent
of welfare reform and applaud the responsible voluntarism of
Ralph and others that supported Michel's assimilation. For me,
the fact that the confluence of uncoordinated policies somehow
worked together to the benefit of an individual and a community
was one of the virtues of American democracy.

Michel's American journey was paradigmatic of the kind of
policy fusion that I believed best suited low-income communities and supported individuals who were striving to better their
lives. After years of sclerosis, federal and state welfare reform
initiatives had now seemingly begun to break rather than foster
cycles of dependency.

As I listened to Ralph and Michel, however, I couldn't stop
myself from wishing that there were more African-American
beneficiaries of these policies. I'd heard rumors that the foreign entrepreneurs who dominated Harlem's small businesses
received special governmental assistance. While I didn't believe

188 FROM HARLEM WITH LOVE

them, I nonetheless clung to my deferred dream that our native sons and daughters would rise up from the underclass and themselves turn the symbols of poverty and dependency into icons of hope and achievement.

Suddenly, a baker's dozen worth of kids out of school rush up to embrace Ralph, who showers grandfatherly affection on all. "I have something to share today, Uncle Ralph," a bald-headed boy announces. Ralph instructs the others to sit before his sidewalk stage.

"'Children of the Sun,'" he proclaims. "By Fenton Johnson." He recites the poem without a note.

> We are children of the sun,
>   Rising sun!
> Weaving Southern destiny,
> Waiting for the mighty hour
> When our Shiloh shall appear
> With the flaming sword of right,
> With the steel of brotherhood,
> And emboss in crimson die
> Liberty! Fraternity!
>
> . . .
>
> We have come through cloud and mist,
>   Mighty men!
> Dusk has kissed our sleep-born eyes,
> Reared for us a mystic throne
> In the splendor of the skies,
> That shall always be for us,
> Children of the Nazarene,
> Children who shall ever sing
> Liberty! Fraternity!

We all applaud the perfect rendition. This moment—and the transformation it represents for 129th Street—stuns me. In less than a generation, a male teen from this block is reciting poetry instead of dealing drugs. Either the Renaissance muse or the Lord or both are sending me a message: It's okay to come back to 129th Street.

I shoot Ralph a glance. "Amazing." He meets my gaze. "Goes to charter school."

"Can you help me with my homework, Uncle Ralph?" a little girl asks. I know it's time to go. I flash Ralph an admiring smile. His endeavors to help educate the block's children evoke the ultimate clash between good and evil—the power of individual compassion versus the consequences of intractable blight. It's a struggle manifest in little efforts against big problems that have played out in the hearts and history of Harlem. Today I'm surprised—discovering on this block dreams being redeemed, not deferred.

Ralph looks up from his brood and beckons me close. "This block won't really change until that corner changes," he whispers, discreetly nodding in the direction that needs no pointing to.

"Yeah. I notice we still got some problems over there."

"You're a big shot now. Can't you do something to help?"

For a moment, I feel like telling Ralph that I have even less influence now than I did in the past—and that wasn't much. But I keep silent.

Then Ralph pulls the ace from his sleeve. "You're a minister. Can't you at least do something about the Church?!"

"Not sure, Ralph." That's the best I can offer him right now.

"Y'know, Joe," he adds piercingly, "we're fighting for Harlem's soul."

I wonder whether Ralph knew Hope Stevens. Decades after my fateful encounter with Hope, the battle cry rings just as true.

I think about saying something affirmative but stay with the perfunctory. I've had more than my fair share of 129th Street warfare.

"Good seeing you, Ralph."

Sensing my trepidation, Ralph shifts gears. "Come to our next block meeting. We can talk about it more."

"Block meeting?" I'm surprised, though to a much lesser degree than I would have been before the muse showed up. I recall the Harkhomes days, when the block association would meet in the Bethlehem sanctuary—residents and homeless people sitting side by side, talking about hope on a hopeless block. I'd always been troubled by the fact that the homeless always outnumbered the residents at those meetings.

"We finally got the block association going again," Ralph asserts. "Rachel's my vice president." Rachel Tew is another long-standing warrior fighting 129th Street's ills.

"And Landis is helping, too." Ralph knew a good report about Landis Farrington would make me smile. A former Harkhomes resident, he and his wife Myrtle are now pillars of the block, I've learned.

I say goodbye to Ralph as the kids engulf him, wondering whether the macro forces (falling crime, a booming New York City economy, welfare reform) conspiring with the micro forces (grassroots groups like Harkhomes, entrepreneurial wonders like Pascal, heroes like Ralph) is really the right formula to reverse the cycle of generational poverty.

Passing through the Dark Corner, I surprise myself again by slowing down. Thinking about the miracle of this transforming block, I peer at No. 60, then study the Church.

What about Ralph's request? I ask myself.

FIFTEEN

Harlem's Not for Sale

"THE KEY TO financial success is implementing the Wealth Tool. For the Wealth Tool develops your ability to . . ." I pause to prompt the summarizing of the basic points of the workshop.

"Maximize resources," several say in unison—more young voices than old.

"Then you must . . ."

"Manage resources." More chime in this time.

"Very good. And remember the Parable of the Talents," I continue my wrap-up. "God gives us time, gifts, and other resources according to our abilities, and He expects us to invest them wisely."

I usually don't make house calls, but Ralph had persuaded me to teach Holistic Hardware to a family who'd been active in his block association, but had children who'd been struggling academically. I hadn't known how extended the family was until I was greeted by a dozen of them—a mix of adults and teenagers—squeezed into their cozy living room.

"Now who can tell me the 4-T principle?"

Twelve-year-old Latisha shoots up her hand. "Teamwork plus Time plus Talent equal Treasury."

"Excellent." I commend her with a thumbs-up, observing the look of total surprise on her mother's face.

Not to be outdone, Jamaal, her teen brother, stands with open Bible in hand. Haggai is the biblical role model. "You want me to read it?" he asks.

I nod my assent, shrouding my smile at such healthy competition:

> Now this is what the Lord Almighty says: Give careful thought to your ways. You have planted much, but harvested little. You eat, but never have enough. You drink, but never have your fill. You put on clothes, but are not warm. You earn wages, only to put them in a purse with holes in it.

His mother high-fives him, the group stands, and I pray. Congratulatory hugs are exchanged. The session went well enough, but I know my mix of inspiration and practical advice only scratches the surface of their needs. Yet sowing aspirational values, even if the seed takes root in just one life, can make a difference. Furthermore, every little bit helps when one is endeavoring to cultivate a harvest from ground that's long lain fallow.

As I say my goodbyes, I'm struck that Holistic Hardware, an extension of my nonprofit activities, is the sole survivor of my efforts in Harlem. My Holistic Hardware work was now primarily directed through a faith-based demonstration program where I was conducting welfare-reform workshops throughout the boroughs of New York City. In one of my sessions in the Bronx, I'd met Bishop Betty Middleton of the Mount Calvary Pentecostal Church. She'd retained me to do some legal work for the church, and I'd discovered that Mount Calvary owned the Church, the half-finished structure at the Dark Corner. In light of Ralph's request, Bishop Middleton and I had started exploring solutions to the eyesore.

As I exit the tenement apartment, I encounter two ebullient twenty-somethings leaving a unit across the hallway, about to knock on the next door. They approach me and ask if I'm a social worker. (My jeans and open-collared shirt make me look more like a caseworker than a lawyer.) I explain to the young social workers that I've been teaching practical life skills to a family with troubled kids. They in turn tell me how they're going door to door to enroll new parents in "Baby College," an outreach of the Harlem Children's Zone, teaching parenting techniques. I ask about its efficacy, thinking about the single mom with a toddler in the group I'd just left. They request an introduction.

I'd met Geoff Canada, the founder of the Harlem Children's Zone, many years earlier at a Robin Hood Foundation breakfast. My Harkhomes and his Rheedlen Centers for Children and Families had been grant recipients. Canada had given the keynote that morning, in which he'd explained that his goal was to reverse the cycle of generational poverty that disadvantaged Harlem's children.

Since that was exactly what I'd been trying to do, I'd conducted some research and had become intrigued by the magnitude of Geoff's vision of a holistic, comprehensive set of youth programs for Harlem. His aim hadn't been to help a few kids, but to uplift all of them. He'd concluded that after-school programs, life-skills workshops, and antiviolence seminars weren't sufficient. One had to rebuild lives by renewing Harlem—apartment by apartment, building by building, and block by block.

Canada's big vision of community revival was not new. Garvey had thought big, as had Father Divine in the thirties, who'd created "heavens" all over Harlem; dormitory-like residences where his members lived inexpensively and worked in his clothing stores and restaurants as long as they worshipped their benefactor. Both these schemes had been short-lived.

Dr. Kenneth Clark's trailblazing work in child psychology had created the philosophical framework for the landmark Supreme Court desegregation decision *Brown v. Board of Education*. Clark had attempted to address the plight of the children of Generation Blight. His advocacy had resulted in the greater integration of city schools, initiatives to enrich the curriculum, and funds for improving schools in Harlem and other disadvantaged neighborhoods.

Clark took his crusade for Harlem's kids outside the school system. He organized Harlem Youth Opportunities Limited, better known as HARYOU, the largest antipoverty program in the nation's history. HARYOU used educational experts to restructure Harlem's schools. It published influential reports like "Youth in the Ghetto." It ran pilot initiatives like Project Uplift and established preschool and after-school programs, as well as remedial training for dropouts. With the endorsement of U.S. Attorney General Robert Kennedy, HARYOU received an unprecedented $110 million as part of LBJ's Great Society initiative.

But Harlem showed little if any improvement from this decade-long federal funding in job training, housing, public safety, and health care. By the 1960s, between 75 and 80 percent respectively of Harlem students tested below grade level in reading and math. Adam Clayton Powell Jr. intervened, and he and Clark warred over control of the program. A compromise forced the joint administration of the government financing through Powell's pet project, Associated Community Teams. Thus HARYOU-ACT was born.

The arrival of Richard Nixon in the White House shifted priorities to law and order and foreign policy, and HARYOU-ACT, like other inner-city initiatives, was axed. Critics charged that the vast sums of taxpayer dollars directed to HARYOU-ACT did little more than foster dependency and cronyism. The demise of HARYOU-ACT (along with the Great Society) gutted urban policy on the national level. Instead, attention turned to local antipoverty efforts.

Enter Geoff Canada with the Harlem Children's Zone, the biggest Harlem community program since HARYOU-ACT. I was rooting for him, because in some ways the circumstances confronting African-American families had become even more challenging than those that frustrated Clark a generation earlier. Welfare reform now dictated that single mothers should work regardless of whether it would complicate child care. Parental discipline and support continued to remain poor. And the incarceration rates for African-American men continued to rise, leaving black males without the hard or soft skills to compete for jobs in an increasingly global economy. Meanwhile, black youth were being drawn to gangs as parental surrogates and sources of income.

Canada believed in investing in Harlem kids from birth to college, with the broadest intervention coming early in the child's life. The "zone" itself constituted a large swath of Harlem, in which he sought to create a safety net of educational, medical, and social services, targeting the kids who were most at risk. Holistic Hardware was rooted in accountability, the very thing Geoff stressed. I was teaching people who were struggling with their brokenness the importance of taking ownership of a problem, encouraging them to set high standards, and applying successful strategies to achieve them. Canada furthered this method by trumpeting values-based approaches at the same time as he erected neighborhood-wide support systems to help kids and their parents attain their goals.

• • •

Heartened by this unexpected supplementary resource, I return to the apartment with the Harlem Children's Zone workers and initiate a fruitful exchange with the surprised family members. The single mom shows an interest in Baby College, and the workers show an interest in Holistic Hardware. I like the collaborative possibilities.

As I leave the building, I cross paths with a woman from the block association. She glares at me and fires some profanity. The meeting I'd recently attended had been a disaster. Ralph had insisted that I present my development idea for the church: to demolish the eyesore and build a twelve-story, market-rate condo. I shared with them a rendering of the new building and argued that it was the only way to create the new revenues and facilities that Bishop Middleton and her leadership sought. The economics for a low-rise, low-income project on that site just didn't work.

"Why are you doing this?" someone asked as the opposition to the project simmered. I explained that the only Harlem eyesore better known than the Church had been the Ruins. Situated along the western border of Marcus Garvey Park, the Ruins were a row of abandoned century-old Queen Anne townhouses that had brandished their exposed steel girders at the park for a generation. Vacant since the sixties, this once-handsome block front had been seized by New York State government for an urban renewal project, which never got off the drawing board. A mental-health center had been proposed for the site, but community opposition had prevailed. The neighborhood lost its subsequent battle to block a minimum-security women's prison from one of the site's buildings. During my tenure as housing commissioner, I'd organized a task force of agency heads to study development options for the Ruins. The initiative kindled the project's

FIGURE 27: An artist's rendering of the plans for the Lenox

momentum, resulting in restoration of the buildings and full occupation of thirty-four condominiums with views overlooking the park.

The point fell on deaf ears, as had all my others. What the 129th Street residents failed to understand was that a solution for the Dark Corner was hard to come by. And they were scared of change. The question I'd most feared came from one of the old-timers: "You used to house homeless people on this block," he asserted. "We still got homeless around. Why can't you house them or at least house people who really need housing?"

The applause that followed his question made it clear that any goodwill from my years of service on the block was gone. With my Dark Corner strategy, I'd metamorphosed from a good neighbor to an evil developer as quickly as I'd changed from favorite son to wayward offspring with my Harlem decision two decades prior.

So I'd tried the empowerment argument: "We need to bring the black middle class back to Harlem—better role models for our kids: lawyers, doctors, and bankers instead of drug dealers, street-corner slackers, and gangsta rappers."

"Where are the poor people going to go?" a senior citizen countered.

What if Harlem goes upscale while fostering racial and economic diversity? I thought.

"We need more housing for people who live in Harlem," a twenty-something man offered. "Instead of forcing them out to make room for outsiders."

"No one is living there now," I countered. "No one will have to move if we build it. I'm removing an eyesore and displacing half the rodent population of the neighborhood." *Probably more than half*, I thought, since the rats had already been evicted from the Dirty Alley.

The levity had been ill advised.

"You not helping any," a middle-aged woman fired. "Those rats might start running over to my building if you put them outta that ol' church!"

"You should be ashamed—jumping on the gentrification bandwagon, like all the rest," shrieked another woman.

"Gentrification is about displacement and I'm not displacing anyone," I insisted.

It was as if she hadn't heard a word. "Why don't you go back to the suburbs, and stop trying to turn our beloved black Mecca into a rich white community? People like you who are benefiting the most are the ones who got here last."

What is she talking about? I've been here almost a quarter of a century!

"Harlem's not for sale!" she shouted.

Her tirade drives home an unpleasant truth—once a carpetbagger, always a carpetbagger. It also reveals how infamous I've become in Harlem over the years. I can now add aiding and abetting white interlopers to my crime of smuggling Ivy Leaguers into the community.

Since Ralph had joined the Amen Corner, I decided to shut up and leave. I walked slowly to the door. No one tried to convince me to stay.

Walking through the Dark Corner on the way to my car, I veer out of the way of a group of foul-mouthed teens with ill-fitting clothes (a well-mannered bunch would have stepped out of my way), which strengthens my conviction that Harlem should have at least as many role models speaking the Queen's English, well-groomed and wearing a suit and tie, as those spewing expletives, tattooed-up, and sporting baggy, low-sagging jeans.

I glance back and watch them enter No. 60, which is no surprise.

I walk by Lenox Terrace, the luxury rental of six towers, each with its own terrace, which is the castle for the Clubhouse. Three of the Gang of Four—Rangel, Sutton, and Paterson—live there, as do family members and staff. Rumors abound that Clubhouse membership holds special privileges at Lenox Terrace; that some have more than one apartment; that they may not be using their apartments as primary residences and may be paying lower rents than others tenants with comparable units at the complex. I guess someone could create some controversy or at least embarrassment by poking around this issue. But I've decided to eschew my conspiracy theories and bury such buzz. I've tangled with the Clubhouse before—and lost. I choose to keep my powder dry.

About to get into my car, I spy the Schomburg Center for Research in Black Culture, as well as Harlem Hospital. Harlem's caretaker of cultural health sits on one corner and that of her physical health is across the street. The dynamic duo presents a welcome contrast to the Dark Corner, a stone's throw to the south.

Originating in the Renaissance, the Schomburg was named for Arthur Schomburg, the greatest collector of black literature of the twentieth century. My visits to the library invariably opened up new vistas of history and culture. It's almost like revelations rose from the stacks themselves, and helped turn my scribbling into stuff worthy of the stage and other settings. I keep walking past my car. With bad memories of the block association battlefield lingering, I could use some inspiration today.

Lots of people are up ahead. What's Harlem up to today? If it's another protest against gentrification, I'm going back to the car. I press on to the corner of Lenox Avenue and 135th Street. Two blocks are closed off to cars. Ahead of me is a throng so thick that I must maneuver sideways just to move along the sidewalk.

It's the Harlem Book Fair!

The sight is transformative—blowing away the racist propaganda that argues that blacks don't read. Everywhere I look, children are browsing, listening, playing, and reading around the endless tables that overflow with racks of books. It's a crowd much bigger than the turnout for my Ben & Jerry's giveaway or Bill Clinton's coronation. I'm willing to believe that Harlem likes books more than super-premium ice cream and great white hopes.

Banners from publishing giants such as Random House,

Scholastic, HarperCollins, and Time Warner are on display alongside indie bookstores like Sister's Uptown, forming a new kind of street vendor. Around them are stages presenting panels of poets and publishers, storytellers and celebrities. Are those TV cameras over there? C-Span is covering this? Is that a mouse pad with the image of Frederick Douglass on it for sale?

The Harlem Book Fair, the brainchild of Max Rodriguez, publisher of *QBR: The Black Book Review*, had been launched in 1999. The Harlem Book Fair had been better-timed than the Louis Michaux Book Fair, which had been held at the Schomburg in its former location on 125th Street, but had been felled in the seventies by the Blight. Today's fair clarified for me the connection from first to second renaissance—Harlem's literary soul reincarnated in the bosom of the Schomburg.

I scour the fair for creative clues for my current writing projects. Even though my mentor Tunde Samuel suddenly passed away, I hadn't given up on our vision of *Homegrown: The Musical*. My first play, *Cast Me Down*, matured into my first screenplay, *Booker T.* And two other ideas were finding their way from imagination to script: *Harlem Law*, a teleplay about a black twenty-something lawyer, a master of the universe, who had left his high-flying career on Wall Street to carry on his father's legacy in Harlem; and *Undercover Grace*, a buddy dramedy with a spiritual twist about two ministers who find themselves in a homeless shelter and become crime fighters. I'm keeping my eyes open for Hollywood agents to pitch.

I pass the table for the Harlem Writers Guild, one of whose founders was noted historian and Afrocentric scholar John Henrik Clarke. I'd first learned about the guild, the Schomburg, and the Harlem Renaissance from Professor Clarke himself, when he was a visiting lecturer at Cornell. I could still recall the night in Ithaca when he'd shared his experience of the first reading of Ossie Davis' play *Purlie Victorious* at a guild meeting.

Of course, the Renaissance had been one huge book fair. The luminaries of that era were writers, and they're all on display on this day in Harlem: Claude McKay's *Home to Harlem*; Carter G. Woodson's *The Negro in Our History*; Countee Cullen's *Color*; James Weldon Johnson's *The Autobiography of an Ex-Colored Man*; W. E. B. Du Bois' *Darkwater*; Charles S. Johnson's *Ebony and Topaz*; Zora Neale Hurston's *Their Eyes Were Watching God*; Marcus Garvey's *Africa for the Africans*; Jessie Fauset's *Dead Fires*; Jean Toomer's *Cane*; and the seminal work—Alain Locke's *The New Negro*.

Every movement needs an architect, someone to give it structure and direction. Alain Locke, the first African-American Rhodes Scholar and a Harvard-to-Harlem pioneer, was known as the "Father of the Harlem Renaissance." A professor at Howard University, Locke spent much of his time outside of academia bringing African-American artists, writers, and musicians together to create works that affirmed their own heritage. He was also entrepreneurially minded, promoting the works of his clan of creators to a broad audience, educating white readers about the uniqueness of black culture, and turning them into consumers to help launch the careers of his various artists.

The pinnacle of the Renaissance wasn't a new building, great speech, memorable concert, business venture, or special event. It was a book—*The New Negro*—published in 1925, a collection of African-American writings edited by Locke. "The New Negro" would no longer accept white subjugation, he wrote. Instead, he described "the new spirit" that had arisen among the black masses. Locke's theme was to establish a new black self-identity, transforming African Americans from a stereotype of obsequiousness to one where proud, enterprising, self-confident actors took their place on national and global stages—men and women strong enough to throw off the shackles of two centuries of slavery and another of Jim Crow.

Locke knew that creating cultural strength through intellectual endeavor for political purposes was a new and risky proposition, especially for members of an ethnic group that had been known more for brute force than artistic agility or the pursuits of the mind. Locke's genius was to organize this cultural uprising around a compelling location: Harlem. This was the revolutionary achievement of the Renaissance. Harlem became the locus for African Americans to create their cultural community not because she had any history tied to African Americans: in fact, the opposite was true. Locke and his fellow artistic entrepreneurs *chose* Harlem. Philip Payton and Marcus Garvey may have created a demographic foundation, but it was upon it that Locke and his fellow artists built a cultural movement. Together they used their imaginative powers to write the Renaissance into existence.

What is remarkable is that, although the Renaissance gained renown through the entertainment pizzazz of the Jazz Age, the cultural expressions orchestrated by Locke and projected by Hughes, Toomer, McKay, Cullen, and others defined it—so much so that the Renaissance extended beyond its temporal and physical borders to seed the African liberation movement of the 1950s and the black consciousness movement of the 1960s— through to the redefinition of the entire social landscape of America, which subsequently more truly reflected the egalitarian values on which the nation was founded.

As I reach the end of the two-block-long fair, I find my treasure—a dusty ensemble of antiquated books, magazines, and paraphernalia. It's the Langston Hughes table. And staring at me is an essay by Hughes entitled "My Early Days in Harlem." The introduction helps me to recall the Hughes legend: he'd been the first African American to make a living as a creative writer;

the first with a literary society in his name to study his life and work; and the poet laureate of Harlem who personified the cultural movement that created new definitions of black identity and consciousness.

Hughes begins his essay by reflecting on the moment in September 1921 when he first arrived in Harlem. He emerged from the subway at Lenox at 135th Street "into the beginnings of the Negro Renaissance."

I look over at the very same subway stop and imagine Hughes coming out into a changing Harlem, and myself in the same kind of excitement in the throes of a Harlem that is changing once more. I glance back at the Schomburg, where Hughes's ashes are buried under a floor inlaid with blue stone, representing rivers, evoking his poem "The Negro Speaks of Rivers." I sigh and close my eyes, as the confluence of past and present consecrates the moment. I reflect on my maelstrom of a journey through recent Harlem history, identifying with Hughes' poetic yearning: "My soul has grown deep like the rivers."

As I read his fascinating account, I follow Hughes' footsteps from his rooming at the Harlem Y.M.C.A.; to his visits at the Harlem Branch Library, the precursor to the Schomburg; to his studies at "Columbia College"; to nights out at the "Lincoln Theatre where maybe one of the Smiths—Bessie, Clara, Trixie, or Mamie—was singing the blues." His summary of these halcyon days is simple: "I was in love in Harlem."

A dozen years later, however, love had turned to lamentation. "Adam Powell with a picket sign; me, too. BUY BLACK! . . . The Stock Market crash. The bank failures. Empty pockets. *God Bless the Child That's Got His Own. Depression.* . . . I went to Moscow."

I stare at these words, counting in my head my Harlem years. Have I really lasted longer than Langston? If Hughes bailed out of Harlem to Eastern Europe, then why can't I bail out to Wall Street or White Plains or Stockholm or someplace?

I glance up from the table and look back at the Schomburg—the lively, growing crowd strolling through her shadow as a rite of passage. I'm finally able to return her smile. It's as if this hulk of red brick and mortar had sheltered and nurtured Harlem's literary spirit and is now breathing it forth anew, anointing the community with fresh artistic life, showering future literary legends with the love of learning, and safeguarding this new generation of hopefuls from history's caprice and cruelty.

And with the help of her literary offspring, she's transformed my mood today.

SIXTEEN

Harlem Rocks!

MY THREE CHILDREN and I walk amid the hustle and bustle of 125th Street. The Apollo welcomes us with a new, high-tech marquee. The old sneaker stores, check-cashing spots, and urban fashion shops are still here but are being challenged by the new kids on the block—an array of national retailers. With Mayor Rudy long gone, the coast is now clear: a handful of vendors have come back, having slipped past the city hall of Mayor Michael Bloomberg.

My youngest, six-year-old Laura, holds my hand tightly. "Where are we going?" she asks.

"It's a surprise," I tease her.

"We could've stayed home with Daisy," she complains, referring to our fluffy, taupe, and playful cockapoo puppy, who squeaked and moaned her displeasure when left home alone.

"C'mon, Dad, why don't you tell us?" Jason, my eight-year-old son, interjects. "Why can't we just go to the movies?"

"No, Jason, there's nothing playing that we can see that we haven't already seen," ten-year-old Shelby advises. "We're here now, Dad," she insists. "Game over. Just tell us."

FIGURE 28: My children: (*from left*) Jason, Shelby, and Laura, with Daisy

"It's an adventure," I kid. I playfully walk faster. They dutifully speed up. "The sooner we get there, the sooner you'll know."

It's a day off from school. I've decided to make it an afternoon with Dad in Harlem. The plan for my old stomping ground to be a friendly destination for my suburban children is ambitious. It's the first time all of us have been back to Harlem since we moved to Westchester County when Laura was born. The distance between East Yonkers and West Harlem is measured more in culture than in miles.

"Does Grandma still come to Harlem with you?" asks Shelby, recalling Mother's intrepid days at Harlem Travel. Though she's eternally unhappy about my endless odyssey, she's thrilled about her three grandchildren, especially her namesake. It's as if the youngsters have requited her for enduring my Harlem misadventure.

My sister's marriage also boosted my stock. Lucy married Robert, my former Harkhomes resident supervisor, Holistic Hardware volunteer, Ben & Jerry's manager, and good friend. As I walked Lucy down the aisle, I felt great to have been a part in the evolution of the man becoming her mate. After the ceremony, Mother had put it more bluntly: "If nothing else good comes out of this Harlem experience of yours, at least you helped your sister get a husband!" Coming from my no-nonsense mother, higher praise I wouldn't get.

I am about to answer Shelby when I hear the New Harlem dissenters' anthem—"No Housing! No Peace!" I look across the street and see a placard-carrying group of anti-gentrifiers heading in our direction. I spy in their midst the woman from the 129th Street block association who had cursed me out at the Dark Corner.

I told you not to bring your kids to Harlem.

I endeavor to ignore the indefatigable Mrs. Stokes.

With my anxiety rising, I look down and observe that the laces on one of Laura's sneakers are coming untied. I kneel down to retie them, momentarily ducking out of sight of any would-be detractors. I intentionally fumble through a couple of attempts—"Hurry up, Daddy!"—to allow the protesters to pass.

I'm very aware of the minefield through which I'm leading my peevish little band. This grassroots movement against developers (i.e., guys like me) appears to be growing, as complaints over rising housing costs and escalating commercial rents seem to intensify by the day. As we continue to stroll, I pull the brim of my cap low and flip my collar up high to cover as much of my face as possible, wondering whether my attempt at camouflage is anything more than another silly exercise.

The protestors of the New Renaissance want to reverse gentrification and displacement. Their methods vary. Some are old—protest marches and threatened boycotts have made a comeback. Some are new—online denunciations of public officials and greedy developers. The organizer's tool of choice these days is the town hall; "State of Black Harlem" meetings are used to rally the troops regularly. I don't sense the same intensity in the new protest movement as the old. Harlem just doesn't feel as heated these days. But I've been wrong many times before and could be wrong again. I hope my unsuspecting children don't have to witness one of those angry times in Harlem.

I glance around: Has the danger passed? I notice how quiet my children have become—no chatter, no sibling rivalry, and no more questions. Have their instincts picked up on the proximity of potential peril or have they become engaged by the energy and ethnicity of the thoroughfare?

I point upward as we reach our first destination. Laura sees the sign first: HARLEM LANES.

"We're going bowling," Shelby quickly assesses. A collective "Yeah!" rises as they run inside.

Harlem Lanes is the first uptown bowling alley since the Blight knocked down Lenox Lanes a quarter-century ago. It's the classic New Renaissance enterprise, established by two African-American women, Gail Richards and her niece Sharon Joseph, who garnered a loan from the Upper Manhattan Empowerment Zone to help finance it. The strobe lights, R&B music, urban design, and staff of color give the place a different feel from the comparatively mundane lanes my kids frequent.

"Can we go to the arcade when we're done bowling?" Jason asks. "I see some cool games in there."

"Let's wait and see," I parry. I'm ambivalent. I want them to have a good time but intend to stick to my agenda. My well-laid plan has been in the works for a while.

By our second game, my competitive kids are in full swing, striving to beat Dad. I'm focused on trying to stay ahead.

"I'm hungry," Jason reports.

"Already?" I'm not really surprised.

"Growth spurt," he explains.

We finish bowling, eat a quick lunch, and move even faster past the arcade toward the exit. They're excited now, not knowing where my Harlem train is leading, but fully on board. As we leave Harlem Lanes, I inch ahead and scan the streets. The coast looks clear, but I remain vigilant. I have no need today of drug pushers fleeing the police, helicopters flying low overhead, overzealous cops, or invective-spewing radicals.

We stroll along and the face of New Harlem captures me, putting my worries to rest. The young overburdened welfare moms pushing their overloaded strollers along 125th Street mix with divas sporting designer labels; fashionistas unfurling Afrocentric fare; teens with tattoos, nose rings, and Mohawks; and a handful of Buppies and Yuppies in business suits. They form the multitextured distance that Harlem has covered in a quarter-century—and the miles she still has to go.

New Renaissance commerce presents a more refined panorama than did the retail landscape of the Blight: upscale grocer Citarella; elegant men's grooming salon BBraxton; Harlem Vintage (the neighborhood's first fine wine shop); ethnic-themed bath-and-skin care retailer Carol's Daughter; Tribal Spears Gallery, one of the many magnets for the burgeoning arts scene; and the clothing stores—Bebenoir, H&M, B. Oyama, and the Brownstone. A hot yoga studio, Ottomanelli gourmet market, and a luxury car dealership are on the way. The bodegas, tattoo-and-body-piercing spots, pawnshops, cut-rate stores, and other old-school retailers still hold the lead, but at least their classier counterparts are now in the game.

La Famille had long gone, and an unexpected turf war has broken out between old-school soul-food outlets and those presenting nouvelle cuisine. Sylvia's is still thriving because of tourist traffic, but casualties abound: Wilson's, Wimps, Wells, 22 West, Pan Pan, and most notably Copeland's. This Hamilton Heights landmark had closed recently after fifty fried-chicken-full years, felled by the demographics of incoming Dominicans and whites who had less of an appetite for the traditional Harlem fare.

Louise's, Charles', M & G, and Manna's are among the hard-core holdouts that still offer chitterlings, oxtails, neck bones, pigs' feet, deep fried chicken, and chops, and an overdose of gravy or butter or both on all side dishes. The new-school soul food survivors—Spoonbread, Londells, Amy Ruth's, and Melba's—are being challenged by options offering a more eclectic cuisine: Mobay, Dinosaur, Piatto D'Oro, Creole, the River Room, Chocolat, Settepani, and the Hudson River Cafe. As New Harlem figures out her palate, I'm relieved to no longer have to catch a cab or subway to the Upper East or West Side to find non-greasy, non-fried, or vegetarian cuisine. Harlem now had three Starbucks and three New York Sports Clubs. To get in shape for the New Renaissance, Harlem apparently needed as much exercise as caffeine.

The most upscale strip in New Harlem is called SOHA, the sophisticated sobriquet for South Harlem. Delimited by Frederick Douglass Boulevard between 110th and 125th Streets, this section of Harlem was even scarier than 129th Street only twenty years ago. I'd even vetoed doing HARK outreach in the area because it was so desolate. These days the only outreach going on in SOHA was between Buppies and Yuppies congregating in the trendy spots after work.

Even social services had a New Harlem face. Geoff Canada had moved the "Zone" to a new six-story, $44 million headquarters on 125th Street. Its focus was not retail, office, residential, or hospitality but youth services and education. It even hosted a charter school, which had become a New Harlem brand: of the twenty-five on the island of Manhattan, eighteen were in Harlem.

Major development on Harlem's borders is proceeding at a furious rate. To the west, Columbia University is gobbling up land as part of seventeen-acre, $4 billion northward expansion of its campus into Harlem. To the east, an abandoned factory building is being demolished to make way for East River Plaza, anchored by Target, Costco, and Home Depot—Manhattan's first mammoth big-box-store mall.

And with the New Renaissance market in overdrive, the big boys were now circling Harlem. Vornado Realty Trust was developing a twenty-one-story tower, the community's first major office building in two decades. Kimco Realty was negotiating to acquire a major 125th Street corner property, tear it down, and build a big, mixed-use project. And Starwood was scouting out hotel sites. But as we passed a shuttered storefront, I was reminded of a recent report that described the dozens of black businesses closing due to market forces, with the pace of such closures projected to quicken.

As we walk beneath the Apollo marquee again, the kids recognize the illuminated name of a rapper I've never heard of. I'm badgered with the collective cry, "Can we come to a show?" Since I'm still trying to survive the children's first foray into Harlem, I insist on the pat reply, "Let's talk about it later."

"Where are we going next?" they shout in unison.

I give only a mischievous smile, and the children laugh—a good sign, since our next stop is my biggest hurdle to a fun outing. As we near the destination, I observe a cop patrol, and am pleased at police presence for the first time since my law enforcement encounter (still the euphemism).

"A bookstore?" Laura protests.

"We could've gone to the Barnes & Noble near home," Jason chimes in. "It's a lot bigger."

"Relax, guys," Shelby counsels. "Maybe Dad will buy us something cool in here."

It's Hue-man, Harlem's best bookstore and another New Renaissance paradigm. The store had been founded by four black businesswomen—Clara Villarosa, Celeste Johnson, Rita Ewing, and Marva Allen. The spirit of Madam C. J. Walker lived on. Hue-man features children's books among a variety of black-themed selections. I translate Shelby's hope into a proposition: "I will buy you each one book. And we're not leaving until you each have one. And only one. And no magazines. And no picture books. Only chapter books."

They scatter and leave me to my hidden agenda—a chance to browse. I pick up a self-help book. I wonder whether I should reapproach the owners about carrying my *Holistic Hardware* book and video series, which has been upgraded from VHS to DVD. A prison chaplaincy outreach is using *Holistic Hardware* in correctional facilities in Georgia and Florida, my periodic workshops take me far and wide, and I've been contacted by a Liberian bishop about bringing the program to Africa.

I happen upon *Forever Harlem: Celebrating America's Most Diverse Community* by Voza Rivers and Lloyd Williams. As I thumb through the pages, my mind wanders to the recent meeting I attended of the Harlem Arts Alliance, which Voza chairs. Though not all of his four hundred members had been present, the Riverside Church Theater was mostly full, which was quite remarkable for ten o'clock on a Monday morning.

Voza orchestrated the meeting like a conductor showcasing the cultural symphony of the New Renaissance. A curator of a Harlem-based exhibit introduced several of his artists who had their paintings on display. An actor performed a scene from her new one-woman play. An arts-organization funder discussed two new grant programs. An announcement was made about an upcoming national arts-awards conference. An African-American/Latino string quartet played a jazzy number. Brochures were passed out about the educational initiative of the National Jazz Museum in Harlem. A theater company manager explained how imperative it was she get a new space. A solicitation was made for a fund to support unemployed artists. An activist promoted a rally to lobby for greater public support for the arts. A filmmaker praised Voza's Harlemwood Festival— and on and on it went.

If Voza was the cultural architect of the New Renaissance in the spirit of Alain Locke, then his coauthor Lloyd Williams was its dynamic image-maker, the cheerleader in the spirit of A'Lelia Walker, albeit less ostentatiously and more strategically. Lloyd's brands had become synonymous with Harlem's public image: the Greater Harlem Chamber of Commerce, Harlem Week, the Harlem Visitors and Convention Association, the Harlem Jazz and Music Festival, "You Haven't Done This Town Until You've Done It Uptown," and the National Black Sports & Entertainment Hall of Fame. Through street fairs, block parties, forums, speeches, special events, celebrity appearances, maps, exhibitions, T-shirts, business fairs, and movie festivals—whatever it took—Lloyd had marketed Harlem to counter the negative images of crime and drugs and to tap into the $2.5 billion that New York City's tourists generated annually.

I scan the bookstore and discover my children are still on

their mission. Then a gem appears—*A Tree Beyond Telling: Poems Selected and New* by my favorite Cornell English professor, Ken McClane. McClane had grown up in Harlem and would tell the story about when he was six years old and Langston Hughes had said to his father, "I hate to say this, but it looks like your son is going to be a poet. God help him and you." I used to see Professor McClane on my trips to Ithaca, but since I'd been made a trustee emeritus my upstate sojourns were infrequent. I'd first learned Harlem Renaissance poetry from him, which made him the one most responsible for my irrepressible muse.

I wish I had more time to write. *Undercover Grace*, my *Homegrown* screenplay adaptation, needed another rewrite. Though it won the Christian Screenwriting Competition, with an option from Fox Home Entertainment, and had been plugged by the contest director as "Mel Gibson and Danny Glover as sparring preachers with Hilary Swank as the referee," it continued, like my other scripts, to collect dust on the shelf. Maybe it was time to listen more to my muse, and take one of Ken's workshops and try verse.

I find another treasure, *Against All Odds: A Harlem Story*, by Rev. Walter Wilson, my Harlem mentor. I skim the pages of the book and arrive at a passage that grips me. Writing about a great trial in his life, Walter concludes: "I needed to find a neutral place to consider what was going on and God presented HARK. James O'Neal and Joseph Holland were there when I needed God most."

I sensed the divinity of the moment. I'd failed a lot. My businesses had been shuttered, I'd been defeated politically. I'd experienced embarrassing disclosures and had been in chronic financial distress. I'd struggled long and hard to accept that my endless troubles had been just part of my Harlem destiny. Since I'd come to believe that God had been using these incessant trials to forge my character, I had found myself wishing the Lord would hurry up with my internal makeover or whatever He was doing. But I'd learned to be less impatient and to rejoice at divine outcomes vindicating faithful strivings, like uplifting a Harlem man in need as in my fairway vision of long ago.

My children run up, excitedly displaying their selections. Much to my delight, they were on their Hue-man mission for over an hour. The unique array of books has stumped them; no one is quite sure how to whittle down their choices. I hold my ground and resist their entreaties for an additional book, until Jason spots Walter's 400-page book in my hand and argues that two kids' books equal one of mine. He prevails; they each get two.

We leave Hue-man, and Jason notices its neighbor at the Harlem USA mall, the Magic Johnson cinemas. Jason's the movie buff in the family. He knows all the Shreks, superheroes, and Disney features. He insists we go inside. "Why do they show mostly black movies here?" Jason asks. Relieved that no kid-appropriate films are playing, I do my best to explain how ethnic marketing works.

The mall's newest addition is one of Laura's favorite places— Chuck E. Cheese. I'm watching her, waiting for the smile as we round St. Nicholas Avenue and the familiar mouse-centered sign appears. As we enter the recently opened entertainment center, a grin breaks out from ear to ear.

"Show me some gratitude." I get hugs and "Thank yous."

"I didn't know Harlem had Chuck E. Cheese," Laura remarks.

"I told you it was a surprise."

"Y'know something, Dad . . ."

"Ready to go home?" I tease her.

"I'm really glad we came." She gives me another big hug. "Harlem rocks!"

She and her siblings hustle up the stairs and indulge in tokens, games, and tickets. I grab the only free seat, amused at some parents' efforts to shepherd their children to the exit, until I realize that that will soon be my plight. How the tables turn! My kids' reluctance to visit Harlem has changed to exuberance, presenting a new but welcome challenge. I'd hoped for an uneventful two-hour foray. Now I was plotting how to get them out of Harlem in time for dinner.

Laura approaches with an armful of tickets for me to hold. She calls out above the din. "Dad, can we have dinner here?"

I quickly think about the best way to say no, then change my mind. I recall her comment about the coolness of Harlem.

"Okay, but you only have fifteen—"

She doesn't hear me finish the sentence, running off at her sister's beckoning to play another game. I lean back against the uncomfortable booth and feel an unexpected peace. Nothing has ever signified more to me the extent of this community's change than my little daughter's exclamation about the rockiness of Harlem, rising out of the very ordinariness of the day—just a dad out with his school-age kids. I smile, gratified that the inner torments of Mrs. Stokes have finally been silenced by a gush of girlish glee.

And a little child shall lead them.

I laugh at God's sense of humor, and it's so noisy, no one hears my "Hallelujah!"

Laura rushes back with yet more tickets for me to hold. Her next question is the final nail in Mrs. Stokes' coffin.

"Can we bring Daisy with us to Harlem next time?"

SEVENTEEN

In Unison to Walk

IN THE SPACIOUS living room of Penthouse J of the Lenox, I settle in between my business partner Lew Futterman and managing agent Harriet Kyrous to face several dozen of the new condo owners. Penthouse D down the hall set the record for Harlem condos when it had recently sold for $2.4 million. But unit J is still on the market. So that's where we've gathered for the first annual meeting (as stipulated by the bylaws) of the Lenox unit owners.

I greet the fifty-plus residents and conceal my smile. It's still hard to believe I'm sitting one hundred feet above the Dark Corner, where the Church once stood, in the market-rate condo I conceived. More aliens have landed on 129th Street, and I built their spaceship!

But any pride of accomplishment I might feel was attributable less to my efforts than Harlem's irrepressible housing boom. Economic and Clubhouse pressures forced city hall to auction public land to developers like Pascal for as little as a dollar. The developers used local, state, and federal subsidy programs to build affordable housing for low- and moderate-income Harlemites. Pioneering brownstoners on Sugar Hill and elsewhere recycled underperforming real estate assets from Astor Row to 129th Street and beyond. Harlem was seeing more construction than at any time since the boom that Philip Payton and others had started a century ago.

Instead of using government money to build public housing like the St. Nick, the Kemp-Clinton model was followed: hundreds of millions of dollars of government money had been used to leverage private investment, yielding a profusion of more new housing and encouraging greater population growth in Harlem than in any decade since the 1940s. Whether they rose in empty lots, were placed within the midblock brownstones, or were narrow tenements converted into apartments or condominiums, these buildings ultimately left the city with no more parcels to recycle: Ellington on the Park, 50 West, the Marshall, 2002 Fifth Avenue, the Rhapsody on Fifth, Graceline Court, 10 Mount Morris Park, Strivers' Row lofts, the Fitzgerald, Bradhurst Court, Loft 124, The Sutton, Brownstone Lane, St. Charles Condominiums, Maple Court, the Langston, Renaissance Plaza, Harriet Tubman Gardens, 1400 on Fifth, Rosa Parks, Strivers' Gardens—I couldn't keep count. And Apollo Real Estate Advisors took control of Delano Village, a large rent-regulated housing complex, with the aim of turning it into a market-rate development called Savoy Park.

Even the Dwyer, which I'd saved from demolition all those years before, had risen again. The original building had been razed. A construction worker had tumbled seven stories to his death when the floor above him collapsed, and no lawyer (even one able to stop the brick-wielding Kofi Brown) could keep the once-defiant Dwyer from being bulldozed to the ground. In its place stood the Dwyer Lofts, a luxury condo with designated space for a new cultural center.

Planning for my new project, 5th on the Park, was well underway. Over twice the size of the Lenox, it would be twenty-eight stories—the tallest building in Harlem. It would compete with other epochal uptown developments: Soha 118, defining Harlem's new hot neighborhood; 111 Central Park West, bringing high-rise, midtown-priced luxury to Harlem's gateway; and the Kalahari, asserting an Afrocentric aesthetic. I'm preparing for the new battlefield, as my meeting with 5th on the Park's neighboring block association looms. Maybe I'll leave the rendering at home this time.

I see Carol Griffin, our sales agent, mingling with a couple of prospective purchasers. Manhattan real estate firms had descended on the white-hot marketplace of New Harlem with a policy of "No Broker Left Behind." Companies like Corcoran, Halstead, Elliman, Weichert, Warburg, Greenthal, Century 21, and others had rushed to set up shop, fighting for prime turf with old-guard realtors like Webb & Brooker, Stafford Realty, Giscombe Henderson, Griffin Realty, Myers Smith & Granady, Tridez, and Edwards Sisters. The outcome of this turf battle remained uncertain.

Celebrity, of course, mattered. It was clear that Harlem's fame made it an attractive investment for the Brooke Astors of this world. The area's proximity and ease of transit to midtown and downtown Manhattan, within a vibrant regional economy, also fueled the surge. I doubt that any other urban community in the nation could have commanded this magnitude of collectively channeled capital in a New York minute to turn itself around. Whatever the spark, Harlem's housing market sizzled sooner, and with more heat, than I—or anyone—could have anticipated.

Crash!
"Yes!!"
My exclamation had risen beyond the intended whisper,

FIGURE 29: An artist's rendering of the plans for 5th on the Park

prompting the glance of a curious passerby. I was too excited to be bothered by the unwanted attention on the day that this monument of the Blight was finally brought to the ground. As the demolition crew toppled the stubborn walls of the Church I was strutting along Lenox Avenue humming a favorite hymn, "What a Mighty God We Serve." This must be how Berliners felt when their wall came down.

Crash!! I just saw my mountain move.

With this intractable hulk down, No. 55 and No. 60—the other bullies of the Dark Corner—didn't appear so ominous. I'd dreamed that the new kid on the block, the completed Lenox, would bring the tough guys to their knees. The twelve-story, seventy-seven-unit condo was the first New Renaissance housing development to be built without a public subsidy. Our marketing pitch—value, space, and price over status and stores—had drawn pioneering purchasers uptown. I'd hoped there'd be some new role models and community-oriented souls among them.

As the unit owners settle into their seats, I realize I've gone from constructing lives to constructing buildings. Although this meeting would contain no Bible-based discussions about personal growth, no testimonies would be given, and it was unlikely that anyone would be inspired to break into song, nonetheless—like the gatherings of 419 Convent Avenue a generation ago—a new community of ghetto-busters would be trying to figure out how to live, and to live together, in Harlem.

We'd recently had a kind of HARK reunion at the First Annual Hands of Service Awards, held at Harlem Grace Tabernacle and pastored by Harvard-to-Harlem fellow traveler Dennis Henderson. Dennis presented me with the business-sector leadership award, as Leslie, Jackie, Mimsie, Sylvia, and others from the early Harlem days looked on, beaming. It was especially gratifying to have my pastor, Bishop Carlton Brown of Bethel Gospel Assembly, as a fellow honoree.

I wave at a couple who could have bought an apartment at the Lenox Grand but purchased with us instead. The Lenox Grand was another luxury condo building directly across from us on the west side of Lenox Avenue. That two market-rate residences should be dueling it out in the shadow of the Dark Corner was another sign of the amazing change in Harlem. The handful of jobs that my old businesses had birthed paled in comparison with the dozens of construction and permanent jobs spawned by the Lenox. I clung to the hope that the New Renaissance might be kinder to my entrepreneurship than those dark days of the Blight.

Seeing the real estate deal through had been in some ways as challenging as running a homeless shelter. I'd had to get commitments from lenders and investors, all the while arguing that New Harlem possessed a market for upscale condos that wouldn't disappear with the next protest on 125th Street or uptick in crime. When opposition from both the block associations of 129th (Ralph was unrelenting) and 130th streets stiffened over building height and the lack of affordability, I'd found myself needing to reach out to the Clubhouse to push through my land-use variance application. Manhattan Borough President C. Virginia Fields, Assemblyman Keith Wright, and even my old friendly foe State Senator David Paterson stepped up, not only helping to bring down a despised icon of the Blight but also laying to rest my long-standing conspiracy theory about the Clubhouse.

I sit back and scan the room. The ethnic mix far exceeds my expectations: the black actor, the Asian-American restaurateur, the white theatrical agent, the Latino scientist, the white tax attorney, the Asian-American investment banker, the black speech pathologist, the white couple who own a business, the black chef, the white international attorney, the black engineer. I'm also delighted that my sister Lucy and brother-in-law Robert are among the new Lenox residents.

I see Mary, whose recommendation to the Manhattan Chamber of Commerce resulted in my receiving the community service award at their annual recognition breakfast. Mother had attended, as well as a banquet room full of Manhattan political bigwigs and business leaders. They'd given me a standing ovation after my Harlem history lesson:

> Almost a century ago Harlem was roaring through its first renaissance, but it didn't last, overcome by the Depression of the thirties, the flight of the forties, the heroin of the fifties, the riots of the sixties, the abandonment of the seventies. I arrived in the midst of the crime and crack of the eighties and took part in the brownstoning of the nineties, and then, in the dawn of the twenty-first century—a second Harlem renaissance. But will it last? Will it go the way of its predecessor, a victim of unforeseen, adverse historical forces? Or perhaps endure as a source of permanent progress? I believe Harlem's best hope lies in the handiwork of its businesspeople, its developers, its entrepreneurs, its innovative institution-builders, those who understand that creating a job is an effective social program, those who seek to build an economic base to open wide doors of opportunity, those who make daily sacrifices to make a difference in individual lives.

As I discreetly look around the well-appointed, high-ceilinged penthouse, I do a little racial calculation in my head, endeavoring to fathom the distance that Harlem has traveled from the 1980s, when white people traveled uptown perhaps once a day to score some cocaine, to today, where hundreds of whites are seeking to buy here and live here. Will the Lenox have a smooth racial journey or end up on the rocky road of 2002 Fifth Avenue, a nearby upscale development sitting on the north side of Marcus Garvey Park?

The mostly white residents of 2002 Fifth Avenue had lodged noise complaints against the drummers, who'd been playing in the park on summer Saturdays for thirty years. The drummers became not only a cultural fixture but also community guardians. Their loud, protracted jam sessions had safeguarded playtime for neighborhood kids amid the crack and crime. But an inflammatory email ("Let's get rid of these people") from a 2002 Fifth resident had escalated the conflict into a cultural war between Old Harlem and her new neighbors. I felt that the supposed compromise of moving the drummers to a location in the park farther away from 2002 Fifth was ill-advised, not only because the drummers' beats carried far and wide, but a lot more people wouldn't be happy at the end of it all than were unhappy at the beginning.

Since neither the Blight nor Mrs. Stokes had extinguished my incurable optimism, I expected that the furor at 2002 Fifth would be the exception rather than the rule of New Harlem race relations. For me, the unsung heroes of the New Renaissance would be the community-minded residents (some of whom I could be looking at right now) who would venture beyond the comfort zones of their condos and commit themselves to the much-needed continuous renewal of their neighborhoods.

I exchange a smile with one of the new black residents. I wonder whether he and his wife might herald the return of the black middle class, who flooded out of Harlem half a century ago. Years of alienation in Harlem had shown me that no public or private sector plan existed to bridge the growing divide between the black middle class and those folks left behind in the underclass. I could count on the fingers of one hand my black Harvard-to-Harlem peers who'd stayed for any length of time. I didn't blame them for fleeing the challenge of balancing family and career and endeavoring to make a difference in Harlem. I would've been gone, too, but for my faith in divine purpose, provision, and power.

Whether the Lenox owners wanted to live in Harlem because their apartments offered space, value, and convenience; or whether they were looking for a good investment; or whether they'd bought here because of the community-centered lifestyle their new locale promised, they nonetheless were (perhaps unwittingly) on the front lines of the historical battle over who Harlem was for. The truth is that Harlem had been diversifying for more than half a century, although the nonblack population had only surged in recent years. Would the incoming whites help Harlem reimagine herself as a neighborhood belonging to more than just blacks?

The prospect of a distinctively new uptown racial identity evoked "Tableau," my favorite Countee Cullen verse, where the poet imagines a white boy and a black boy joining hands down the street, daring—in the face of indignant observers—"in unison to walk."

The poem's theme and the pattern of the New Harlem fly in the face of recent findings in social science that suggest that because of the high rate of poverty among blacks and the tendency of black communities to self-segregate, African Americans would remain more isolated from whites in the privacy of their homes and neighborhoods than they had been in the era of Jim Crow. But racial isolation is a two-sided coin. White people, as the minority in a neighborhood of color, would have to deal with the occasional racial epithet. They'd have to get used to buying merchandise or even banking through Plexiglas partitions. They might have to search for conveniently located barbers who cut straight hair.

Of course, these problems paled in comparison to the troubles awaiting middle-class African-American newcomers. Black gentrification seemed more complex than its white counterpart. Long-time locals could either perceive new black residents as potential pioneers or dismiss them as being the same as the white neophytes, potentially more interested in comfortable lifestyles, easy commutes, and property values than in Harlem's well-being. Would black arrivals distinguish themselves by a determination to overcome local fears and help Harlem and its people, with compassionate Caucasians at their side, driven by a love of the destined domain that had drawn them out of a divided past to endeavor together?

Harriet asks for a show of hands to elect the board of managers: a white male contractor, a black female sales rep, a white male product manager, a black male investment banker, and a white female CPA. Lew and I, as the project sponsors, round out the leadership board, which reflects the black/nonblack makeup of the building. I'm encouraged that there are no affirmative-action quotas or politically correct sensibilities that drive these wonderfully diverse determinations.

The whisper around the Lenox is that the investment banker is the favorite to become the president of the new board. Since I cling to my hope of a black middle-class influx, maybe this thirty-something black guy on 129th Street without tattoos and earrings and with suit, tie, and non-sagging pants represents the first ripples of a wave of direly needed role models. Or maybe someone in this room will possess the Solomonic wisdom to weave a new Harlem tapestry out of her twentieth-century black identity and her twenty-first-century ethnic makeover.

As Harriet continues with the minutiae of building management, my mind races to the larger implications of tonight's gathering. Could it be that Harlem—once scorned as an icon of the worst of the ghetto—might become the multiethnic model for twenty-first-century America? Might the New Renaissance be to American multicultural identity what the Renaissance was to African-American self-identity? That one of the community's worst blocks has been transformed in less than a generation offers a promise for Harlem's leadership in forging new strategies to address the legacy of America's travails with race.

Of course, one would have to be Pollyanna to believe that racism has vanished. Open animus may have been replaced by unspoken bias, but racism doesn't shirk from daring to speak its name. Within walking distance of the Lenox, an African-American professor of racial justice at Columbia College found a noose hanging from her office door. In Brooklyn, a noose was sent to an African-American high school principal. On Long Island, a black construction worker discovered a noose hanging at a job site, while in upstate New York, a noose was hung from an African-American chaplain's office door. In New Rochelle, a black middle school custodian found three nooses over several months. On his first day on the job, one was slung around the head of a stuffed monkey. Similar incidents occurred in Illinois, Indiana, Texas, Louisiana, Florida, Pennsylvania, Connecticut, and the Carolinas. Since more than 70 percent of the 5,000 victims of lynching between the Civil War and the Civil Rights Act were African American, these incidents ripped the scab off this long-festering American wound, demonstrating the intractability of American racism, twenty-first-century racial progress notwithstanding.

For me, these episodes set the contest for America's racial consciousness in sharp relief. In one corner was the Noose, aided by Jim Crow and the Blight; in the other was Harlem, seeking through reconciliation to combat bigotry, tokenism, and oppression with the still untested strategy of judging someone by the content of their character and not the color of their skin. Would Harlem's New Community—first-born of Martin Luther King's "beloved community"—be powerful enough to overcome the Noose?

Harriet opens the floor to questions. Why did she do that?

Not so fast, Joe, I can hear Ralph's voice echoing. . . .

How could I forget about the undertow?

I wish Ralph could have experienced the not-so-dark Dark Corner, but he'd lost his battle with diabetes. He would have been thrilled to look from his chair in front of No. 26 toward Lenox Avenue and not have to wag his finger at his favorite scapegoat—the Church. Naturally, he would have chastised me for helping tip the racial balance of Harlem. I'd like to have proved him wrong by getting as many blacks as whites in the Lenox. And he would have laughed at the irony of integrating "the city," as the block's most upscale building went up on the "black side" of 129th Street.

Sure enough, Harriet's offer calls forth a cacophony of complaints: traffic jams in the parking garage, some of the staff's limited English, too many elevator breakdowns, unresolved punch lists, noisy roof vents. . . .

Then the question I fear most: "What about that corner?"

This is not good. I should've been out of here twenty minutes ago to not be too late to make my pitch to the Metropolitan Black Bar Association. My best hope of meeting my racially balanced condo sales goals is to present to black professional groups—and pray for open minds. Now I've been cornered by an old nemesis.

I knew very well which corner they were talking about. Too

many kids are hanging out inside the laundromat and outside the barbershop. The clamor from late-night street parties is penetrating the building. There are rumors of drug activity reinfecting the intersection, as well as reports of periodic violence. Police sirens have been blaring, and through the night residents can hear gunshots echoing ominously close to the building. And No. 60 still casts its shadow over the block, ever the magnet for troublemakers. The mustiness lingers, and the breeze that blows along the block still has a wintry chill. The Dark Corner dies hard.

"We didn't sign up for this," says the crowd.

I rub my forehead and promise to arrange a meeting with the 32nd Police Precinct.

This gloomy corner of the Blight, which I thought had suffered a fatal wound, rears its ugly head.

The meeting ends. I'm encircled by the disenchanted. I grudgingly give up going to my downtown gathering.

It's going to be another long night on 129th Street.

EIGHTEEN

I, Too, Sing America

I LEAVE MY Sugar Hill brownstone office and hustle to my car. I have a couple of chores to do before I pick Jason up from Pop Warner football practice. As I walk down the hill, I glance over at Hamilton Grange, which had recently been relocated to St. Nicholas Park. This was surely a good sign for Harlem: the abode of her most famous former resident rising where drug lords used to tread.

These days I spend a lot of time at the garage at the Langston, one of the New Renaissance mixed-use landmarks on 145th Street, which houses upscale condos, as well as my preferred New York Sports Club and a favorite Starbucks. It's where I'm forced to park my car because spots on the streets in Harlem are now as precious as they are in the rest of Manhattan. The mix of blacks, whites, Hispanics, and Asians sipping pricey beverages and kickboxing, spinning, training, and crunching takes the diversity I saw at the Lenox to a whole new level: poetic justice in a building named after a beloved hero of Harlem.

• • •

It's Election Day, and my car radio is reporting that a large crowd has formed at African Square in front of the Powell Office Building. I'd learned that returns were being played on a big screen in the Langston Hughes Auditorium at the Schomburg, and rumors had reached me about "watch night services" taking place in churches across the community. I decide to detour to 125th Street for a peek, unable to resist my inclination to watch history unfold in Harlem.

I park not too far away and approach the growing throng. Before this night is over, the street festivities might surpass Harlem's celebration of Joe Louis beating Max Schmeling seventy years ago. In the crowd, I can discern reflections of the Garvey gatherings, the Malcolm X masses, the Al Sharpton rallies of the eighties and nineties, and even the Clinton coronation. What's different today is that Harlem's historic ill temper is not on display. Though I doubt Harlem's angry days are gone for good, an Obama victory tonight is likely to extend its good mood at least through Inauguration Day.

Not everyone is preparing to celebrate. A homeless man lies asleep next to a brownstone stoop. I'm particularly sensitive to social dislocations since I traveled to Liberia. Bishop Emmanuel Jones had invited me to Monrovia to conduct a series of Holistic Hardware workshops and for the dedication of the Joseph Holland Christian Institute, a residence and school for the orphans of Liberia's civil war.

Bishop Jones, who'd found his Christian calling as a teenager in a refugee camp, provides leadership for eighty-six churches and parachurches throughout Liberia. He'd discovered Holistic Hardware on the Internet, and I schooled him through our online correspondence, then made my first trip to West Africa to help him implement the program to address the rampant drug addiction, homelessness, and prostitution in the aftermath of one of the longest civil wars in African history. As I'd completed

FIGURE 30: Ministers after a Holistic Hardware workshop, Monrovia, Liberia

the life-skills training for a group of the bishop's ministers, the miracle of this motivational teaching rising from 129th Street to help the downtrodden in Africa hadn't been lost on me.

Of course, African Americans have a strong connection with Liberia. Free blacks first resettled there in 1820 as an early step in the policy of repatriating former slaves to Africa, which was considered condescendingly acceptable in the early decades of the American republic. This colony of black Americans founded the nation of Liberia in 1847. Its capital city, Monrovia, was named after the United States' fifth president, James Monroe. Black nationalists in America, Marcus Garvey among them, had long regarded Liberia as the destination for their nation-building aspirations. These were abandoned, for the most part, unfulfilled.

Liberia had been relatively stable for most of its history, supported by U.S. corporate investments in its plentiful natural resources—timber, iron, precious metals, and rubber. However, the protracted civil war of the last quarter of the twentieth century had devastated the country, killing half a million of its three million people and completely destroying the country's infrastructure. The pervasive poverty that marred the idyllic coastline far outstripped Harlem's destitution during the Blight. Roads had huge craters in them. Most of the homes, including the bishop's, were without electricity and running water. I visited several houses that were shacks with two families crammed into space the size of my daughter Shelby's room.

Unemployment levels were at 90 percent, and to keep order a United Nations peacekeeping force had deployed tanks and armored cars at checkpoints across Monrovia. In some areas, such as the West Point slum, the beach waters served as a bathtub, outhouse, and cemetery; children died there every day, since life expectancy in Liberia was a mere forty-two years. I found myself often glancing at the heroic, thirty-something Bishop Jones and wondering whether he'd be gone by forty, too.

Liberia's dire circumstances brought to mind the history I'd read about the slave trade and its consequences for those of African descent. In spite of centuries of slavery, Jim Crow, and the Blight, blacks in America were generally better off; while colonialism, post-colonialism, and civil wars had left blacks in Africa generally worse off. It was not a happy comparison.

Bishop Jones shared his vision for taking Holistic Hardware all over Africa. He organized four regional coordinators to spread the message throughout Liberia, invited pastors to the workshops from Sierra Leone and Ghana, planned outreach to Nigeria, Guinea, and the rest of West Africa, before launching east and south. I'd started to tell him that I needed to finish battling the Blight back home before taking on post-colonialism in an entire continent. Before I could demur, he asked me to organize a black business delegation to return to meet with Africa's first female head of state, "Iron Lady" Ellen Johnson Sirleaf. So I decided to hold my tongue, not wanting to quench the enthusiasm of the visionary. After all, others had done the same for me.

As we listened to Bishop Jones describe his vision for Holistic Hardware Africa, I nodded at my brother-in-law Robert, who'd accompanied me on the trip. He returned my smile, sharing my understanding that the struggles for justice and equality from one continent to another weren't beyond God's sovereignty. The bishop's militia of ministers reminded us of the host of witnesses back home, who'd been steadfast at the grassroots—the unsung heroes of Harlem's safe passage through its traumatic history. The preachers hadn't left when most had. They'd kept the community from sinking beyond the point of no return. They'd reached out beyond the four walls of the church to shield Harlem from the disintegration of the Blight. They'd provided homes for the hopeless, food for the hungry, interventions for the addicted, and programs for youth. I was heartened to be a part of God's army fighting for the needy on both sides of the Atlantic.

As I move through the throng in Powell Plaza, I see a couple of young black men—adorned with tattoos, rings in their ears, and sporting bling and baggy pants—waving the American flag. Waving the American flag? They bob and weave to their own improvised beat: "O-ba-ma. Yes we can. O-ba-ma. Yes we can." I overhear some middle-agers crooning, "We Shall Overcome." I pass a man buzzing the Stevie Wonder classic, "Signed, Sealed, Delivered" which strikes me as a bit premature. Although Obama used it as his campaign song, he still has quite a distance to travel to reach 270 electoral votes.

A woman, who's dancing with everyone, grabs my arm and pulls me into a community bop. I do a couple of swift spins through the crowd, and exit as ungracefully as I entered. I hear an elderly man reciting pieces of the Langston Hughes classic, "I, Too, Sing America," the poetic monologue of a black man depicting his transition from eating alone in the kitchen "when company comes" to the future time when "I'll be at the table." The old man seemed to be saying—and all of Harlem seemed to be shouting along with him—that we had finally made it to the table, and it was time to "sing America." Though I wonder whether the rising expectations of his poetic elation can be fulfilled, there's no doubt that the muse brought its A-game today.

A biblical reference comes to mind, which puts the collective bliss in historical context.

Seek the peace and prosperity of the city to which I have carried you into exile.

Jeremiah's words to the Israelites in exile in Babylon must have been heeded, it seems to me, by my ancestors and by countless slaves, former slaves, and their progeny. Seeking peace and prosperity rather than revenge and destruction, they'd kept on singing America—or at least trying to—through centuries of de jure then de facto captivity and deferred dreams. How else could one explain the universal joy that's emerging this evening in the Harlems of this nation, but that it rose from a profound sense that the persevering faith held by African Americans in America's promise of equality and justice may finally in some manner have been vindicated?

The stadium-style Jumbotron screen, set up in the center of Powell Plaza, is turned to CNN. (It's no surprise that Fox News isn't the network of choice in the heart of Harlem.) Spectators cheer as the huge monitor flashes that Obama is ahead in Pennsylvania, Ohio, New Hampshire, and other battleground states.

I'd seen the enthusiasm as early as six-thirty this morning, when my Yonkers polling place had had longer lines than I'd ever experienced. It usually took me two minutes to vote; this time, casting my ballot had been a thirty-two-minute adventure. Some parents had brought their children along to see history. A woman who'd recently relocated to the area had argued with an election official about not being allowed to vote. As I jogged back home, I figured that if it took me sixteen times longer to vote in my predominantly white, suburban neighborhood, then turnout would be huge elsewhere, especially in the Harlems of America.

On my way to work I observed Harlemites waiting, evidently without complaint, in lines that stretched blocks from their polling place. I paused to take in the spectacle and conjectured that it might take them ninety minutes to exercise their democratic right. That turned out to be a gross underestimate. I found out later that a friend had endured three-and-a-half hours in a queue outside a Harlem school.

I sensed that such dedication from minority and young voters—among them many first-time participants—would be decisive and quell the cynics, who'd predicted that Obama's historic candidacy would be derailed by some inevitable, inscrutable conspiracy or the mysterious "Bradley effect" (whereby white voters would tell pollsters that they would vote for an African American but then not do so in the voting booth).

What turned out to really matter in the election—more than Bush's mistakes, McCain's miscues, Palin's misfirings, and even more than Obama's masterful organization and oratory—were the post–Labor Day manifestations of the worst economic crisis since the Depression, which brought to an end seemingly unstoppable economic growth, wiped out hundreds of thousands of jobs, and consumed trillions of dollars of stock market retirement funds.

Whatever the proximate causes of the meltdown, it was clear that the fundamental problem was that too many people had succumbed to greed and shirked personal responsibility. The result was a breakdown in values. Immediate gratification and risky speculation displaced personal sacrifice and patient investing. People had lived well beyond their means and had bought homes without having to put any actual money toward them. Retail bankers had made fortunes by extending loans to those who could never pay them back and investment bankers had pocketed bigger bonuses by bundling such loans into dubious financial instruments. Rating agencies and government regulators had turned a blind eye to transactions that had layer upon layer upon layer of bad debt.

The meltdown made a rocky time in Harlem even rockier. Bad news erupted on Memorial Day earlier this year. A fight over girls in Marcus Garvey Park had turned into a shooting rampage. Bullets had flown across the neighborhood, up Lenox Avenue and past 129th Street. Seven people were shot, all of them in their teens or early twenties. The incident brought back to the surface the old fears of a return to the violent, angry days of the Blight.

In the days leading up to Halloween last month, a turf war between the Bloods and the Crips gangs terrorized Harlem, as threats and counterthreats were made about killing thirteen teenage girls. Illicit street activity intensified at the Dark Corner to such an extent that the residents of the Lenox lobbied hard, and successfully, to have NYPD officers patrol the area daily, leading to a thirty-foot-high police lookout tower ensconced right outside. And the violence hit way too close to home, as a stray Dark Corner bullet invaded my sister's fourth-floor residence, piercing her bedroom wall a few feet above where she sleeps.

Inevitably perhaps, the credit crisis and its consequences slowed the New Renaissance. Vacant buildings and lots and unfinished or unsold construction projects dotted the Harlem landscape. The long-awaited office tower at 125th Street and Park Avenue, which was to house Major League Baseball's new TV network, was abandoned and the impending hotel developments were stalled.

Some Harlem leaders cheered the cooling off of Harlem's hot housing market as a brake on gentrification. I didn't share their enthusiasm. Since potential buyers couldn't get mortgages, the Lenox never sold out and sales at my new project 5th on the Park stalled. It may have been true that when downtown caught a cold, uptown got pneumonia. Now that downtown had got pneumonia, I thought, what was to happen uptown?

On this election night nobody in the 'hood cares about my concerns for the future of the New Renaissance, or what might happen to New Harlem's commercial and housing markets if countless jobs are lost in the region and elsewhere. Nobody's interested in my worry that the recession might do to New Harlem what the Great Depression did to the Renaissance. Instead, with tambourine in hand, a man grooves to McFadden and Whitehead's "Ain't No Stopping Us Now," which blares from giant speakers. The woman who was my impromptu dancing partner a few minutes before is now shaking cowbells. She joins the man's groove, while others chime in. Soon they become a troupe, prancing in the plaza.

An elderly black woman wearing an Obama hat sits at the edge of the bleachers erected for the occasion. This area will be jammed with cheering fans later tonight, as if the Super Bowl or the World Series were being played in the heart of Harlem. The woman has a handkerchief in her hand, and dabs her eyes again and again. Surprised by a stranger's reassuring hug, she looks up. "I'd never thought I'd see the day," she exclaims.

I wish Mother had still been around to experience this moment. We'd lost her suddenly; she'd been stricken by an accidental fall in her apartment. I'm still recovering from the loss of much more than maternal support. After some initial resistance, she became a vital emotional, financial, and practical resource, her pontifications notwithstanding. I couldn't have survived Harlem without her.

A lifelong Republican, Mother once dreamed with me about seeing a President Colin Powell, and had even fancied President Condoleezza Rice. These imaginings had invariably been attended with stories about our roots.

My great-great-great-great-grandmother had been born a slave on a plantation in Marietta, Georgia. She'd been taught to read as she traveled the world with her slave master's daughter who'd married a seaman. This gift of reading was surreptitiously passed through the generations. My great-great-grandmother, who worked as a chambermaid in an Atlanta hotel during Reconstruction, and was raped by a white hotel guest; her daughter became one of the early graduates of Spellman College. Her daughter, my grandmother, who'd lived to the age of 103, loved to tell us about the years of study under her mentor, the legendary black leader Mary McLeod Bethune, which led to her trailblazing career as a New England educator. Mom always concluded these reflections with her hope that a first president of color would destroy the legacy of second-class citizenship.

But she never saw this day.

An energetic street vendor hawks an array of Obama T-shirts. On this historic night, you can get a rhinestone-highlighted "deluxe" for fifty dollars. For a T-shirt? On 125th Street? Obama merchandise is already a cottage industry—framed photographs, wallets, key chains, earrings. A young, ebullient white woman shows off a book she's just purchased—*Obama: The Historic Campaign in Photographs*—which takes the meaning of hot-off-the-press to a whole new level.

A technician checks the equipment on the platform. I know who's coming to bring this celebration to a climax. Yes, it's none other than the Clubhouse, basking in Obama's triumph: former mayor David Dinkins, Councilwoman Inez Dickens, Assemblyman Keith Wright, now Governor David Paterson and, of course, orchestrating the show, just as he did for the Clinton coronation, Congressman Charles Rangel.

It was a good year for the Clubhouse, with an unexpected political prize—the New York statehouse. The demise of scandal-plagued Eliot Spitzer had catapulted the lieutenant governor, Paterson the son, into the political stratosphere, becoming New York State's first African-American governor. His unlikely ascension was followed by the challenge of how to handle the crumbling state budget, which had been undermined by the explosive Wall Street crisis. With the favorite son of the Clubhouse now running the state, Obama soon to be running the country (although Hillary Clinton had been the Clubhouse's first choice), and Rangel reelected for the umpteenth time, the Gang of Four and its political clan were sitting pretty.

As I pull myself away, I pause to appreciate a saxophonist tuning up with "When the Saints Go Marching In." Other instruments will later join him for an impromptu midnight "victory lap" through the streets of Harlem. The brass band–led procession will be so loud as they march up Lenox Avenue and cross 129th Street that Lucy and Robert, asleep in their condo at the Lenox, will be awakened by Harlem's biggest election night party ever.

I finally wade out of the multitude in Powell Plaza. I glance at my watch. Lingering any longer will leave my tired, hungry son high and dry at the practice field. I check the Jumbotron one last time. Obama's lead stretches past the point of a miraculous McCain comeback. Two men—one white, the other black—share a congratulatory hug, and no one seems to heed their ecstatic exchange but me. From the Lenox to African Square, the interracial embrace of the New Renaissance keeps showing up. An elderly man exclaims: "We ain' never got our forty acres and a mule but now we gettin' fifty states and the Big House." Hyperbole aside, his is the high note among Harlemites, certainly in concert with countless celebrants across the nation.

I rush back to the car and ponder the reaction of someone I hadn't thought about for a long while. If Mrs. Stokes were still around, I wonder what she'd say now. I know what she'd say tomorrow. But what about now? Perhaps she'd say nothing—nothing at all. And maybe tonight, for a moment, she would sing America, too.

But then I notice that homeless man still sleeping in the shadows of the stoop. Will the Obama presidency make a difference in his circumstances? I guess his presence is just Mrs. Stokes' way of resurrecting the message that she, like the Blight, is a die-hard. In her inimical style she's letting me know that, after all the history-making and hoopla, she won't be singing tonight.

NINETEEN

Climbing Toward the Higher Ground

I **WALK OUT** of Uptown Grand, the supper club Lucy, Robert, and I started, hoping that the afternoon sunshine will bring light to today's dilemma—which creditors to pay. Our vision had been to combine fine dining and live music for an inspirational mix of entertainment and culinary excellence in the heart of Harlem. We saw locals and tourists, churchgoers and jazz lovers coming together, and the entertainment excitement of the Renaissance returning to life.

Economic reality had quickly challenged that business vision. We'd unwittingly launched in the teeth of the Great Recession of 2008, which, like the Great Depression and the Blight that preceded it, had upended uptown's entrepreneurs. With a paucity of patrons, we trimmed staff and endeavored to diversify our revenue stream. Then unanticipated problems emerged, taking the restaurant from upstream currents into treacherous rapids.

The drumbeats emanating from the Powell Office Building Plaza provide a much-needed diversion from the business blues. Fifteen years after their uprooting, the street vendors of 125th

Street have returned in full force, but they've evolved since those volatile days. More are selling fruit, bootleg movie DVDs, cell phone covers and holsters, and knock-off sunglasses and wallets rather than the old-school music CDs, paperback black books, oils and incense, cheap cologne and cheaper perfume that were so redolent of my early Harlem experience. A man with a MICHAEL LIVES T-shirt walks by, and I recall brighter Uptown Grand days.

The aftermath of Michael Jackson's death in 2009 had boosted customer traffic and Uptown Grand's weekly sales. I'd seen 125th Street shut down for protests, ice cream giveaways, police investigations, the Clinton coronation, and the Obama celebration, but never for a party masquerading as a memorial service. I'd been astonished that Harlem had turned out in greater numbers for the king of pop than it had for the king of politics a few months before.

Masses of people jammed the sidewalks on both sides of the closed 125th Street. My plan to be an anonymous observer was spoiled when a police officer recognized me and escorted me down the street to the ceremony. Sizing me up as someone who'd grown up with the Jackson Five just like him, a middle-aged man turned up the volume on his boombox to blast the oldie but goodie "ABC." I stopped to sing along with him, relieved that he was more out of key than I was.

The new electronic Apollo marquee brightened the overcast day: MICHAEL JACKSON: A TRUE APOLLO LEGEND 1958–2009. I swerved to elude a school-aged Michael Jackson look-alike, wearing the familiar fedora and white glove, moonwalking down the center of the street, to the cheers of the crowd on both sides. My celebrity hadn't yet faded from the publicity push to open the restaurant, and I'd been ushered through the throng into the Apollo's renovated lobby, struck by how far the theater had come since its shuttered days a quarter-century ago.

It has been a rocky road for the Apollo and the Clubhouse. When Percy Sutton revived the Apollo in the eighties, he'd been unable to make it work as a for-profit performance venue. Fifteen hundred seats were no longer a big enough draw for the major stars. So Sutton sold the Apollo to a state agency, created a nonprofit foundation to operate it, and retained ownership of *Showtime at the Apollo*, with contractual rights from the new foundation to produce the TV variety show.

The battle that opened up proved that the Apollo remained Harlem's most valuable asset and brand. Frank Mercado-Valdes, a trailblazing television syndicator, made an offer to produce *Showtime*, bidding significantly more for the production rights than Sutton's group had been paying for them and bringing Emmy-winning Suzanne de Passe in as his producer. The board of the Apollo Foundation foiled this bid, which precipitated a state investigation. The result was a New York State attorney general's suit that accused the foundation's board of failing to collect millions owed to it by Sutton's group.

The litigation was settled and resulted in a changing of the guard. In 1999, the chair of the foundation's board, Charlie Rangel, was replaced by Time Warner CEO Richard Parsons, who was joined by new board members, Beverly Sills, Quincy Jones, and George Wein, and a new president, Jonelle Procope. The new high-profile leadership raised $54 million of a planned $96 million capital campaign and launched an array of trailblazing programming: *Blueprint of a Lady: The Once and Future Life of Billie Holiday*; its first Broadway-caliber musical, *Dreamgirls*; the flashy fusion *The Apollo Circus of Soul*, with the ringmaster's signature chant, "Get your circus on!"; and shows featuring legends Stevie Wonder, Aretha Franklin, and Paul McCartney.

Approaching the auditorium on the day of Michael Jackson's commemoration, I heard Rev. Al Sharpton's booming preacher's cadence: "Before Michael, we were limited and ghettoized. But Michael put on a cutaway military jacket, pulled his pants leg up, put on a white glove, and smashed the barriers of segregated music. He isn't 'Jacko.' He wasn't a freak. He was an innovator. Without him, there would be no Oprah, no Tiger, no Obama."

Flanked by Spike Lee, Congressman Rangel, and other dignitaries, Al looked trimmer than in the days of our regular dealings when I'd been Governor Pataki's top black aide. He'd reinvented himself, from the bouffant-haired, round-bellied chameleon who'd championed Tawana Brawley in her controversial rape claims in 1987, to the svelte champion of the black grassroots and adviser to the president.

Sharpton's transformation from protester to pragmatist signified the transition in black politics since Obama's election. This philosophical power struggle pitted the old-school generation of protest candidates, with their race-based approaches like the Gang of Four and Rev. Jesse Jackson, against the post-racial candidates who emphasized broad social remedies, like President Obama and my Harvard Law School classmate, Massachusetts Governor Deval Patrick. The protesters advocated a black agenda that evoked the injustices of the civil rights movement, whereas the pragmatists premised their ideology on class rather than racial consciousness. Sharpton's uniqueness retained the style of the former while embracing the stratagems of the latter.

The deejay blasted "I Want You Back," amplifying Sharpton's oration. The "mourners" were partying, clapping, laughing, and singing—Charlie Rangel among them. It had been a rough year for the congressman. A plethora of ethics inquiries (which ultimately would lead to him being censured by the House of

Representatives) had encouraged five rivals to challenge him for his seat. One was Adam Clayton Powell IV, the son of the Harlem legend whom Rangel had defeated forty years earlier. The congressman's ethics problems wouldn't dissuade voters from electing him to a twenty-first term. But his censure would lead to speculation about who would succeed the battle-weary warhorse.

Governor David Paterson would decline to seek reelection after mismanaging the search to find someone to replace Hillary Clinton as the junior senator for New York and the emergence of his own set of ethical issues. Though the Clubhouse still had political muscle through rising stars Manhattan Democratic leader Assemblyman Keith Wright, entrepreneur-friendly State Senator Bill Perkins, and New York City council power-house Inez Dickens, it was no longer the unrivaled center of the African-American political universe—eclipsed nationally by Obama's Chicago and locally by a younger generation of elected officials from Brooklyn and Queens, who were seeking to shift the balance of black political power from uptown to the outer boroughs.

Nonetheless, the Clubhouse legacy of public-sector largesse lived on in Obama's administration. Whereas President Clinton proclaimed that "the era of big government is over," the financial debacle of 2008 not only swept Obama into power but provided an opening for government to take center stage. George Bush's Troubled Asset Relief Program (TARP) and Obama's huge stimulus package had put on the back burner the policy of government working with urban entrepreneurs and community organizations—the strategy that turned Harlem around. My concern was that Harlem would get thrown under the bus as governments slashed spending to balance budgets. I continued to hope that political leadership might reduce debt by replacing government bureaucracy with more efficient, cost-effective grassroots partnerships that empowered lives and communities, attaining a balancing of fiscal and social responsibility.

I cross the street and close in on the half-dozen drummers at the heart of African Square. I squeeze onto the bench next to one of them, under the life-size statue of a striding Adam Clayton Powell Jr. The lead drummer flings his dreads about in sync with his finger taps and palm strikes.

I scan the crowd and see two-dozen men hanging around— some grooving to the rhythms, some just sitting, like me. With the national unemployment rate stuck at over nine percent, I'm surprised that the number of idlers isn't higher. I wish the buildup of the drumbeats could drown out the nagging fear that things in Harlem—and for black America—have taken a turn for the worse. Forty-four million Americans now live in poverty, with more than a quarter of African Americans below the pov-

FIGURE 31: The Adam Clayton Powell Jr. statue in African Square

erty line—the highest number since record keeping began fifty years ago. A third of all black children grow up poor, an astonishing 70 percent born to unwed mothers. It's a statistic that further vindicates FDR's prophetic 1935 speech and Moynihan's once-controversial 1965 report.

As expected, downtown's meltdown hit Harlem hard. Credit for small businesses dried up, retail jobs shrank, and rehab work on brownstones slowed. Support for Harlem's vibrant nonprofit sector from Lehman Brothers, Bear Stearns, Merrill Lynch, AIG, and others collapsed along with several of those corporations. Even Harlem's Children Zone, the flagship of uptown community organizations, had considered cutbacks in light of Lehman's failure to fulfill a three-million-dollar pledge. Washington Mutual had been the primary sponsor of *Amateur Night at the Apollo*—until it, too, went bankrupt.

Even good news was combined with bad. The Starwood brand Aloft, the first hotel in Harlem in over forty years, opened, although the offices of the Clinton Foundation closed for a new spot downtown. More charter schools had emerged, but the ghetto-chic baggy pants of more black male teens sagged around their hips, which suggested to me lack of self-pride and an unhealthy valorization of prison culture. Columbia University launched its multi-billion-dollar new campus, but the storied Riverton Houses had experienced foreclosure. Big box stores Costco, Target, and Best Buy had opened on the East River, but mom-and-pop storefronts on the avenues had shuttered. The new hotspot Red Rooster had hosted President Obama for a high-priced fundraiser, but homicide continued to be the leading cause of death for young black men, and a gang shooting in Morningside Park left some new Harlemites ready to flee.

Perhaps most extraordinary of all was an outcome that would have been unthinkable in my early Harlem days. African Americans had been leaving Harlem in record numbers, and their exodus and the white influx had meant that African Americans were no longer the majority in greater Harlem, the area bordered by both rivers and from 155th Street in the north to 96th Street in the south. In 1970, blacks had made up almost two-thirds of the greater Harlem population. By 2010, African-American residents of the area hovered around 40 percent of the total population.

Even north of 110th Street between 5th and St. Nicholas avenues, where blacks were still a clear majority, the racial transition was pronounced. In only a decade, the black population declined by more than 30 percent, while the proportion of whites living in the area more than doubled and the numbers of Hispanics increased by over 25 percent. Central Harlem now had the fewest black residents since the 1920s.

Most had gone south. Nigh on a century after the Great Migration, where blacks had gone north and west in huge numbers to escape Jim Crow, a reverse migration had begun. To be sure, this process had been going on since the 1960s, resulting in well over half of all African Americans in the United States living in Southern states (still a far cry from the 90 percent who had lived below the Mason-Dixon Line before the Great Migration). So rapid was the Harlem exodus that it began to be conceivable that Harlem itself might return to the demographic makeup it had before the Great Migration. More likely was that a good number of African Americans would remain—some in public housing, others drawn by the unquenchable cultural allure of Harlem—keeping alive my dream of Harlem as a paradigmatic mosaic of urban diversity.

As more drummers bang away, an elderly man is caught up in the spirit and puts on a dance show. A crowd gathers and cheers his signature moves, admittedly more Fred Astaire than Jay-Z. My smile vanishes as an African-American woman in business attire approaches me. I don't recall her name or whether we've met, but I dread the inevitable question.

"How you making out?" Her question is loaded with more than a greeting. These days, everybody in Harlem knows my woes.

"Pretty good under the circumstances," I reply curtly, hoping to nip any further exchange in the bud.

"You should never have done business with that man," she replies. I nod at the not unexpected unsolicited advice, and say nothing. "Good luck," she says, and walks away.

"That man" was Thomas Lopez-Pierre, a resident of greater Harlem and licensed real estate broker, who'd invested $50,000 in Uptown Grand and had then become the business partner from hell. I had structured his deal as a win–win. His investment would help the business pay outstanding bills, and he'd become a minority partner with a projected two-year payback. But I rushed through my due-diligence research on him, a mistake that came back to haunt me.

Only six months into the two-year deal, Lopez-Pierre had demanded full repayment, something we were under no obligation, let alone ability, to fulfill. To coerce us into paying him, he launched an online smear campaign via emails and blogs with allegations worthy of a scandal sheet, and incendiary titles such as "Joseph H. Holland, Esq., Leading Harlem Black Republican, to be Sued for Fraud." Though characterizing me as a leading Republican was a stretch, it was somehow more disparaging in his view if the public knew that the alleged misdeed had been perpetrated by a Black Republican—so weird a political animal that it couldn't be trusted anyway! (Of course, he never sued me for fraud or anything else.)

In his widely disseminated email blasts, Lopez-Pierre also vilified my sister Lucy (who suffered from multiple sclerosis) as a drug addict, and my brother-in-law Robert (a deacon at our church) as a pedophile. He falsely accused me of prevarication and embezzlement, of committing adultery and then covering it up, of consorting with drug dealers and loan sharks, and of being a police informant against the gangs. One of his cyber assaults—"Joseph H. Holland, Esq. Defrauds Investors (Harvard Law School Graduate)"—hit a very deep nerve. "With your Ivy League degrees," he wrote, "all you have become is a Harlem street lowlife and a church hustler. It is sad because people tell me that your father was a great man. If your father was alive today I think he would be very disappointed in you—you think?" I really wish he had left out the dig about Dad.

Harlem had schooled me over the years that in the rough-and-tumble world of its business and politics, ad hominem attacks were not unusual—and I'd had my fair share before. But these emails and the controversy they stirred were driving restaurant customers away; they didn't want to be around such craziness. I changed the operational model of the Uptown Grand from restaurant to event space to keep the doors open. It barely stanched the bleeding.

Lopez-Pierre's most menacing email included the following: "I hate you more than I love life." Since I'd survived the drug wars of 129th Street, it took a lot to rattle me. But the night after reading this, I turned to Jesus' Sermon on the Mount: *Blessed are you when you're insulted, persecuted, when all manner of evil is said about you falsely because of me. Rejoice and be glad, for in the same way they persecuted the prophets of old.* Memorizing this New Testament verse helped me find sleep that night, but I was still searching for the joy in this adversity.

I'd pressed the authorities to intervene. Lopez-Pierre was finally arrested and an order of protection was issued; but he posted bail and escalated his smear campaign, using his right to free speech as a legal shield. He eventually pled guilty to aggravated harassment and stalking and received a year's probation with community service. This slap on the wrist hardly broke his malevolent stride, as he began to reveal his underside: "i have decided to make a deal with the devil to secure justice," he wrote all in lower case, " . . . i have made a pact with the devil. . . . i have been praying to the devil to give me justice."

This bizarre confession put Lopez-Pierre's malevolence in perspective, personifying his malice, declaring his allegiance in the eternal struggle of good versus evil. It had taken me decades to overcome Mrs. Stokes' internal assaults. But now I was confronted with a different kind of adversary, aligned with principalities of iniquity.

The situation reached its nadir in an above-the-fold, front-page story, complete with pictures, and titled HARLEM RUMBLE, published in the *Amsterdam News*, the leading community weekly. In my interview with the *News* reporter before publication, I'd challenged him to fact-check the Lopez-Pierre allegations before going to print—to no avail. The story possessed all of Lopez-Pierre's prevarications for the non-cyber world to behold. To rub salt into the wounds, the *News* publisher had appeared on a popular cable news talk show and brandished the headline. I'd come to Harlem as a justice seeker, but was now branded as a brawler.

I stand to shake off the burden of these reflections, ready to leave the now-crowded scene. Grooving with the pounding of the drums, I look up at the statue and see the inlaid words of Adam Clayton Powell Jr.:

> Press forward at all times
> Climbing toward the higher ground
> Of the harmonious society
> That shapes the laws of man
> To the laws of God.

Powell's message invoked a recent sermon by my pastor, Bishop Carlton Brown. "Love is God's greatest law," he'd preached. "It is not *eros*—the erotic feelings of romantic love. Nor is it *philos*—the friendship of brotherly love. God's love is *agape*—unconditional love, the John 3:16 kind of love, the I Corinthians 13 kind of love, when you love even if your act of love doesn't benefit you in any way. You just keep giving, expecting nothing in return."

I pause in the providence of the moment, discerning that this *agape* love is the devotion that God had brought me to Harlem to learn. Through three decades of vicissitudes—with many ups as well as my current downs—I'd felt God's love, constraining, protecting, sustaining, and delivering me. It is the kind of love that creates opportunity rather than dependency, that refines in the crucible of daily crisis, that fosters a noncontingent commitment instead of fair-weather forays. It's love as rugged thanklessness: the ability to keep on serving even when there's persecution instead of prestige, grit instead of glory.

The confluence of the words of Powell and Brown helped me to comprehend that this recent drama was just another Job-like trial I had to endure to demonstrate loyalty to my very own love assignment—the cause of Harlem's uplift.

A teen dancer leaps in tempo with the jam session. I turn to head back to work, resolved to press on. I find myself tapping steps to the pulsating rhythms. The music crescendos; my revelation soars.

Had it really taken me seven times longer than my lousy bet to learn to love Harlem . . . to learn that Harlem's meaning to the world is really about love?

The Great Depression had dealt Harlem a near-knockout blow, but it had come back. Now the Great Recession had knocked her second Renaissance down, but she was still not out. Harlem pressed on, and did it with love, offering a vision of community that could overcome the legacies of hate and could rise up from generations of despair and embrace promise with mountains of adversity looming ahead. I felt like we'd been together, climbing toward the higher ground.

For decades, Harlem had endured intractability and blight, and yet had remained welcoming, affirming, and inspiring, a beacon of cultural light amid the economic and social gloom. The community had been compelling because of something more than famous people, historic places, and notable events. Folks had come to Harlem for more than the cool scene or the soul food; activists had rallied for something greater than their own political advance; and newcomers arrived to experience something more precious than real estate values.

They landed on 125th Street and its surroundings because of Harlem's singular character and culture—of values that were rooted in the simple injunctions of a loving God to care for your neighbor as yourself and faith in the beloved community. Love is really about service and Harlem has been serving the world as a village of possibility and promise for generations. What happens to a dream deferred? (My curiosity about that query helped to draw me here in the first place.) Harlem proves that as long as one holds on to it through the trials and travails, it evolves into the sustaining hope that, some day, the dream will no longer be deferred.

Throughout my inner-city journey, malefactors had endeavored to place Harlem under the yoke, keeping it from rising again. Harlem and I have endured a hater's hall of fame: from the detestable drug dealers and sleazy slumlords of the eighties; to the reckless radicals, overzealous cops, and irresponsible demagogues of the nineties; to the violent gang leaders, profane protesters, noose-hanging racists, and cyber-character assassins of more recent times.

Their persistence notwithstanding, I'd been persuaded that

the force of their hatred was no match for the power of Harlem's love, which gathered and galvanized entrepreneurs, community builders, politicians, doctors, activists, lawyers, reconcilers, preachers, neighbors—all those willing to sacrifice for personal and community renaissance.

I turn to leave, the battle cry of the African Square drums resounding in my ears. Soon I'm out of earshot. But the battle for Harlem's soul rages on.

ACKNOWLEDGMENTS

MY LIFE AND WORK in Harlem has found support on so many shoulders, beginning with those who made the trek from Harvard to Harlem with me: James O'Neal, Leslie Byrd, Jacqueline Patton, and Dennis Henderson, and our fellow traveler from Brown University, Mimsie Robinson. I'm thankful for our initial partnership, for it spawned several generations of fellowships that sustained my journeying.

Because of their foundational influence over the years I extend a big spiritual hug of thanks to my church families and their leaders from whom guidance flowed: Rev. Eleanor Bunyan of Bethlehem Pentecostal Church; Dr. A. R. Bernard Sr., of Christian Cultural Center; and the late Bishop Ezra Williams and Bishop Carlton Brown of Bethel Gospel Assembly. Succor from extended family members Here's Life Inner City, the Christian Community Development Association, and the Voice of Pentecost Churches (Monrovia, Liberia) has also been vital.

Nothing has been more essential than the devotion of my beloved sister, Lucy, and her husband Robert.

The manuscript matured from inchoate meditations to historical narrative through the invaluable input of my editor, Martin Rowe of Lantern Books, and through the inspired counsel of my friend and colleague Paul Liben.

Every effort has been made to locate owners of images and illustrations that aren't clearly in the public domain. Any copyright holder who has inadvertently not been properly credited or who may have responded to the author after the deadline of publication will be acknowledged with gratitude in future printings.

And last but certainly not least, my greatest thanks goes to the Lord God Almighty—my Provider and Deliverer—of Whose glorious design this book prays to be a part.

Joseph H. Holland is a graduate of Harvard Law School and has a master's degree in history from Cornell University where he followed in his father's footsteps as an All-American football player. A lawyer, ordained minister, activist, actor, playwright, and entrepreneur, he is the author of the critically acclaimed play *Cast Me Down* and the true-to-life drama *Homegrown*. He is also the creator of *Holistic Hardware: Tools that Build Lives*—a book, DVD, and series of workshops that foster life-skills among the homeless. Holland serves as an emeritus member of the Cornell Board of Trustees and holds an honorary degree from the City University of New York Law School. *Photo: Guy Gerrard.*